Principles
of Argumentation
and Debate

PRENTICE-HALL INTERNATIONAL, INC., *London*
PRENTICE-HALL OF AUSTRALIA, PTY., LTD., *Sydney*
PRENTICE-HALL OF CANADA, LTD., *Toronto*
PRENTICE-HALL OF INDIA (PRIVATE) LTD., *New Delhi*
PRENTICE-HALL OF JAPAN, INC., *Tokyo*

Principles
of Argumentation
and Debate

Glenn R. Capp

Director of Forensics
Professor and Chairman
Department of Oral Communication
Baylor University

Thelma Robuck Capp

Associate Professor of Speech
Baylor University

Prentice-Hall, Inc.   *Englewood Cliffs, New Jersey*

05688

Current printing (last digit):

11   10   9   8   7   6   5   4   3

© Copyright 1965 by Prentice-Hall, Inc.
Englewood Cliffs, N.J.

Printed in the United States of America [70558-C]

Library of Congress Catalog Card No.: 65-16583

To the memory of *Dr. L. W. Courtney*
colleague, co-author,
and friend of debaters everywhere

Preface

Facility in argumentation requires a knowledge of principles, study of model arguments, and guided practice. This text stresses principles but also outlines a program for cooperative group study and practice.

Part I shows why the debater must first become a scholar—an investigator, a searcher for factual information, an evaluator. He must know all sides of the subject before he can advocate one side intelligently. A program of study that employs discussion enables a large number of students to cooperate in becoming informed on the subject prior to debate.

Part II presents in two concise chapters the procedural principles of advocacy and the proposition. The simulated procedural principles of educational debate have few direct parallels in life situations of advocacy. They come partly from the procedures employed in courts of law and partly from those used by deliberative bodies. Knowledge about these principles must precede participation in debate because it gives purpose and direction to the study.

Part III, "Preparing for Argumentation and Debate," receives major emphasis because we believe that proper preparation constitutes the most important requirement for intelligent advocacy. The seven chapters take the student step by step through the process of preparation in the approximate order in which he encounters the problems. He begins by finding and evaluating his material; then he moves through successive steps to analyze the proposition, find and evaluate his evidence, formulate his arguments, build and brief his case, and prepare for rebuttal and refutation.

Some subjects which might be treated independently are integrated into other chapters so that the material can be better understood. For example, fallacies form a part of the chapters on evidence, reasoning, and refutation. The study of strategy, with emphasis upon thorough preparation, is diffused throughout the text. Ethical and emotional proofs, although not developed in separate chapters, permeate the discussions of both preparation and presentation.

Part IV develops those principles of presentation applicable to oral argument: delivery skills, principles of oral argument, attitudes of debaters and listeners, ethical factors in advocacy, rhetorical principles applicable to argument, stage conduct, and delivery mannerisms. The persuasive factors of advocacy are applied to the principal audiences: public, tournament, and television.

The oral assignments employ progressive stages designed to utilize discussion for preparation for debate. They conclude with a classroom tournament in which each student participates in at least four debates. The collateral readings provide a wide range of supplementary materials, including the latest texts as well as some of the better older volumes. The appendix, a printed version of a television debate, should be assigned for analysis following a study of the text.

This text is based in part upon *Practical Debating* by Luther W. Courtney and Glenn R. Capp, published by J. B. Lippincott Company in 1949. It includes several new chapters, a revision of other chapters, and a rewriting and updating of all the material. Grateful acknowledgment is made to the J. B. Lippincott Company and to the late Mrs. L. W. Courtney for permission to use the older volume as desired. Our debt is great to the late Dr. Courtney, to whom we affectionately dedicate this volume.

We are indebted to our many students, past and present, and to our colleagues on the faculty for their encouragement and helpful suggestions. Lastly, we express appreciation to the many publishers and individuals for permission to quote brief excerpts from copyrighted materials. These sources are listed in footnotes throughout the text.

G. R. C.

T. R. C.

Contents

I   Discussion as Preliminary to Debate   **1**

   1   *The Relation of Discussion and Debate to Problem Solving, 3*

   2   *The Use of Discussion in Preparing for Debate, 19*

II   The Processes of Argument and Debate   **39**

   3   *Applying Debate Procedures, 41*

   4   *Selecting and Phrasing the Debate Proposition, 54*

III   Preparing for Argument and Debate   **65**

   5   *Finding and Evaluating Material, 67*

   6   *Analyzing the Proposition, 82*

   7   *Applying and Evaluating Evidence, 102*

   8   *Reasoning Logically, 122*

   9   *Applying Deductive Forms, 138*

  10   *Briefing the Debate Case, 152*

  11   *Preparing for Rebuttal and Refutation, 167*

IV   Presenting the Debate   **187**

  12   *Presenting the Debate Case, 189*

  13   *Adapting Debates to Public Audiences, Tournaments, and Television, 211*

Appendix   **223**

   A National Television Debate, 225

   Index, 239

Principles
of Argumentation
and Debate

I
Discussion as Preliminary to Debate

1
The Relation
of Discussion and Debate
to Problem Solving

Among famous Americans, former President Franklin D. Roosevelt stands out for his effective use of discussion and debate. Whether or not one agrees with his political philosophy, almost all will agree that he used discussion and debate extensively and effectively to foster his program. From his early life experiences, four events indicate how discussion and debate relate to problem solving and how they combine to serve a free society.

The first event concerns his school debates as a student in Groton, Harvard, and Columbia. A letter to his mother dated February 28, 1899, shows his enthusiasm for securing material: "I am to debate next Monday evening. . . . The subject is: Resolved that the United States and England should guarantee the integrity of China. We are *Con,* against it, and if you happen to see any articles about it one way or the other we would be pleased to have them." [1]

How did Roosevelt prepare for his educational debates? First, he and his fellow debaters exchanged ideas and evidence through informal discussion, which served as a cooperative means for preparation and a supplement to individual research and study. After careful preparation, discussions were held to determine such questions as: "What issues should comprise our case?" "What arguments should be included under each issue?" "What evidence should be used for each argument?"

Differences of opinion arose at these discussion sessions, but compromises were reached through cooperative deliberation and

---
[1] Elliott Roosevelt, *F.D.R.: His Personal Letters* (New York: Duell, Sloan & Pearce, Inc., 1947), I, 272.

informal argument. In upholding their side of the proposition in the debate, Roosevelt and his colleagues were no longer tentative and in doubt. They knew exactly what arguments they planned to use and how they intended to develop them; now they advanced the arguments to prove their predetermined cases. This first incident reflects three steps in the use of discussion and argument for educational debates: (1) Through cooperative deliberation, the debaters used discussion to help prepare for their debates. (2) Again through discussion and informal argument, they decided on their case. (3) Finally, through debate, they became all-out advocates of one side of the proposition.

In 1907, Roosevelt joined the law firm of Carter, Ledyard, and Milburn of New York City. When assigned a case for trial, he arranged conferences with his client to determine the facts. Next followed conferences with members of his law firm to decide how he should plead the case. Differences arose in these discussions, but through compromise, a plan of action was determined. Finally, defending his client in court, Roosevelt no longer considered how to plead or establish his case; rather, he presented the strongest case possible for his client in keeping with the decisions arrived at in the prior conferences. This second incident shows three distinct acts of discussion and argument in preparing for legal debates: (1) Through discussion with his client, Roosevelt ascertained the facts. (2) Through discussion with his fellow lawyers, he decided on his case. (3) Through debate, he argued his case before the jury and judge.

In 1910, Roosevelt announced his candidacy for the New York Senate. He first decided on his staff and campaign managers and then called them together for a series of conferences in which discussion was used for exchanging ideas and planning the campaign. The resultant plans were developed through the sharing of information and group problem solving. Finally, during the campaign, he presented his case and answered his opponent's arguments. This third incident in Roosevelt's life emphasizes how discussion and argument apply to political debates: (1) He used discussion with his staff to discover the facts and decide on the campaign issues. (2) He used discussion and informal argument with his managers to decide how to advance his position. (3) Finally, he used debate when he presented his stand on the issues and refuted his opponent's charges.

Roosevelt won his race for the New York Senate and soon became the leader of a group of eighteen senators called "the mutineers," so termed because of their opposition to Tammany Hall's political machine. An opportunity to display their forensic skills came early in 1911 when Tammany Hall's "Boss" Murphy supported "Blue-Eyed Billy" Sheehan to succeed Republican Chauncey M. Depew as United States senator. At this time United States senators were chosen by the state legislatures. The insurgent Democrats strongly opposed the selection of Sheehan and began their campaign to defeat his appointment with regular meetings at Roosevelt's home, where they first discussed the issues and facts of their case. Next, they discussed the arguments that they planned to use in opposition to Sheehan's election. Finally came the debates on the Senate floor in which Roosevelt and his colleagues argued the cases that they had formulated. So intense was the fight that the debates dragged on at intervals for three months and through sixty-four ballots before a compromise candidate was elected. This fourth incident shows how problem solving goes through three stages in legislative debates: (1) Discussion was used to exchange views on the issues of the controversy. (2) Discussion and informal argument were used to decide the arguments and strategy for the forthcoming debates. (3) Debate was used to defeat the proposal on the Senate floor.

These four events indicate factors important to students of argumentation: (1) the stages of problem solving and resolution of conflict, (2) the areas for applying discussion and debate to life situations, (3) the values derived from a study of debate, and (4) the requirements for developing facility in oral argument.

Stages of Problem Solving

Some controversy prevails as to whether debate is primarily an investigative-evaluative procedure or a propagative method. One school of thought states that the debater should be primarily an objective analyzer, a searcher for factual information, a seeker for the best solution. Others believe that the debater should be primarily a subjective analyzer, a searcher for favorable evidence, an advocate of one solution. The controversy cannot be resolved into an "either-or" proposition. Rather, problem solving should be looked upon as involving progressive stages. First, the debater seeks objective analysis and understanding; second, he evaluates the best arguments on all sides; and finally, he becomes an advocate of one particular side.

Discussion as a preparation process

As a debater, first approach your subject objectively and dispassionately. Become an investigator, a seeker, an analyzer. You cannot become a truly effective advocate unless you know all sides of your subject thoroughly, opposing arguments as well as your own. At this stage, you ask, "What does the proposition mean?" "What fundamental issues apply?" "What is the factual evidence?" You must be objective before you can be effectively subjective.

Discussion as a cooperative endeavor can be invaluable in preparing for all areas of debate. It is not a substitute for independent investigation and research, but instead an additive factor in preparation whereby the participants can pool their facts and reflective thoughts.

Discussion as a problem-solving method

The second stage of the foregoing incidents shows why you must make preliminary decisions before formulating a case of advocacy: for educational debates, decide upon the best arguments and evidence for the cases; for courtroom debates, agree on how to plead the case; for campaign debates, determine the issues of the platform; for legislative debates, decide upon the strongest arguments and evidence. All these decisions can be reached through concessions and compromise, often without formal debate and vote. This stage concerns such questions as "What should be done?" "What constitutes the valid arguments for our side?" "What is the best evidence to prove the case?"

The methods employed in this stage are a combination of discussion and debate: through discussion, the debaters exchange ideas and information; through informal debate, they decide on arguments and evidence for their cases. The attitude of the participants at this stage distinguishes their methods from those of formal advocacy. They have a questioning attitude: "What is the best case?" In formal debate, they have a positive attitude: "Ours is the best case."

Debate as a conflict-resolving process

There comes a time when the debater must cease his investigation; he must become an all-out advocate, a propagator of ideas. He must marshal his best arguments and evidence to prove a case for his side.

Almost everyone will agree that discussion constitutes the best approach to problem solving, but realistic people will also agree that not all problems can be solved that way. Our feelings may be too strong to permit concessions; our personal interests may prevent compromise. Some problems must be submitted to a third party for solution—the jury, the legislative body, the electorate, the judges. These situations call for advocacy; opposing debaters present the case for their side to a third group for decision. The advocate asks not "What are all the facts?" but "What are the facts favorable to my cause?" and not "What are all the arguments?" but "What arguments favor my position?" Thus, the debater on the platform becomes an advocate, not an investigator.

Strife as a conflict-resolving method

If the foregoing methods for solving problems and resolving conflicts fail or are not available for use, belligerent methods will be employed—labor will strike against management, industry will boycott labor, individuals will resort to mob violence, and nations will go to war. The resort to violence will become less frequent as the peaceful methods—discussion and debate—are perfected. A healthy attitude toward problem solving consists of a high regard for the methods of discussion and debate and active vigilance in seeking ways to improve them.

Areas of Application [2]

Studies in discussion and debate are not ends in themselves, but they offer training for life situations of cooperative deliberation and advocacy. To insure the equitable solution of problems, skilled

---

[2] Based on Glenn R. Capp, "Discussion and Debate in Life Activities," *The Bulletin of the National Association of Secondary School Principals*, 38, No. 199 (January, 1954), 67-70.

arbitrators and advocates become essential. Certain situations, especially, demand people skilled in these processes.

Courts of law

Courts of law provide the nearest approach to justice that we have been able to devise. They make possible a means for free people to settle their own disputes. Such people believe the courts, with all their shortcomings, to be superior to dictatorial decrees.

Courts of law make liberal use of both discussion and debate. A citizen recently summoned to serve on the jury panel for the week was listening to the judge's instructions concerning the jury panel's rights and obligations when some lawyers entered the courtroom and called the judge aside. Upon returning to the jury panel, the judge announced that the case on docket had been settled and that the jury was dismissed.[3] The litigants had settled their differences outside of court by use of discussion; without discussion the trial would have been inevitable. The compromise was effected by lawyers skilled in cooperative deliberation. Numerous cases are settled outside the court through the methods taught in college classes in discussion and debate. One prominent attorney reported that he settled more than ninety per cent of his legal cases outside the courtroom.

. Some legal disputes cannot be settled without debate. As long as people govern themselves, conflict arises. A person involved in conflict has the right to have his side of the controversy presented to a jury that he has helped select. To withhold this right is to deny the democratic process, and unless skilled advocates represent both sides, injustice may result. Discussion and debate classes afford invaluable training for this life situation. Walter Lippmann sums up the matter in these words: "We may picture the true spirit of freedom as existing in a place like a court of law, where witnesses testify and are cross-examined, where the lawyer argues against the opposing lawyer before the same judge and in the presence of one jury." [4]

---

[3] See Glenn R. Capp, *How to Communicate Orally* (Englewood Cliffs, N.J.: Prentice-Hall, Inc., 1961), p. 307.

[4] Walter Lippmann, "The Indispensable Opposition," *Atlantic* (August, 1939), p. 188.

Legislative assemblies

Policy-making groups constitute a second important field where discussion and debate perform essential functions. Legislative bodies provide the nearest approach that we have found for securing equitable public policies. The other possible approaches are anarchy on one end of the continuum and dictatorship on the other, both untenable in a free society. Anarchy is characterized by skepticism, doubt, confusion, and disorder—the absence of organized authority; dictatorship is characterized by force, orders, commands, and blind obedience—complete authority. In both extremes discussion and debate are not needed to solve problems. Democracy, the common-sense middle ground, makes use of both discussion and debate as the principal methods by which people govern themselves. Many public policies can be settled in conferences, through agreement, by utilizing discussion principles. If disagreement becomes too intense to permit agreement through discussion, the problem must be submitted to a third body for decision through debate. College classes in argumentation and debate provide the training for organizing thoughts, weighing evidence, and analyzing problems so essential for decision in policy-determining groups.

Political campaigns

Since 1832, when the national party conventions were established in the United States, political campaigning has been an important type of debate. Platform committees spend long hours in discussion and informal debate to determine the party issues. Debate continues at the conventions in the adoption of the party platform and the selection of candidates. Then the standard bearers wage vigorous campaigns for votes. The majority of campaign speeches take the form of indirect debates; rather than meeting on a common platform, the candidates answer campaign claims and promises made by opposing candidates in previous speeches.

There have been notable cases of face-to-face debates in which the candidates met on a common platform. The famous Lincoln-Douglas debates, with slavery as the primary issue, during the senatorial campaign of 1858 were the first between major national candidates. William Jennings Bryan won the Democratic nomination at the 1896 national convention partly because of his effective debating on the issue of bimetallism. More recently, John F. Kennedy and Richard Nixon engaged in a series of four face-to-face debates over national television networks in the presidential campaign of 1960. Political experts predict that such debates will play an increasingly important part in future campaigns. Although President Lyndon B. Johnson and Senator Barry Goldwater did not meet in face-to-face debates in the 1964 presidential campaign, they used television extensively for indirect debates in waging their campaigns. Television debates serve well in acquainting the electorate with the personalities of the candidates and the issues of the campaign.

Everyday activities

The necessity for discussion and debate may be found in the everyday activities of the citizens in a democracy—the student presents his case for a stronger student government, the minister advocates the adoption of the church budget, the school superintendent presents his proposal for expansion, and the housewife presents her arguments for new draperies. The citizen in a democracy gets much of what he wants through conferences, utilizing discussion principles. If he fails with discussion methods, he has the alternative of presenting his case before the body that has the power of decision. Training in debate for such situations is invaluable.

Educational institutions

Beginning in the latter part of the nineteenth century, intercollegiate debating has become a part of the programs of almost all colleges and universities. Thousands of students now receive training for cooperative deliberation and advocacy in college classes and through intercollegiate forensic programs.

McBurney and Hance emphasize the importance of this training as follows: "Legislative, political, and judicial debates occupy the time and attention of some of our greatest minds and affect the lives and well-being of millions of people. . . . We believe that any realistic conception of democracy must admit a place for the trained advocate." [5]

Values of Debate Training

The values of training in argumentation and debate do not end with the college class or with the close of the intercollegiate debate program. On the campus, on the streets, in church, in society, in business, and in politics, a person is constantly confronted with the necessity of influencing human behavior. The extent of that influence will be determined in part by his ability to investigate a question thoroughly, to think clearly, to reason logically, and to present views clearly and convincingly. Seven rewarding benefits bear special emphasis.

Background knowledge of current problems

The first value of a study in argumentation and debate comes from the knowledge acquired on current problems. Almost any former college debater will say that of all his college studies, he remembers most clearly the information he worked out for himself in preparing for debates. To argue intelligently, one must obtain a fundamental understanding of current economic, social, and political problems. The procedures of debating a national topic many times each year stress the necessity of thorough knowledge; those who attempt to get by with only a surface understanding are soon exposed. This creation of interest in and understanding of current problems leads to intelligent citizenship.

Critical decision making

Almost all citizens in a free society must make countless decisions each day. Some decisions relate to inconsequential personal matters; others decide our destiny. Some people decide matters quickly, without a careful weighing of the issues and evidence available to them. Emotional impulses, habitual patterns of thinking, customs, and traditions play a large part in their decisions. Others delay making decisions, attempting to justify their habits of indecision

---

[5] James H. McBurney and Kenneth G. Hance, *The Principles and Methods of Discussion* (New York: Harper & Row, Publishers, 1939), p. 277.

by an exaggerated thoroughness in weighing all the evidence. Critical decision making lies between these extremes. The critical thinker carefully analyzes and weighs the available evidence and decides resolutely on the basis of fact and reason. He varies his standard of evaluation to meet specific problems rather than deciding all matters by set patterns. The preparation for advocacy, both individually and through discussion with others, gives valuable training in critical decision making.

Investigation of a subject

A third value of a study of argumentation and debate comes from the training it provides in research. One cannot prepare adequately for debate without learning how to use the library and how to find material from other sources. Finding material constitutes only part of the problem; a debater must also analyze the material—decide what it means and how it applies to the proposition. Since everything he reads cannot be accepted at face value, the debater must learn to make discriminating choices, to evaluate what he finds. The ability to separate the important from the trivial, to distinguish the objective from the subjective, and to differentiate between the reliable and the unreliable marks the successful debater. Such training becomes valuable in later life regardless of one's vocation.

Logical reasoning

The proper discovery, analysis, and evaluation of the material provides the evidence for logical support. After finding the evidence, one must decide what conclusions can be drawn from it. The process of drawing inferences from evidence constitutes reasoning. In *inductive reasoning,* the reasoner examines specific cases and from them draws a general conclusion about the entire class. In *deductive reasoning,* the reasoner starts with a general statement and draws a conclusion about a specific case. (Reasoning may also take the form of analogy, sign, and causal relation, processes that are explained in Chapters 8 and 9.) Failure to reason logically causes the reasoner to commit a fallacy or make an error in the reasoning process.

Evidence and reasoning are the components of logical proof, the basic appeal in argumentation and debate. Thus facility in logical reasoning is essential to successful debating and an asset to anyone in a free society.

Formulation of a case

As already noted, almost all citizens must at times present a case for or against a proposal. The professor must convince his department head; the department head must convince the dean; the dean must convince the president; the president must convince the board of regents; the board of regents must convince the legislators; the legislators must convince their constituents. How well each builds and presents his case helps determine his success in any stage of advocacy.

A case of advocacy consists of the best arguments and evidence for the side of a proposition that one champions. Time limitations prevent the debater from presenting all the valid arguments and evidence on his side, so he must learn to be selective, to evaluate his reasons and facts for the most reliable and convincing materials. The arguments must be logically organized to be readily understood since haphazard arrangement may prevent an otherwise acceptable case from accomplishing its purpose. The ability to formulate a logically arranged case of valid and convincing arguments serves any citizen well, and it becomes an essential factor in the training of the advocate.

Oral presentation of ideas

Arguments may be presented in either written or oral form. This text stresses oral presentation, the form used in almost all college debates as well as in the preponderance of life situations. Although many factors of communication are common to both written and oral forms, oral discourse requires special methods that can be developed in part through college debating.

Acceptable oral communication includes reasonable poise and confidence, an adequate and colorful vocabulary, a forceful and pleasant voice, and a coordinated body—in short, the coordinated use of mind, body, and language for the purpose of communicating ideas, information, and emotions. Through participation in classroom and intercollegiate debates, one learns how to present arguments effectively through oral communication.

Establishment of ethical standards

A final benefit derived from a properly conducted study of argumentation and debate accrues from the ethical standards it teaches. A debater establishes proper attitudes toward research early in his study because he soon learns that inadequate knowledge and faulty analysis are intellectually dishonest. He learns to be sure of his facts before he speaks and to present the most fundamental arguments for his side.

A thorough study of subjects for debate discourages dogmatism. We often express our most extreme opinions about subjects of which we know the least, whereas a fundamental knowledge about all sides of questions of public policy usually reveals a more equal balance of evidence and arguments than we originally expected. Extensive research teaches the debater to become cautious of extreme statements and unsupported assertions. He soon learns that the most fundamental case is the case most likely to win; he learns to avoid shallow thinking and to concentrate on logical argument and valid evidence.

Sophistic devices are poor substitutes for valid arguments. Questionable practices consist of unusual interpretations of the proposition, surprise cases outside the scope of the proposition, inadequately stated issues, prejudiced and incomplete evidence, and evasion of basic arguments. A debater learns to look upon debate as an educational activity in which fundamental knowledge, mature thinking, and fair play count more heavily than questionable strategic devices.

Requirements for Successful Debating

Debating is an exacting activity that requires hard work and a dedication to purpose. It presupposes a desire to improve background knowledge, to learn about the principles of argument, and to develop communicative skills. Given the proper desire and motivation, what are the requirements for debating effectively?

Study of principles of argumentation

The rhetorical principles of argumentation and debate constitute a body of information that can be learned and practiced. The potential debater must acquaint himself with these principles as a basis for the acquisition of skills. Those principles, in the approximate order in which they will be encountered, are listed here for an over-all view and are developed in detail in subsequent chapters.

Principles of Argumentation

Processes	1.	The procedures in educational debate.
	2.	The proposition for argumentation.
Preparation	3.	The materials of argument.
	4.	The analysis of the subject.
	5.	The evidence of argument.
	6.	The reasoning process.
	7.	The ethical and psychological proofs.
	8.	The argumentative case—constructing and briefing.
	9.	The refutation of opposing arguments.
Presentation	10.	The principles of delivery.
	11.	The application to life situations.

Application of principles to current topics

Principles of argument should not be studied in a vacuum; rather, direct application of the principles to current topics should be made as each principle is considered. The current national debate topic serves well for this purpose, or the class may select its own proposition. For example, as you study principles of analysis, analyze the chosen proposition; as you study evidence, find and evaluate evidence on the subject; as you consider principles of case construction, build cases for and against the selected proposition. This practical approach makes the principles meaningful and prepares for the practice debates to follow.

Analysis of current and historical debates

You can learn a great deal by observing debaters in action and by analyzing published debates. Listen to debates held on college campuses, on television, in legislative assemblies, and in public forums. Listen critically; analyze how the speakers applied the principles of argument and oral presentation.

An analysis of published debates permits a detailed study of all the principles of argument except presentation skills. Start by reading such masterpieces as the Webster-Hayne debates in 1830, the

Lincoln-Douglas debates in 1858, and the Kennedy-Nixon television debates in 1960. Next, study published intercollegiate debates of recent years. Representative volumes include Egbert Ray Nichols, ed., *Intercollegiate Debates* (New York: Noble and Noble, Publishers, Inc., 1919–); *University Debater's Annual* (New York: H. W. Wilson Co., 1914–); James H. McBath, ed., *T. V. Championship Debates* (Portland, Me.: J. Weston Walch, Publishers, 1964); and Russel R. Windes and Arthur N. Kruger, eds., *Championship Debating* (Portland, Me.: J. Weston Walch, Publishers, 1961). The last volume contains nine of the final rounds of the National Debate Tournament held annually at the United States Military Academy, together with critiques by experienced directors of forensics in American colleges. By listening to and reading significant debates, you can observe how successful debaters utilize principles of argumentation and thereby improve your own knowledge and skills.

Engagement in practice debates

Debate is a doing as well as a knowing activity—no amount of knowledge about argumentation will make you an effective debater until you put your acquired knowledge to use by directed practice. Practice sessions may take at least three forms: (1) After completing the necessary research for your case, practice presenting your arguments and anticipated refutation before an imaginary audience. Practice aloud, preferably in a classroom or auditorium, and speak extemporaneously, without stopping to correct errors, as if you were speaking to a real audience. If possible, record your practice sessions and study the recordings for errors. (2) Engage in practice debates with members of your class or debate club under simulated conditions of public debates. Ask your forensic director or an advanced student to serve as a critic, and follow each practice session with a critique in which you and the critic discuss the strengths and weaknesses of your arguments. If possible, have some of your practice debates before your class or debate club. (3) Engage in debate tournaments, both intrasquad and intercollegiate. The stimulus of competition that the tournament engenders provides a strong incentive for self-improvement. Ask the judge for criticisms, or, if written criticisms are provided, study them carefully. Measure your progress by the improvement that you make, not necessarily by how many debates you win or lose.

In short, you can improve your skills in debate by learning the principles of argumentation, applying them to the proposition for debate, analyzing oral and written debates, and engaging in directed practice. Your progress may seem slow at first, but leading citizens in almost all life activities can testify that persistency in applying these suggestions is rewarded.

Summary

Problem solving can be effected through various stages by the use of discussion and debate: (1) Use discussion as a preparation process. (2) Use discussion principles to attain compromises. (3) Use debate to submit a problem to a third party for decision. (4) Avoid strife as a conflict-resolving method.

Training in discussion and debate serves well in preparing for several life activities: (1) in courts of law, (2) in legislative assemblies, (3) in political campaigns, (4) in everyday activities, and (5) in educational institutions.

Training in argumentation and debate gives the student (1) a background knowledge of current problems, (2) training in critical decision making, (3) knowledge of how to investigate a subject, (4) experience in logical reasoning, (5) training in how to formulate a case, (6) skills in presenting ideas orally, and (7) concepts of ethical standards.

To learn to debate effectively (1) study the principles of argumentation, (2) apply the principles to current topics, (3) analyze current and historical debates, and (4) engage in directed practice.

Oral Assignment

Review a magazine article on the subject selected for class debates for oral presentation in class. Each class member should take notes on the articles reviewed. This exercise serves as a cooperative means of preparation by the class members. Observe the following procedures:

1. State the author's name, the magazine, the title of the article, and the date of publication.
2. Review the article. Give the arguments and the most pertinent evidence for each point.
3. Evaluate the article and advise the class members if they should read it.

4. Limit your review to five minutes.
5. Remain on the platform no longer than two minutes for questions from the class members.

Collateral Readings

Braden, Waldo W., and Earnest Brandenburg, *Oral Decision Making,* Ch. 1. New York: Harper & Row, Publishers, 1955.

Crocker, Lionel, *Argumentation and Debate,* Ch. 1. New York: American Institute of Banking, 1962.

Ehninger, Douglas, and Wayne Brockriede, *Decision by Debate,* Chs. 1, 2, 3. New York: Dodd, Mead & Co., 1963.

Freeley, Austin J., *Argumentation and Debate,* Ch. 1. Belmont, Calif.: Wadsworth Publishing Co., Inc., 1961.

Huber, Robert B., *Influencing Through Argument,* Ch. 1. New York: David McKay Co., Inc., 1963.

McBurney, James H., and Glen E. Mills, *Argumentation and Debate: Techniques of a Free Society,* Ch. 1. New York: The Macmillan Company, 1964.

2

The Use of Discussion
in Preparing
for Debate

We learned in Chapter 1 that discussion serves as a problem-solving procedure and works together with debate for the peaceful settlement of disputes. Discussion also performs a useful purpose in learning groups, especially in preparing college debaters on the proposition for debate. This chapter will show how discussion may be used as a cooperative method for group participation in analyzing a subject. First let us consider the pattern that discussion takes.

Pattern for Discussion

Discussion is a collective approach to problem solving and learning situations by a group under shared or directed leadership. It defines and analyzes problems and tests suggested solutions.

By its nature, discussion is a slow and tedious procedure operating largely through trial and error. It must allow the participants time to pool their ideas and facts, consider their differences, and evaluate possible solutions. The participants may digress, discuss one phase of the subject too long, or spend time on inconsequential matters. The logical pattern for discussion attempts to overcome these inherent weaknesses. Although no panacea for the weaknesses of discussion, it serves to give order and arrangement to the process. If all participants keep the logical pattern in mind, the chances for a productive discussion will be enhanced.

McBurney and Hance list five steps in the pattern of discussion:

1. Defining and delimiting the problem.
2. Analyzing the problem.

3. The suggestion of solutions.
4. Reasoned development of the proposed solutions.
5. Further verification.[1]

The steps in discussion center around analysis and investigation, both of which logically precede debate. Discussion sometimes ends before there is an attempt to gain acceptance or rejection of a particular solution. A decision may not be reached through discussion because of differences of opinion. In debate, the weighing of advantages against disadvantages of a proposed solution takes place. One possible solution to a problem takes the form of a proposition, the issues of which opposing teams attempt to sustain or to overthrow. Debate, then, may be said to take up where discussion leaves off.

The steps in the pattern for discussion may be restated for learning groups as follows:

1. Define, explain, and narrow the subject.
2. Diagnose the problem by analyzing its cause-effect relationships.
   a. Consider the effects of the problem, the conditions that exist.
   b. Discover the causes that gave rise to the problem.
   c. Consider criteria for judging solutions.
3. Analyze and evaluate proposed solutions.
   a. Explain each proposed solution.
   b. Consider the advantages of each solution.
   c. Consider the disadvantages of each solution.
4. Seek agreement on a proposed solution.
   a. Explain the selected solution.
   b. Consider its advantages.
   c. Consider its disadvantages.
5. Examine procedures for initiating the proposed solution.
   a. Discuss practical problems in instituting it.
   b. Determine how problems created by the new policy may be overcome.

Let us consider the steps of the pattern to see how they apply to learning groups.[2]

Define, explain, and narrow the subject

Attempt first to locate and understand the problem. Define and explain terms that may prevent a common understanding, since

---

[1] James H. McBurney and Kenneth G. Hance, *Discussion in Human Affairs* (New York: Harper & Row, Publishers, 1950), pp. 11-13.
[2] Based on Glenn R. Capp, *How to Communicate Orally* (Englewood Cliffs, N.J.: Prentice-Hall, Inc., 1961), pp. 310-17.

some terms may have different meanings to different people.

Discussions sometime fail to realize their maximum usefulness because the group attempts too much for a single session. On topics broad in scope, several meetings, on different phases of the subject, may be necessary. At the beginning of the discussion, decide what terms in the subject mean, how the scope of the subject may be limited, how irrelevant and extraneous matter may be disposed of, and how the purpose of the discussion may be achieved.

Diagnose the problem

After securing a meeting of minds on the meaning and scope of the problem, analyse its cause-effect relationships to determine its nature and extent. Do existing conditions constitute a problem? How serious are the conditions? What facts reveal their significance? An objective analysis will reveal the factual conditions of the problem. This analysis should precede a consideration of solutions so that the participants will understand what conditions need correcting.

Next consider what factors brought these conditions about. A temporary solution only extends the problem; to effect a lasting solution, the conditions that gave rise to the problem must be attacked. Discussions must consider causes as well as effects.

As a third step, decide on criteria to evaluate and measure the adequacy of possible solutions. Each proposed solution can then be considered in light of the criteria agreed upon; agreement on these criteria may pave the way for a mutually satisfactory solution.

Analyze and evaluate proposed solutions

This step considers the many possible solutions, not simply those solutions favored by various members. What are the possibilities? Among the possible solutions, which one is best? Consider and explain each possible solution in detail. How would it operate? What are the principles that underlie it? Follow explanations by a consideration of the possible advantages and disadvantages of each suggested solution, and then seek agreement on the best solution. Although these procedures do not ensure agreement, they do improve the chances for it.

The attitude of the participants determines the success of this stage of the discussion. Do not assume that you must champion a solution because you suggested it. Rather, your attitude should be: "Here is a possible solution. What do you think of it? How does this proposed solution compare to the others that have been suggested? What are its advantages and disadvantages?" An objective, weighing attitude at this stage paves the way for the next step.

Seek agreement on a proposed solution

After considering possible solutions, the participants try to agree on one of the solutions evaluated or to compromise on two or more of them. Discussions sometime break down at this point because the participants cannot compromise their differences. Their convictions on the problem may be too strong to permit compromise; personal bias or prejudice may also impede agreement. The chances of agreement will have been improved, however, by a prior consideration of the meaning and scope of the problem, an analysis of the cause-effect relationships, and an objective consideration of the workings, advantages, and disadvantages of each possible solution. Discussion participants may reach the solution phase too soon; they may seek agreement on solutions before the problem has been properly diagnosed or before other possible solutions have been examined, and such action decreases the chances of agreement.

Examine procedures for initiating the proposed solution

When the participants agree on a solution, they next consider how to put the solution into operation. The practicability of instituting the solution should be considered first. What steps should be taken to initiate it? How effective would it be in solving the problems discussed in the analysis stage? This phase of the discussion attempts to spell out a step-by-step procedure of execution.

Next, consider what new problems may arise as a result of the adoption of the proposed solution. How can these problems be avoided? The total effect of the change must improve conditions—otherwise, there can be little justification for change.

In short, the pattern for discussion gives direction to the process. If followed unobtrusively, it should make possible an orderly discussion. Each of the steps is illustrated later in this chapter.

Types of Discussion

The technical aspects of the different types of discussion must be understood for effective use in preparing for debate. The following four types are most frequently used in preparing debaters as a group: (1) the informal discussion, (2) the panel, (3) the symposium, and (4) the lecture forum.

Informal

Of the four types listed, debate classes probably use informal discussion most frequently because it permits participation by all members of the class or squad, pooling the information of the entire group.

Although this type does not require strict rules, there are certain procedures that constitute an orderly meeting. The leader usually announces the topic and gives a brief background of the general nature of the subject, stresses the importance of the topic, and creates a pleasant atmosphere. He may then ask questions or present a hypothetical problem to start the discussion. His opening remarks should clarify the subject and motivate the group to constructive participation.

After starting the discussion, the leader directs it, makes brief summaries at the conclusion of each step, prevents useless arguments, keeps down strife, and makes a full summary at the end. The good leader makes no attempt to monopolize the activities; rather he attempts to keep it moving constructively through the steps in the pattern for discussion.

The success of a discussion depends largely upon the preparation of the participants. Unless careful preparation precedes the discussion, the result will be a "pooling of ignorance." To insure adequate preparation, each participant should make an outline before he comes to the meeting.

The form for the outline need not be formal or technical; it should follow the pattern outlined in the preceding section of this chapter. Under the heading "define, explain, and narrow the subject," list how you think the topic should be interpreted and restricted. Under the division "diagnose the problem," include the results of your analysis of the problem: the evidence of existing conditions, the causes of those conditions, and the criteria that you deem advisable in judging a solution. In the third division of the outline, list, explain, and give both the advantages and disadvantages of various possible solutions to the problem. Then, for your fourth point, designate what solution you personally think should be adopted, explaining your solution and stating why you consider it a workable plan. Finally, explain how you think the solution can be instituted.

Do not feel that you must defend the conclusions set forth in your outline. If, during the discussion, former conclusions seem wrong, accept what most nearly complies with the findings of the group. Make discussion a process of thinking together, a cooperative rather than a competitive endeavor.

The panel

In the panel, a small group of participants and a chairman conduct a discussion for the benefit of an audience. The panel and the audience form co-acting groups. For the best effect, the group should be seated in a semicircle or around three sides of a table so that each member of the panel can see both the audience and his fellow members. The participants do not make speeches; they engage in the discussion much as if there were no audience present. Each speaks informally when he feels that he has something to contribute or when he wishes to ask a question. The panel defines and limits the scope of the problem, discusses its effects and causes, sets up standards for judging solutions, proposes solutions, discusses the advantages and disadvantages of each one, attempts to agree on a tentative solution, and makes suggestions for putting the solution into effect.

After a pattern of thought has been established and the chairman has summarized the discussion, the audience takes part. Any member of the audience now has the right to ask questions or to make brief comments, addressing the panel as a whole or any individual member. The open-forum period permits expression of views that may aid in the clarification of the topic.

The symposium

The symposium differs from the informal and panel discussions in that it makes use of prepared speeches. The symposium may be divided into two classes—the unrestricted and the restricted.

In the unrestricted symposium, a number of persons, limited by the time allotted, give speeches expressing their own views on the topic. The speeches usually contain analyses of the problem and suggested solutions. After the speeches, members of the audience participate in an open forum conducted by the group leader. If the symposium is used in the classroom or debate meeting, the student speeches should be limited to five or six minutes to give an opportunity for several students to speak and to permit time for an open forum.

The unrestricted symposium for classroom use is valuable because it permits the debater to propose his own solutions to problems, although this may result in duplication of ideas and materials, with several students presenting similar analyses and solutions. An unrestricted symposium on the topic "What should be done about the veto provision of the United Nations?" could take the following form: The first speaker would discuss how the United Nations came into being. The second speaker would explain the veto provisions of the United Nations. Then four speakers would discuss what they individually think should be done about the veto. The seventh and final speaker would summarize the discussion and discuss what he considers to be the future of the veto power.

In the restricted symposium, speakers talk on assigned topics. After the question is divided into its logical parts, different topics are assigned to the participants, who prepare their assignments in advance of the discussion. The subject should be divided so as to allow presentation of all its phases. For example, suppose the question selected is stated as follows: "Should the veto power of the United Nations be abolished?" The subject may be divided into seven topics:

Speaker I: Events leading to the formation of the United Nations.
Speaker II: The framework of the United Nations.
Speaker III: An analysis of the problems presented by the veto provision of the United Nations charter.
Speaker IV: Arguments for abolishing the veto power.
Speaker V: Arguments against abolishing the veto power.
Speaker VI: Methods of revising the veto power.
Speaker VII: The future of the veto power.

At the conclusion of each speech, the speaker may be questioned by other members of the symposium. When all speeches have been concluded, members of the audience question the participants and make comments.

The lecture forum

The lecture-forum method consists of a formal lecture followed by an open forum. Following the lecture, the chairman takes charge, comments on important phases of the speech, and opens the meeting for general discussion. Questions from the audience usually come readily after the first question, for one question and the comment upon it by the speaker naturally stimulate others to take an active part. The chairman should therefore be prepared to ask the initial question. He directs the questions along the lines most likely to help the majority of the group; he discourages embarrassing or irrelevant questions and encourages all listeners to participate.

If the lecture is given before a class in debate, each student should come prepared to ask questions that will clarify his particular problem; thus the greatest good will be derived from hearing the authority. The properly conducted lecture forum proves a timesaver in preparing a group to debate. For most questions chosen by national debate committees, several competent lecturers can be found in the community; often the director of the forensic program gives the first lecture.

Suggested Discussion Series

The types of discussion described in the foregoing section may be employed for a series of meetings designed to acquaint all members of a class or forensic program with the proposition for debate. Each member should conduct his independent investigation of the topic during the series of discussions. The discussions supplement independent study; they do not supplant it. Start by working out a practical series for the program. The number of discussions employed will depend upon such factors as the time available, the number of participants, and the organization of the class or the extracurricular activity. For best results, arrange a minimum of twelve discussions, employing the four types already explained. If the series can extend over a period of at least three months, the debaters will have time to conduct their independent investigations between sessions. As a result of the series of meetings and individual research, each member of the group should become well informed on the question. Although the order for employing the four types may vary, the following step-by-step plan offers a practical approach.

Informal discussions

An early problem facing the debater is where to find material. A modified version of the informal discussion offers an excellent method for cooperation by members of the class or debate squad in locating the best materials. In preparation for this first meeting, each member plans to review and evaluate a magazine article or a book pertinent to the topic. Each participant gives the source of his article, presents its outline, relates factual materials of general use, and evaluates his article. All members of the class or squad will thus acquire information and will exchange leads to the more important articles and books on the subject. The reports may be followed by a general discussion to clarify these background materials.

Informal discussion, explained in the preceding section, may be used at the next group meeting. Since all members participate, the general outline for the program should be explained well in advance of the meeting. Suppose, for example, that the topic concerns whether the federal government should provide an opportunity for all qualified high school graduates to attend college. The following skeleton outline with pertinent questions applies:

Topic: What is the responsibility of the federal government for providing higher education for qualified high school graduates?
   I. Define terms and limit the scope of the problem.
      A. What does "providing higher education" mean?
         1. Does it mean scholarships, loans, or federal schools?
         2. Does it mean tuition expenses, living expenses, or all expenses?
      B. What is a "qualified high school graduate"?
         1. What standards of scholarship qualify a student and how can these standards be applied?
         2. What criteria for determining economic need can be applied?
      C. What does "higher education" mean?
         1. Is it limited to liberal arts colleges or does it include professional schools or trade schools?
         2. Is the education limited to undergraduate study?

II. What is the problem and what conditions give rise to it?
   A. How many students fail to go to college because of financial reasons?
   B. What effect does the failure to educate qualified students have upon the individual and upon the nation?
   C. Are finances the real cause for the failure of qualified students to attend college?
      1. Is lack of motivation a contributing cause?
      2. Is lack of counseling a contributing cause?
   D. What criteria should govern a solution to the problem?
III. What are the possible solutions to the problem?
   A. Would a program of federal scholarships suffice?
      1. How would this plan work?
      2. What would be its advantages and disadvantages?
   B. Would an expanded program of federal loans solve the problem? (Explain, give advantages and disadvantages.)
   C. Would an expanded junior college program meet the need? (Explain, give advantages and disadvantages.)
   D. Should the federal government establish federal colleges and universities? (Explain, give advantages and disadvantages.)
IV. What solution would prove best?
   A. How would the solution work?
   B. Would it solve the problem?
   C. What would be its advantages and disadvantages?
V. How could the proposed program be instituted?

Such a discussion will acquaint each student with the background of the problem and enable him to define the terms of the topic. He will likewise develop standards for determining the worth of the proposed solutions, receive information concerning the major issues, and gain sufficient knowledge to attack other plans that might be advanced.

Lecture forums

Some groups prefer the lecture forum to the informal discussion for the first meeting in the series. As a general rule, however, greater good will result from having the informal discussions first, for thereby the student will acquire background knowledge and will encounter problems about which to question the lecturer. Since unprejudiced men are not always available, it may be wise to have several lecture forums that cover all attitudes toward the subject. For example, on the topic of federal scholarships, invite a school administrator, a businessman, and a lawyer. A lecture on the general subject by an expert without special interests makes a good start; later lectures on the different phases of the subject and by special-interest representatives will permit detailed development of varying points of view.

The following questions may prove helpful as topics for several lecture forums on the problem of federal support of education: Can the states solve the problem? Would federal aid mean federal control? How would the program be financed? Can private financial enterprises solve the problem? Can the colleges and universities provide adequate scholarships and loans?

At the conclusion of a lecture, the chairman takes charge, summarizes briefly what has been said, and then calls for questions from the debaters. The open-forum period following the lecture should be informal enough to allow free discussion.

Panels

The panel proves especially valuable when experts participate. If experts are available for the initial panel, students will gain useful information about the debate subject and at the same time observe procedures for use at subsequent meetings in which they will participate. For the same reasons, the earlier student panels should be composed of the more experienced debaters.

The panel also offers opportunity for student participation where groups are too large for informal discussion. The subject for debate can be divided into several questions suitable for a series of panel discussions. For example, the proposition that the federal government should provide the opportunity for higher education to all qualified high school graduates offers the following discussion topics:

1. What problems are created by failure of qualified high school graduates to attend college?
2. What conditions give rise to our failure to extend higher education to all qualified students?
3. How can private industry help solve the problem of non-college attendance?
4. How can our colleges help solve the problem of non-college attendance?
5. How can the problem of non-college attendance best be solved?

A good panel chairman directs the discussion so that it follows the logical pattern in an orderly procedure, as explained in the beginning of this chapter.

Symposiums

Both the restricted and the unrestricted symposium may be used in the discussion series. The following plan can be used for a restricted symposium:

> *Topic:* Should the federal government guarantee a higher education to all qualified high school graduates?
>
> *Speaker I:* A survey of the history of federal participation in education.
>
> *Speaker II:* The problems created by failure to educate qualified high school graduates.
>
> *Speaker III:* A survey of arguments for federal aid to qualified high school graduates.
>
> *Speaker IV:* A survey of arguments against federal aid to qualified high school graduates.
>
> *Speaker V:* Can the problem be solved without federal aid?
>
> *Speaker VI:* The outlook for solving the problem.

The two speakers who survey the arguments pro and con do not debate. The purpose of the discussion is to explore the problem, to obtain information, and to review the arguments on the proposed solution.

The unrestricted symposium should be conducted by at least four speakers, each giving his own views on the topic and how it can be solved. After each speech and at the conclusion of the discussion, the speakers may exchange views and ask questions, as do the speakers of the restricted symposium.

When the purpose of the meetings is to train debaters, all discussions should be on the national topic chosen for the year's debates. Let the topics be stated in question form rather than as propositions. Following the series of discussions and individual research, each member of the debate class or squad should be ready to engage in practice debates.

Effective Participation

The success of the series of discussions depends in part on effective participation, which in turn depends on (1) the attitude of the participant, (2) the number of his contributions, and (3) the value of his contributions.

Attitude of participants

The attitude of the conference participants should be characterized in four ways.

Cooperative Attitude. Each participant should put
the common good of the group above his own selfish interests; he
should be willing to sublimate personal desires for group interests;
he should desire to share his ideas and information with fellow
members of the debate program. In policy-making groups, the goal
of discussion is to compromise differences and arrive at solutions
that represent the consensus of the group. In learning groups, the
goal is to pool the information and ideas of the participants for
the benefit of all. A self-centered, individualistic, and competitive
attitude defeats cooperation.

Sharing of Responsibility. Each participant assumes
his part of the responsibility by (1) adequate preparation and (2)
active participation. Discussion permits a pooling of information
and ideas; but to have information to share, each participant must
make proper preparation. The discussion will be no more productive than the ideas expressed by the participants.

When engaging in discussions, participate actively; do not withhold ideas because you have not had time to think them through
thoroughly. Contributing ideas may sometimes come from an im-
pulse. Such ideas may not reflect the maturity of judgment of those
that are thought through in advance, but they may prove to be just
what the group needs to settle a problem or to move forward with
it. Express tentative opinions for the group's consideration and
raise questions to get others to clarify their ideas.

Objective Attitude. Do not feel that you must continue to uphold a point of view because you advanced it originally.
New facts or opinions may cause you to change your original position. Your purpose is to help the group solve its problem, not to
make your own ideas prevail. You should defend any position that
you consider valid, but remain willing to modify your position.
Keep to the issue and avoid subjective statements designed to
belittle persons associated with the issue or other members of the
discussion group. The objective attitude minimizes digression and
dissension and furthers an orderly procedure.

Active Listening. This attitude constitutes an essential part of the give-and-take processes in discussion. You cannot

contribute effectively to the point at issue unless you understand what others have said about it. A good listener responds overtly to what others say, asks questions for clarification, and thinks before expressing agreement or opposition. If you spend your time thinking of what you plan to say next while others speak, your contribution may not be applicable. Adapt your contributions specifically to what has gone before; listen to understand.

Number of contributions

There appears to be a correlation between the number of times a person speaks in discussion and his general worth to the group. To help determine this matter, some experiments were conducted during practice discussions among forensic groups. The number of times that each participant talked was tabulated. A panel of speech teachers scored each participant on a qualitative rating scale marked (1) superior, (2) good, (3) average, (4) fair, and (5) poor.

The experiments showed in general that those who talked the most received the highest qualitative scores. There were, however, several individual exceptions. Some persons participated actively but had little to contribute, and others felt a compulsion to pass judgment on what everyone else said. Some were free in expressing opinions but had little factual information to substantiate their assertions. A few had competitive attitudes and attempted to argue each point. In spite of these exceptions, a majority of those who took the most active part made the highest scores on the qualitative rating scales. A participant can hardly speak too often in a discussion as long as he makes worthwhile contributions. Beware, however, of monopolizing the discussion; all members of the group should be given a chance to participate. Contribute actively, but also respect the rights of others.

Value of contributions

Effectiveness of participation in discussion can be measured not only by the number of contributions but also by their value. Value depends upon a factual basis for statements and the logic of conclusions.

Sometimes discussions fail to produce constructive results because no one has gone to the trouble to learn the facts. Little can be accomplished, for example, by arguing about how many students fail to go to college because of financial reasons. Such questions should be investigated, not argued, because no amount of argument will change the facts or appraise the participants of them. If someone knows the facts, the discussion can proceed without argument.

Statements of judgment and conclusions from the facts also count heavily in discussion participation. What do the facts mean? What conclusions can be drawn from them? Suppose the evidence shows that a significant number of high school graduates do not go to college. How do these facts constitute a problem? What harm results to the nation and to the individual? An accurate interpretation of the evidence forms the basis for logical reasoning, an essential part of effective discussion participation.

Leading Discussion

The discussion leader not only prepares the subject for the discussion but also plans means for keeping the discussion moving constructively. To be successful, he must know his duties and understand the methods of procedure.

The leader's duty

A good discussion chairman is a democratic leader who works with the group in attempting to analyze and solve problems and who is neither too dictatorial nor too willing to let the discussion drift along without proper guidance. He works out an outline but permits deviation from it if circumstances indicate the need. He plans the possible course that the discussion will take and attempts to keep the discussion moving constructively, discouraging personal encounter by keeping the discussion on the issues. He asks discerning, thought-provoking questions that tend to draw out facts and opinions from members of the group, but at the same time he attempts to distinguish the essential from the nonessential and discourage uninformed opinions.

The creation of a cooperative atmosphere conducive to the exchange of ideas and information is the leader's responsibility. If he has ideas and facts he does not hesitate to contribute them, but he does not take sides on controversies that arise. Nor does he dominate the discussion or permit others to do so. In short, he attempts to be objective, patient, stimulating, and impartial, measuring his success by how well the discussion goes, not by what type of an impression he makes.

The leader's methods of procedure

The procedural methods for discussion should not be formal or stilted. The parliamentary rules of legislative groups do not apply to discussion groups; informal procedures serve best. The leader cannot let the meeting drift along without any direction, however, because he is largely responsible for the progress of the discussion. His methods of procedure may be summarized as follows:

Starting the Discussion. The leader begins the discussion by introducing the panel members to the audience and stressing the purpose and importance of the topic. The introduction need not be long, but it should include any background about the origin and history of the problem necessary to a better understanding of it. If the discussion is one of a series on the same problem, the leader summarizes briefly the accomplishments of previous sessions and states the purpose and scope of the present meeting. At the end of his introductory remarks, he raises the question of the definition and limitation of the problem. Other panel members then express their views about the meaning of the topic. These procedures apply specifically to the panel and informal discussions; in the symposium and lecture-forum types, the leader acts as chairman, but the same principles of friendliness and cooperation apply.

Keeping the Discussion Moving. Once underway, the discussion must be kept moving toward its goal. Two devices serve the leader well for this purpose: (1) summaries and (2) questions.

Summaries within the discussion have four primary uses. (1) The summary may be used to keep the discussion moving in an orderly manner. If the discussion has gone so far that no one seems to know where it is, or has gotten off on side issues with a resultant loss of direction, a summary will bring it into focus and back to the main issues. (2) The summary may be used when the group has been discussing a single topic too long and should move on to another phase of the subject. During the summary the leader should indicate what has been accomplished and at the end, direct the discussion to a new topic. The summary then serves as a transition from one phase of the subject to another. (3) The summary may be used to delay proceedings if the discussion gets too heated and tends to get out of hand or if the group seems to lose perspective. The leader may channel the discussion in other directions and not permit it to return to the topic that gave rise to the dispute. (4) The leader may use the summary when he is uncertain of what to do next or uncertain about the best procedure to follow. Usually, during the process of summarizing, a new direction will occur to him.

With skillful use of the question, the leader can draw out members of the group, secure needed information, and keep the discussion moving. At times talk may lag and the discussion may seem to bog down. When this condition arises, the leader should ask inferential questions, not those that can be answered briefly. The following questions illustrate this method as applied to the question of federal aid to qualified high school students.

1. What experience have other countries had with this problem? How did they solve them?
2. When did this condition come about? What caused it to happen?
3. What do you think is the best solution to the problem? Why?
4. Can you give an example of scholarships with unusual stipulations? How widespread is this practice?
5. What other solution can you suggest? What would be the advantages and disadvantages of it?

These types of questions serve to keep the panel talking. During his preparation, the leader should formulate such questions for each stage of the discussion.

Keeping Down Conflict. Personal conflict and bickering may prevent the harmonious atmosphere desirable for discussion. The leader should not stifle honest differences of opinion, but he should not allow unpleasantness and should never permit conflicts to get out of hand. If the leader can keep the discussion on the issues of the problem, the occasion for personal conflicts will be lessened. If he knows that personal differences exist on certain matters, he should delay their discussion until after the participants have discussed other matters upon which prejudices do not exist, so that the participants may learn to work together before the disputatious questions arise.

Encouraging Participation. All panel members should be encouraged to participate. The leader should remember, however, that a person talks best when he wants to talk, not when the leader calls on him. Avoid the *what-do-you-think-Mr. Smith* type of question; raise problems and ask questions that will move the participants to want to talk.

The leader may encounter and have to deal with (1) individuals who talk too much, and (2) individuals who do not talk enough. What can the leader do if a person tries to monopolize the discussion but has little to contribute? As a leader, you should not embarrass such an individual because his embarrassment may affect the atmosphere of the meeting and cause others to decline to participate. Unobtrusively suggest that the function of good discussion is to have all participate. If Mr. Smith continues, interrupt him, turn to the group, and state that you would like others to discuss Mr. Smith's idea. After one member concludes, direct the discussion to another without letting it return to Mr. Smith. Or, you may listen to Mr. Smith and then, without commenting on what he said, introduce a new idea. Ask others to give their opinions of the new idea. In short, lessen Mr. Smith's opportunities to speak without embarrassing him.

Occasionally the leader encounters a panel member who declines to speak. This person may have much to offer but because of his retiring nature, remains silent. The leader should unobtrusively try to bring such a person into the discussion. For example, he might turn to him and say, "John, I recall that you wrote a term paper on the subject of federal aid to education. What did you find about the adequacy of present scholarship programs?" This method points up John's qualifications to speak and brings him into the discussion on a point about which he has special information. The leader should then keep John talking by asking several follow-up questions. Once he has made an original contribution, the reticent person will usually continue to participate actively.

Concluding the Discussion. The leader should conclude the discussion at the scheduled time or when the panel ceases to make progress. He should give a brief summary, clarify questions that remain unsolved, and thank the discussion members and audience for their participation. He then opens the meeting to questions and comments from the audience and continues to preside during the open forum. If there are to be future discussions on the subject, the leader announces plans for the next discussion before concluding the meeting.

Summary

Discussion serves a useful purpose in preparing a class or debate squad on the proposition for debate. It offers a cooperative means for pooling information and ideas. The pattern for discussion, giving order and arrangement to the process, includes five steps: (1) define, explain, and narrow the subject; (2) diagnose the problem by analyzing its cause-effect relationships; (3) analyze and evaluate proposed solutions; (4) seek agreement on a proposed solution; and (5) examine procedures for instituting the proposed solution.

Types of discussions applicable to group preparation fall under four headings: informal, panel, symposium, and lecture forum. These types may be employed for a series of meetings designed to give members of the debate group a background on the debate subject. Each member will conduct his independent investigation of the subject during the period of the series of discussions.

Effective participation may be measured by (1) the attitude of the participant, (2) the number of his contributions, and (3) the value of his contributions. He should have a cooperative attitude, participate actively, and give reasons and facts for his statements.

The leader should be democratic as he guides the discussion through the steps in the logical pattern. His duties are to (1) start the discussion, (2) keep it moving constructively, (3) keep down conflict, (4) encourage all to participate, and (5) conclude the discussion. He performs an indispensable part of the discussion process.

Oral Assignment

Come to the class prepared to participate in an informal discussion on the subject selected for classroom debates. In preparing for the discussion, observe the following procedures:

1. Make an outline for the discussion in which you follow the logical pattern.
2. Include in the outline factual data that may be helpful in the discussion.
3. Keep the outline during the discussion as a guide, but do not attempt to force the discussion to conform to your outline.
4. Hand in your outline at the end of the discussion.

Collateral Readings

Braden, Waldo W., and Earnest Brandenburg, *Oral Decision Making*, Ch. 8. New York: Harper & Row, Publishers, 1955.

Capp, Glenn R., *How to Communicate Orally*, Ch. 15. Englewood Cliffs, N.J.: Prentice-Hall, Inc., 1961.

Ewbank, Henry Lee, and J. Jeffery Auer, *Discussion and Debate*, Ch. 2. New York: Appleton-Century-Crofts, Inc., 1951.

Keltner, John W., *Group Discussion Processes*. New York: David McKay Co., Inc., 1957.

McBurney, James H., and Glen E. Mills, *Argumentation and Debate: Techniques of a Free Society*, Ch. 6. New York: The Macmillan Company, 1964.

————, and Kenneth G. Hance, *Discussion in Human Affairs*. New York: Harper & Row, Publishers, 1950.

II

The Processes of Argument and Debate

3
Applying Debate Procedures

Although educational debate provides excellent training for life situations of advocacy, the procedures have but few parallels in present-day forums. Except for face-to-face debates between political candidates, public debates before interested organizations, and television debates, few life situations follow the simulated procedures of college debates. Concepts for procedural methods in educational debating come partly from the rules of procedure in courts of law and partly from parliamentary rules of legislative groups—the two principal forums for advocacy in a free society. With a minimum of adaptation, the student trained in educational debate can apply his training to life settings of advocacy.

Based upon legal and deliberative advocacy, procedures in college debate require that both the affirmative and the negative teams present cases for their respective sides. Each side must defend its case against attack by the opposing team and also attack the contentions of the opposition. Since debaters must accept these obligations, they should understand general procedural methods.

Burden of Proof

Burden of proof constitutes an integral part of all forms of advocacy. Almost all the procedural methods of life debates arise from this principle.

Explanation

Burden of proof means the obligation to prove a case. In a properly worded proposition, the affirmative has the burden of proof because it advocates a change. It must present the proposed change as preferable to the existing order, and must show that the proposed change will not usher in new evils. The affirmative cannot satisfy its obligation of burden of proof by showing the proposed change to be only as good as the existing order; it must prove its superiority. An improved condition is the only justification for going to the expense and trouble of making the change. A recognized principle in criminal law regards a man as innocent until proved guilty. This principle holds with any existing order —social, economic, or political; the order should not be condemned without cause.

Requirements

Any burden involves an obligation, that is, a requirement must be met. What obligation arises from the affirmative's burden of proof? There is one predominant requirement—a case that will overcome this burden. A prima-facie case, one that will convince the average reasonable and prudent person that the proposed course should be taken, must be advanced. The constructive case must overcome the natural advantage in favor of the existing conditions. The presumption of the argument favors the negative at the beginning of the debate just as the presumption favors the defendant in a court case or the opponent of a proposal in a legislative group; the affirmative must overcome this presumption.

That the presumption favors the negative may be illustrated as follows: When the affirmative and negative meet for a debate, the negative initially prevails because the existing order is considered best until proved otherwise. Suppose, however, that the chairman permits only the affirmative to present its constructive case and then calls for a decision. Assuming that the affirmative succeeds in presenting a prima-facie case, which side should win? The affirmative, because it has overcome its original burden of proof. The affirmative thereby shifts the presumption from the negative to the affirmative.

Suppose further that the debate runs its full course and the arguments of each side exactly balance—neither side gained over its position at the beginning. Which side should receive the decision? The negative wins because the affirmative failed to establish a case preferable to the existing order, failed to override the presumption in favor of the negative, and thereby failed to overcome its burden of proof.

Application

The principle that burden of proof rests on the affirmative may be illustrated by using a proposition: *Resolved, That the non-Communist nations of the world should establish an economic community.* The issues of this resolution may be stated as follows: (1) There is a need for a change in international trade alignments. (2) A non-Communist economic community would meet the need. (3) A non-Communist economic community would be desirable. These issues, essential to a prima-facie case, must be upheld in the constructive speeches, and they must be resubstantiated in the rebuttal speeches if the negative side successfully contests them.

In the first place, the affirmative must show a need for change because of the inadequacies of our present system of trade relationships. Unless this fact can be established, there is no need to proceed to the remaining issues. Probably the negative will admit the weakness of the present system and suggest some modification to correct such admitted weakness. In this event the affirmative would gain the first issue without contest and should centralize its efforts on the remaining issues. If the negative contests the issue of need, however, it becomes a point of controversy throughout the debate and a factor in determining the winner.

Whether the affirmative gains the first contention by argument or by admission, it still faces the necessity of showing that its proposal of an economic community by non-Communist nations will remedy the defects of the present system. The negative must meet this issue either by argument or admission. If the negative admits that a non-Communist economic community can remedy the shortcomings of the present system but fails to show a more desirable remedy for removing the acknowledged defects, it makes no progress. If the negative proposes some modification, the debate still centers on the second issue. Which plan would be superior as a means of fulfilling the need that both teams admit exist—the affirmative proposal of an economic community or the negative proposal of modification of the present system? Should the negative succeed in showing its proposed modifications superior, the negative would win despite its admission of the first affirmative issue. Also, it would be possible for the negative to admit or lose the first two issues and still win by proving that the affirmative proposal would cause new evils, more serious evils than those it would correct. Thus, the third issue of desirability could become the deciding factor. This example illustrates the importance of understanding the principles of burden of proof. If the negative can successfully overthrow any one real issue, it prevails. The affirmative must establish each fundamental issue in its case.

Burden of Rebuttal

Closely related to burden of proof is burden of rebuttal—the obligation of a team to respond to an argument. This burden may shift from one side to the other throughout the debate; it rests originally with the negative because the affirmative has the first constructive arguments. Once the affirmative presents its prima-facie case, the negative must answer it. If the negative succeeds in making a successful rejoinder, the burden of rebuttal then shifts to the affirmative. The failure to answer a prima-facie argument automatically concedes the point to the team advancing it. This obligation to respond extends throughout the debate and presents an important factor in determining the relative effectiveness of the opposing teams.

The principle of burden of rebuttal does not indicate the manner in which an argument should be answered; it does infer the necessity for a prima-facie answer. The admission of an argument constitutes as much a reply as presenting counterevidence, pointing out fallacious reasoning, or exposing insufficient evidence. Consider the example of the proposition that a non-Communist economic community should be established. In answer to the affirmative contention of the need for a change, the negative may make at least one of three replies: (1) It may deny that any need exists and present evidence and reasoning to show the adequacy of existing conditions. (2) It may argue that although a need exists for improving international trade relationships, conditions do not constitute a need for changing the principle of the present system. (3) It may admit the need for a change and present some other method for meeting the need. Any of the three responses, if properly constructed and effectively presented, shifts the burden of rebuttal to the affirmative.

Burden of rebuttal relates closely to prima-facie case, presumption of the argument, and burden of proof. Consider this relationship in a typical debate. Two teams meet to discuss a proposition: *Resolved, That the power of labor unions should be substantially decreased.* Possible issues may be stated as follows: (1) The evils of labor unions demand a change. (2) Limiting the power of labor unions will remedy these defects. (3) Decreasing the power of labor unions constitutes the best plan for improving capital-labor relationships.

The proposition calls for a change in the power of labor unions. Since the presumption of the argument rests with the negative at the beginning of the debate, the affirmative must present a prima-facie case for the proposal that the power of labor unions be decreased. This case must show sufficient reason on each of the three issues to justify the proposed change. The affirmative has the burden to overcome the presumption.

If the first affirmative speaker advances effectively the first two issues, for example, he shifts the burden of rebuttal to the negative on these issues. The burden of proof on the entire case still rests with the affirmative, as it does throughout the debate; the negative assumes the burden of rebuttal only. If the first negative speaker responds effectively to the issues advanced by the affirmative, the presumption of the argument will again be with the negative, and the affirmative will assume the burden of rebuttal.

The second affirmative speaker faces two duties: (1) the obligation to answer the negative's refutation on the first two issues and (2) the need to complete the affirmative's prima-facie case. If he performs these two duties effectively, the burden of rebuttal again shifts to the negative on all three issues. This process extends throughout rebuttal speeches; burden of rebuttal shifts to the opposing team as each speaker succeeds in transferring the presumption of the argument on any given issue in favor of his team. Effectiveness in overcoming the burden of rebuttal helps determine the winning team.

The third issue on the labor union proposition involves another important point closely related to burden of rebuttal. The negative assumes a burden of proof when it presents a counterplan or alternate solution. This principle does not contradict a previous statement that the burden of proof never shifts from the affirmative. When the negative presents a counterplan, both sides have a burden of proof: the affirmative on the entire case, the negative on its counterproposal.

For example, the negative might advocate that the power of labor unions be increased. Inasmuch as this proposal calls for a change from the status quo, the negative assumes a burden of proof. The issue of need for a change is automatically admitted and the debate narrows to a contest between different solutions. The affirmative continues with its original burden of proof and the negative assumes the burden of proof on its counterplan. To win, either team must show its proposed solution to be superior both to the status quo and to the solution proposed by the opposing team.

Rights That Accrue from Burden of Proof

For every burden, equity gives corresponding rights or advantages. The affirmative has a twofold privilege that offsets the responsibility of burden of proof: the right to interpret the proposition and the right to declare the main issues.

Interpreting the proposition

The affirmative side has the right to define terms and interpret the proposition, but it also has the responsibility of making a reasonable interpretation. Debates sometime result in a quibble because the affirmative gives a misleading interpretation, one that could not reasonably be expected from the statement of the proposition. The affirmative should not attempt "to catch the negative off guard" by suggesting a meaning contrary to logic. To insist that some word has a meaning contrary to that usually given by informed people leads to a quibble over the meaning of terms rather than to a debate on the issues. For example, suppose that in the proposition, *Resolved, That the non-Communist nations of the world should establish an economic community,* the affirmative defines "economic community" as a loose treaty among existing regional economic communities. Has the affirmative really proposed a significant change? No, because an economic community requires more than a treaty agreement. It presupposes an organization with sufficient powers to bring about a significant change from the status quo. Abuse of the affirmative's right of interpretation results in poor debates.

In reaching a correct interpretation, it must be considered that every proposition involves a principle. For example, the proposition that the federal government should aid state schools by annual grants for building construction has the underlying principle of federal versus state support of education. Although the affirmative may favor partial support by the states and school districts, it must contend for the principle of federal aid. On the other hand, the negative may advocate any number of reforms, such as improved tax programs, economy in administration, and greater cooperation between states; but it should not include an extension of the principle of federal aid. To insure a good debate, the proposition must be interpreted to bring out the basic principles inherent in the resolution.

Declaring the main issues

The main issues inhere in the question; they are not a matter of arbitrary choice. They must be discovered through study and analysis, and there can be no productive debate until they are found and set forth. The affirmative must assume this responsibility. If the affirmative fails to set forth one or more of the inherent issues, the negative should introduce them. Any essential issue introduced by the negative must be met by the affirmative. To win the debate, the affirmative must have the advantage on all real issues. The right to set them forth, regardless of arrangement, is an affirmative privilege not to be denied by the negative.

Corresponding Negative Rights

If the affirmative should give an unfair interpretation of the proposition, the negative may assume any one of several positions, depending upon the circumstances of the debate and the nature of the interpretation. If possible, the negative should accept the affirmative's interpretation even though the definitions may appear improper. Such acceptance prevents quibbling and insures a debate on the resolution rather than about its meaning. If, however, the affirmative's definitions seem unreasonable, the negative should state its objections immediately and request the affirmative to change its interpretation in accordance with the negative objections and the statement of the proposition. Such objections should be based upon reason and not upon mere preference. If the affirmative refuses to change, the negative may debate the proposition as defined, but should continue to point out the unwarranted interpretation. Such procedure permits a debate on issues, and at the same time gives the negative psychological advantage because of its willingness to continue the debate in spite of the affirmative's objectionable interpretation.

As a last resort the negative may refuse the affirmative's interpretation. It should then define the meaning of the proposition and continue the debate according to its own definition. Under this circumstance, the debate must be decided on the reasonableness of the opposing interpretations, not upon the issues of the question. Such a procedure, if widely followed, would surely bring educational debate into disrepute.

Processes of Debate Procedure

The procedures for educational debate call for a threefold process, the parts of which must be clearly distinguished.

A threefold process

Debate consists of building-up, tearing-down, and rebuilding processes. The building-up process comes in the constructive speeches. Each team must present positive cases capable of proving its side of the proposition. The cases depend upon the development of the main issues. In policy propositions, these issues involve the need for a change, the practicability of the proposal, and the desirability of the proposed change.

Each side must also refute the opposing team's case. Refutation is the process of destroying opposing arguments. It has limited use in the constructive speeches for answering opposing arguments necessary for a continuation of one's own case. However, it is used extensively in the rebuttal speeches.

Finally, each team must rebuild its own case against the attacks of the opposing team. This rebuilding process comes primarily in the rebuttal speeches. The dual purpose of any rebuttal is first to tear down the opponent's case and second to rebuild one's own case. At the conclusion of a debate, the winning team must have its own case established and the opposing case destroyed or definitely weakened. Effective debating includes all three processes.

New issues in rebuttal speeches

The entire constructive case must be presented in the constructive speeches; no new issues may be introduced in the rebuttal speeches. The principle of no new issues in rebuttal speeches must not be confused with that of no new material. New material or evidence may be presented in the rebuttal speeches on main issues already introduced in the constructive speeches. If new material could not be presented in rebuttal speeches, there would be only a rehashing of evidence already given. New supporting material and new alignment of argument in rebuttal speeches are essential because they aid in the tearing-down and building-up processes. The only limitation is that no new issue, necessary to the establishment of the original case, be introduced in the rebuttals.

Affirmative and Negative Positions

The affirmative and negative positions on the proposition must be clearly distinguishable as upholding the opposing principles inherent in the proposition.

Affirmative

The stand of the affirmative depends largely on the statement of the proposition. Although the affirmative has the right to interpret the proposition, it has no right to make any changes in it. The affirmative must set forth the essential significance of the question at issue.

The following resolution may be used to illustrate this principle: *Resolved, That the federal government should adopt a uniform retail sales tax.* The statement obligates the affirmative to uphold the federal retail sales tax as the best means of raising additional revenue. The affirmative has considerable latitude in determining how much additional revenue may be needed and how much can reasonably be expected from a sales tax. It may favor measures such as rigorous economy in government and increased penalties for delinquent taxes in addition to an increased sales tax. The statement of the proposition, however, requires the affirmative to advocate the retail sales tax as the primary source of gaining additional revenue, and this obligation holds despite the affirmative's right to interpret the proposition. The affirmative must show (1) a need for more revenue, (2) that a federal sales tax would prove practical in providing the needed revenue, and (3) that the sales tax would not be accompanied by more evils than it would remedy.

Negative

The negative may assume any one of four possible positions: (1) The negative's case may consist entirely of refutation. (2) It may uphold the status quo. (3) It may uphold the status quo with modifications. (4) It may present a counterplan. Which procedure should be followed? There can be no stock answer to this question because the procedure will vary with each debate proposition. The negative should analyze the proposition carefully before deciding. A few suggestions about each attitude follow; these suggestions apply regardless of the proposition.

Pure Refutation. This procedure consists of an entirely destructive case. The negative may refuse to take a stand either for the present system or for any substitute; its case consists entirely of countering the affirmative's main contentions. For example, on the federal retail sales tax proposition, the negative's main contentions could be: (1) There is no need for additional revenue. (2) A federal retail sales tax would prove impractical. (3) The proposal would be undesirable. Although this attitude is within the realm of debate ethics, psychologically it may prove unwise. Few audiences react favorably to pure refutation, an entirely destructive attitude. An audience would not, however, resent refutation prefaced to show that the proposed destruction will ultimately prove to be constructive.

Status Quo. The extreme position in upholding the status quo contends that all is satisfactory. This stand denies the affirmative's indictment of the present system; for example, the existing tax program is satisfactory. In most instances such a contention is unnecessary and may actually prove to be dangerous. A more logical position contends that although minor evils exist, the status quo is sound in principle and can remedy its own shortcomings. Furthermore, the negative may show the impossibility of devising a perfect plan and argue the superiority of the present system over the changes suggested by the affirmative. When taking this position, the negative usually contends that the affirmative has exaggerated the evils and accompanies such reasoning with a strong defense of the status quo.

Status Quo with Modifications. The negative may concede inadequacies in the status quo and show that certain modifications will remedy present evils; for example, the present tax structure is adequate if we will practice economy in governmental administration. The negative that takes this stand usually presents some definite modification and shows that its proposal does not change the fundamental principles of the present system. Such a contention should be prefaced with a clear exposition of the principles of the status quo. Any admitted weakness should be attributed to the way the system operates, not to its fundamental principle. Whether or not this negative attitude should be used extensively depends upon the strength of the affirmative's indictment. If the weakness is not inherent, the negative may use this position to advantage.

A negative team shows poor judgment when it contests any issue upon which the affirmative has a strong advantage from the very nature of the issue. Rather, the negative should concentrate on those issues in which it has an inherent advantage. If it appears difficult to uphold the present system, the negative can well afford to argue for the status quo with modifications.

The Counterplan. If the negative finds it inadvisable to undertake pure refutation, to uphold the status quo, or to argue for modification of the present system, it may present a counterplan, for example, a proposal that the federal government levy a tax on real property. The counterplan offers a solution that differs in principle from both the status quo and the affirmative proposal; the federal government does not now levy taxes on real property. This somewhat extreme type of negative case often proves to be the least satisfactory. It automatically admits the need for a change and thus resolves the debate into a comparison of two proposed solutions. The negative in offering a counterplan loses the presumption of the argument and assumes the burden of proof on the alternate solution. Furthermore, the negative must prove that its counterplan is superior to the affirmative's proposal. The counterplan is usually the most difficult type of case to uphold.

Summary

The general theories and principles of educational debate enable the college debater to engage in formal argument intelligently. The affirmative has the burden of proof in debate with its off-setting advantages—the right to interpret the question and to declare the main issues. The interpretation should be reasonable; the issues presented must be fundamental.

The burden of rebuttal means the obligation to answer a prima-facie argument. This burden is on the negative after the affirmative presents a prima-facie case, but it may be shifted to the affirmative upon effective refutation. The entire constructive case should be presented in the constructive speeches; no essential issue should be withheld until the rebuttal speeches.

The affirmative position in a debate must uphold the essential features called for by the proposition. Negative teams have a choice of four different positions: (1) to argue pure refutation, (2) to uphold the status quo, (3) to uphold the status quo with modifications, (4) to present a counterplan. The proposition to be debated determines the choice; the choice should always be based upon reason, not mere preference.

Oral Assignment

Divide the class into several panels with no more than seven people on a panel. Each panel should elect its chairman. Assign each panel the topic "What is the problem relative to the question chosen for classroom debate?" At the next class period the panels should conduct their discussions simultaneously. The panels may be assigned to various parts of the classroom or to separate small rooms if they are available. Each participant should prepare an outline for the discussion. The chairman should be assigned to make a five-minute report on the conclusions reached by his panel at the next class session.

Collateral Readings

Courtney, Luther W., and Glenn R. Capp, *Practical Debating*, Ch. 2. Philadelphia: J. B. Lippincott Co., 1949.

Crocker, Lionel, *Argumentation and Debate,* Ch. 4. New York: American Book Co., 1944.

Ehninger, Douglas, and Wayne Brockriede, *Decision by Debate*, Ch. 7. New York: Dodd, Mead & Co., 1963.

McBath, James H., ed., *Argumentation and Debate*, Ch. 7. New York: Holt, Rinehart & Winston, Inc., 1963.

McBurney, James H., and Glen E. Mills, *Argumentation and Debate: Techniques of a Free Society*, Ch. 2. New York: The Macmillan Company, 1964.

Windes, Russel R., and Arthur N. Kruger, *Championship Debating*, pp. 23-33. Portland, Me.: J. Weston Walch, Publishers, 1961.

4

Selecting and Phrasing the Debate Proposition

Subjects for argumentation and debate take the form of propositions that specify a particular course of action. Topics for discussion may be stated in question form; for example, "What should be the foreign trade policy of the United States?" Subjects for narration or description may be expressed in phrases, for example, "The foreign trade policy of the United States." Propositions for debate call for a resolution, for example, "Resolved, That the United States should join the European Common Market."

A national proposition for intercollegiate debate is selected each year by a five-man committee consisting of one representative each from Delta Sigma Rho-Tau Kappa Alpha, Pi Kappa Delta, Phi Rho Pi, the American Forensic Association, and the Speech Association of America. The member appointed by the Speech Association of America represents those colleges not affiliated with national forensic organizations. A national topic facilitates the scheduling of debate tournaments and public debates, but debating need not be restricted to this topic. Variety in the use of topics adds interest and educational values to forensic programs and classes in argumentation. For an understanding of the proposition for argumentation, consider the (1) types, (2) characteristics, and (3) requirements for phrasing.

Types of Propositions

Three types of propositions predominate—policy, value, and fact. Since the method of arguing each type varies, consider the following explanations of the types.

54

Policy

A proposition of policy proposes a change in an existing political, social, or economic order. It exemplifies the type of questions debated in Congress or in any deliberative assembly. Policy propositions raise the question "Should this action be taken?" "The federal government should decrease the income tax" is an example. A sound case of fundamental arguments may be assembled to show that either the income tax should or should not be decreased. Public opinion differs concerning the merits of lowering the income tax rate. Some tax authorities commend this form of taxation, others oppose it. The aims of debate on propositions of public policy should be to determine which side offers greater advantages to the general public. There is no such thing as "the truth" concerning questions of policy because truthful arguments exist on both sides. The following are additional propositions of policy:

> Resolved, That the United States should extend diplomatic recognition to the Communist government of China.
> Resolved, That the federal government should establish a national program of public work for the unemployed.
> Resolved, That the non-Communist nations of the world should establish an economic community.

Value

A proposition of value relates to the worth of a proposal, asking whether it is good or bad, right or wrong, sound or unsound; for example, *Resolved, That socialism is superior to communism*. This proposition questions the worth or value of existing orders; it does not suggest a change. Propositions of value, like propositions of policy, demand no such thing as ultimate truth. Our sense of values change; what we consider truth today might not be considered truth tomorrow. For a profitable debate, standards for evaluation must be agreed upon early in the debate; otherwise, the opposing teams may not debate the same principles. Nonetheless, sound arguments may be marshaled on either side of propositions that question the worth of things. The following are examples:

> Resolved, That capital punishment is justifiable.
> Resolved, That segregation in public schools is an unchristian practice.
> Resolved, That the use of nuclear weapons in warfare is justifiable.

Fact

A proposition of fact argues the truth or the falsity of a statement. It asks the question "Is this true?" The purpose in debating resolutions of fact is to secure acceptance or rejection of a statement of alleged fact. Truth exists in propositions of fact although its determination may be highly improbable if not impossible. An example is the proposition *Resolved, That the European Common Market has promoted economic recovery in Europe.* It cannot be denied that either the European Common Market is or is not responsible for improved economic conditions among its member nations. The fact of improved economic stability exists; the cause for the condition may be strongly disputed. Whether we can prove or disprove the assertion does not alter the possibility of presenting the cases for and against such a fact in formal debate. Obviously, only questions of fact that remain unsettled may be debated profitably. The following are propositions of fact:

> Resolved, That a compulsory automobile insurance program improves traffic safety.
> Resolved, That the foreign aid program of the United States prevented the spread of communism.
> Resolved, That war causes an increase in the crime rate of a nation.

Questions about which people could never agree even in part should not be debated, nor should questions of fact capable of proof by concrete evidence or by direct testimony. For example, whether our national budget for defense has increased in recent years offers no grounds for debate because factual proof may be found by examining the national budget and other available documentary evidence.

Propositions of policy usually make better questions for educational debate than either those of value or of fact. They are more realistic because they relate to present-day problems, those debated in life situations of advocacy by policy-determining groups.

Characteristics of a Good Proposition

As a college student in a course in argumentation and debate, you may be asked to select your own topics for practice speeches. As an intercollegiate debater, you may be asked to vote on the national proposition to determine your school's vote. Knowledge of what constitutes an acceptable proposition may serve you well. Consider the following characteristics.

Current interest

The old questions that involve discussion of obscure philosophical or theological opinions no longer interest people. Whether or not ten thousand angels can stand on the point of a cambric needle matters little to the average man. The justice of some proposed welfare measure or the practicability of some plan to control nuclear testing commands more attention than does the discussion of the physical characteristics of angels.

The problem of world trade has been selected five times since 1930 as the national debate topic. Each time current changes in world trade relationships called forth the proposition. For example, emphasis on the European Common Market motivated the selection of a world trade proposition again in 1962–63. The movement toward economic communities gave an old problem current interest and afforded the opportunity to have debates on a current problem that interested audiences. Usually, propositions related to the life of today should be chosen for public debate and for classroom assignments in argumentation and debate courses.

Continuous interest

Propositions for intercollegiate debate call for a reasonable assurance of continuous interest, since those questions settled before the end of the debate season cannot retain interest. For example, during a presidential campaign two problems that may command attention are plans for electing a president and the question of the national debt. Which of these will continue to be important? The national debt constitutes an ever-present problem; the November elections settle the choice of president for the next four years. On the other hand, if a choice must be made between a question of an international trade policy and a temporary debt-retirement program, the trade policy topic would appeal to more people because of the far-reaching consequences involved.

Several years ago an intrastate debate league chose a proposition calling for a reduction in the state sales tax. Before the end of the debate season, the state legislature passed such a proposal, thus decreasing the interest in and timeliness of the subject. It may sometimes prove wise to sacrifice timeliness in order to secure stability.

Provision for a broad background study

A good proposition has sufficient scope to command thorough analysis and research over the debate season. Those who debate whether or not the United States should decrease the federal income tax would hardly restrict their study to the income tax alone. The proposition affords opportunity for study of the larger problems of taxation and fiscal policy. In addition to elementary texts on economic principles, study could be made of the better treatises on taxation, fiscal policy, national debt, inflation, and related subjects.

The question of a federal scholarship program for superior students would prove interesting for a classroom assignment in a course in argumentation, but it may be too narrow in scope to challenge college debaters over an entire debate season. Conversely, the problem of international trade would probably be too broad in scope for a class assignment, but it affords a good basis for profitable study throughout the forensic year. Good propositions demand inquiry into related fields; they thus contribute to the general culture of the student.

Adaptability to the participants' ability

A good proposition is not above or below the intellectual ability of the student. For example, a question involving a fundamental knowledge of law should not be chosen for college undergraduate students since they are not likely to understand it fully. To debate intelligently that Congress should have the power to override decisions of the Supreme Court requires a thorough knowledge of our political and legal systems. The proposition would serve as a challenging subject for law students. Beginning college students are not likely to have the necessary background to understand the full implications of the question, however, and to require them to debate questions beyond their capacity encourages sophistry.

Such subjects as world trade relationships, the United Nations, the welfare state, and labor-management problems offer broad fields for study within the ability of undergraduate students.

Propositions such as compulsory health insurance, federal aid to education, and the sales tax are good topics for classroom debates, but they may not prove sufficiently challenging as national questions. In short, good propositions enlist the interests and best efforts of debaters without requiring them to debate subjects beyond their ability.

Phrasing the Proposition

A proposition may meet all the requirements for a good subject and still not make a suitable proposition because of improper phrasing. The following suggestions should be considered when a proposition is phrased.

Use a complete sentence

We argue for or against, not about, a proposition. The proposition should be stated in a declarative sentence with two terms and a copula. The subject is one term; the verb is the copula or connecting link; and the word or words after the verb make up the other term. For example, one does not debate about world trade. The following resolution, however, is debatable: *Resolved, That the non-Communist nations of the world should establish an economic community.* "The non-Communist nations" is the subject or first term, "should establish" the verb or copula, and "an economic community" the object or second term.

As stated in the introduction, for purposes of formal debate the proposition should be stated in the form of a resolution, such as *Resolved, That the United Nations should be given control of nuclear power.* For discussion, an informal question serves best; for example, "How can nuclear power be controlled?" The differences are attributable to the inherent natures of discussion and debate. Discussion should consider the various solutions to a problem; debate should weigh the arguments on the two sides of one proposed solution. The resolution indicates clearly the affirmative and negative positions in the argument.

Provide a debatable resolution

A good proposition should have a balance of arguments to prevent giving either side an initial advantage. For example, "the federal government should adopt a uniform retail sales tax" would be more equally balanced than "the federal government should retire its national debt by a uniform retail sales tax." Both pertain to the same question and would involve the same principles, but the latter statement puts too great a burden upon the affirmative because methods other than a sales tax would be necessary to retire the debt.

Resolutions that do not have acceptable standards for comparison make poor propositions, for example, *Resolved, That medicine has done more than law to advance civilization.* The statement gives no criteria for decision. Both the medical and the legal professions have accomplished much in their respective fields, but the two areas are hardly comparable. A similar proposition is *Resolved, That Lincoln was a greater president than Franklin Roosevelt.* Since the two men lived in different periods and faced different issues, no common standard for measurement prevails. Propositions that have no criteria for judging the truth or falsity of the basic principle involved prove unsuitable.

Phrase the proposition affirmatively

Debate propositions are phrased so that the affirmative advocates the change and the negative opposes it. Consider *Resolved, That the United States should retain its present reciprocal trade agreements with foreign nations.* The affirmative must argue against a change before the existing program is indicted. The negative must assume the burden of proving the inadequacy of the status quo, and the affirmative has the presumption in its favor from the beginning. This arrangement is comparable to asking the defense counsel in a criminal lawsuit to present the defense before the state presents the prosecution. The following affirmative statement avoids this confusion: *Resolved, That the United States should discontinue its present reciprocal trade agreements with foreign nations.*

Propositions do not necessarily have to contain a negative term to violate this principle. For example, the proposition *Resolved, That the United States should not join the European Common Market* is clearly a negative statement. The proposition *Resolved, That the United States should continue its present trade policy with the European Common Market* is also negative because it does not require the affirmative to indict the present system nor to assume the burden of proof.

Include only one central idea

Improperly phrased propositions may contain two or more proposals, for example, *Resolved, That the United States should decrease the tax on income and adopt a sales tax.* This resolution places upon the affirmative the double duty of showing (1) that the income tax should be decreased and (2) that a sales tax should be adopted. The negative side might reasonably concede the proposal to decrease income taxes and contest the adoption of a sales tax. There would be little need to counter both parts of the proposition. A similar condition would result with the proposition *Resolved, That the United States should extend diplomatic recognition to Communist China and vote for her acceptance into the United Nations.* It might be possible to establish a case for recognition and fail to prove a case for membership in the United Nations.

Certain propositions that approach a dual nature may be acceptable for formal debate, such as *Resolved, That the President of the United States should be elected for a single term of six years.* The two ideas "single term" and "six years" have long been associated as a single idea as opposed to a four-year term with no provisions against re-election. A good proposition is *Resolved, That the federal government should own and operate the railroads.* Since ownership presupposes operation, the proposal need not be classified as dual. The same could not be said for *Resolved, That the federal government should own and operate the railroads and coal mines.* An acceptable case might be advanced for nationalizing one industry but not the other.

Avoid ambiguous terms

Terms capable of more than one interpretation will lead to confusion and result in quibbling. Consider the following: *Resolved, That the income tax is superior to the sales tax.* The term "superior" is ambiguous. Does it mean that one tax is more equitable, more productive, easier to administer, or that it fits better into our present tax program? The proposition could arouse more discussion over the meaning of "superior" than on the issues of the question because no acceptable standard of measurement of the term exists.

Another proposition ambiguously stated is *Resolved, That the federal government should aid private colleges and universities.* What is meant by "aid"? Does it mean that the federal government should provide funds for buildings, promote scholarships for superior students, grant additional tax concessions, or make other provisions to encourage private schools? Valuable time would be consumed in reaching an understanding of the term.

The term "economic community" in the 1962–63 national proposition, *Resolved, That the non-Communist nations of the world should establish an economic community,* caused confusion when affirmative teams neglected to define the term clearly in the opening speech. Definitions of this term varied all the way from a "loose treaty agreement" to a "world government with police powers." The first negative speaker often wasted valuable time refuting a principle different from that presented in the second affirmative speech. Then the negative often charged the affirmative with failure to propose a significant change. The result was a loss of time in an effort by the affirmative to justify its interpretation. Some teams debated the meaning of the term rather than the issues of the proposition.

Avoid prejudiced terms

A proposition contains a prejudiced term when it assumes a point that should be in dispute, for example, *Resolved, That the brutal sport of boxing should be declared illegal.* If the statement of the proposition assumes boxing to be brutal, the negative has the incongruous position of upholding a brutal sport; the term "brutal" assumes a point that should be an issue in the debate. The same is true of the word "inequitable" in *Resolved, That the inequitable income tax should be abolished.* "Inequitable" is clearly a prejudicial term, the use of which gives the affirmative an advantage from the mere statement of the proposition.

Such terms as "fair employment practices," "right to work laws," and "diplomatic recognition," as used in former national questions, were unfortunate because they evoked emotional responses in uninformed people from the mere use of the terms, although the terms had specific meanings apart from the emotional connotations.

Restrict the scope

Acceptable subjects may result in poor debates because the phrasing of the proposition fails to narrow the debate to the time limit. The subject of world trade constitutes an excellent study for debaters; the entire field of world trade is, however, too broad for a debate limited to one hour. For example, *Resolved, That the United States should revise its world trade policies* has no limits. Propositions that properly limit the subject are: *Resolved, That the United States should abolish all tariffs; Resolved, That the United States should join the European Common Market;* or *Resolved, That the non-Communist nations should adopt a policy of free trade.* The following proposition is too broad: *Resolved, That the United States should reform its tax program.* The proposition *Resolved, That the United States should adopt a sales tax* is suitable for debate because it properly restricts the field of taxation. Instead of phrasing the proposition *Resolved, That the American system of education should be reformed,* restrict it to *Resolved, That the federal government should guarantee an opportunity for higher education to all qualified high school graduates.*

Summary

Care in the selection and in the phrasing of the proposition is essential to intelligent debating and profitable classroom assignments. Propositions arise from questions of policy, of value, or of fact. Propositions of policy propose a change in a prevailing social, economic, or political program; propositions of value question the worth of a proposal; propositions of fact seek to determine the existence of alleged facts. Propositions of policy make the best debate questions because they are more frequently debated in life situations.

The following characteristics of a good debate question should be observed: (1) It has current interest. (2) It has continuous interest. (3) It provides for a broad background study. (4) It is adapted to the participant's ability.

The following rules govern the phrasing of debate propositions: (1) Use a complete sentence. (2) Provide a debatable resolution. (3) Phrase the proposition affirmatively. (4) Include only one central idea. (5) Avoid ambiguous terms. (6) Avoid prejudiced terms. (7) Restrict the scope.

Oral Assignment

The chairmen of the panel discussions of the last period should report on the conclusions reached by their panels—time limit, five minutes. Class members should take notes. An open forum should follow the reports.

Collateral Readings

Abernathy, Elton, *The Advocate: A Manual of Persuasion,* Ch. 2. New York: David McKay Co., Inc., 1964.

Courtney, Luther W., and Glenn R. Capp, *Practical Debating,* Ch. 4. Philadelphia: J. B. Lippincott Co., 1949.

Crocker, Lionel, *Argumentation and Debate,* Ch. 2. New York: American Institute of Banking, 1962.

Freeley, Austin J., *Argumentation and Debate,* Ch. 2. Belmont, Calif.: Wadsworth Publishing Co., Inc., 1961.

Huber, Robert B., *Influencing Through Argument,* Ch. 2. New York: David McKay Co., Inc., 1963.

McBurney, James H., and Glen E. Mills, *Argumentation and Debate: Techniques of a Free Society,* Ch. 3. New York: The Macmillan Company, 1964.

III
Preparing for Argument and Debate

5
Finding and
Evaluating Material

A leading forensic director, asked what he considered most important in successful debating, answered, "Know more about the subject than your opponent." Thorough preparation may not be the most interesting part of debating, but it often proves the most rewarding. Almost all successful debaters testify in later life to the value of habits of research acquired from college forensic work. In a survey of fifty former college debaters, this factor was listed among the five most important benefits derived from debating.[1] Representative replies follow: C. J. Humphrey, a prominent lawyer, stated, "Debating taught me early that hard work, diligence, and preparedness often offset the initial advantage of better speakers who are not prepared." Dr. Ralph Phelps, President of Ouachita College, stated, "First, it taught valuable lessons in research. This included a knowledge of sources, digging deeply into a problem, and organization of facts thus found." The Reverend J. W. Bruner, a successful minister, stated, "I would also emphasize that the reading and research . . . broadened my thinking and helped to make me at least conversant on many subjects which I would not have explored otherwise." Frank M. Rosson, Vice-President and General Counsel of the Government Personnel Mutual Life Insurance Company, stated, "It is my firm opinion that the study and preparation of debate cases were of inestimable value in the planning and preparation of law cases and briefs in my later years. . . . The same mechanics employed in the preparation of debate cases I found could be carried over in the preparation of cases on appeal in the appellate courts." In short, finding and eval-

---

1 Edna G. Allen and Glenn R. Capp, "As the Debaters See It," *Speech Activities,* VI, No. 4 (Winter, 1950), 150-53.

uating material result in successful debating and make permanent contributions in later life.

Sources of Material

Before studying the procedure for gathering material, examine the sources from which the debater may draw. Consider the following primary sources.

General knowledge

Instead of going immediately to the library in search of arguments, think first about the proposition—consider its meaning, how it may be narrowed, what fundamental principles inhere, and what the main arguments might be. As a basis for such reflective thought, your general background of information will be helpful. Because of the vastness of modern means of communication, you perhaps have a greater knowledge of current subjects than you may realize; you need only to think reflectively to recall the information. To make a tentative evaluation of material, start by listing the possible arguments on both sides of the resolution. First impressions will undergo changes after further investigation, but putting thoughts on paper stimulates thinking and leads to additional research. Re-examining what has been read, studying new material, and revising initial arguments will enable you to analyze the question and arrange your thoughts logically.

In planning your study, understand the distinction between direct and indirect preparation. The latter comes through experience, travel, association with others, general study, and observation; the former consists of specific research, reflective thought, and reasoning. Both types of preparation are essential, but the debater with a background of general knowledge has the initial advantage.

Consider the following suggestions for developing a general background:

1. Read a newspaper daily. Not all items found in the papers prove helpful, but the general trend of domestic and world affairs, editorials and syndicated columns, the financial section, and special features serve the debater well. Keeping up with current problems pays rich dividends for developing a background of information.

2. Read a news magazine each week. The leading news maga-

zines are *United States News and World Report, Newsweek,* and *Time.* These magazines summarize and synthesize current happenings and keep you abreast of national and international affairs. You can get a broader understanding from the news magazines than from the daily papers alone because news magazines give analytical and extensive accounts of current events.

3. Read some of the better magazines each month, for example, *Harper's, Atlantic, Scribner's, Review of Reviews, Fortune, American Economic Review, Vital Speeches, Academy of Political Science, Survey Graphic,* and other periodicals in special fields of interest. Such magazines ordinarily contain articles based on extensive research that give needed facts and stimulate thinking. Read articles that represent varying points of view; for example, magazines like *The Nation, The New Republic,* and *The Reporter* give a liberal point of view to offset the conservative flavor of some of those magazines already listed. Digest magazines sometimes prove helpful in spite of their condensation, but it is best to read the original articles.

4. Read good books regularly. A regular habit of reading books will add to your background of information. Try to achieve a balance between classical and contemporary books, fiction and nonfiction, prose and poetry. The book review sections of the news magazines and such publications as the *New York Times,* the *Saturday Review, Harper's,* and *Atlantic* will provide information about the leading current books; for information about the classics, consult such books as May Lamberton Becker's *Adventures in Reading,* Francis Xavier Meehan's *Living Upstairs: Reading for Profit and Pleasure,* and John O'Donnell's *Much Loved Books.*

Conferences or interviews

Helpful material may be obtained from interviews or conferences with informed persons, and the college campus offers a fruitful source for such interviews. If, for example, the debate question pertains to the Supreme Court, a professor in political science could be interviewed about the function of our court system. A professor of law could give information on how our courts operate. Interviews with the president of the local bar association, with some prominent attorney or judge, or with an official from the state bar association would be profitable.

Interviews will be most productive after you have studied the subject sufficiently to ask discerning questions. Plan the interview carefully to get the desired information in a minimum of time. Try to obtain information not readily available by reading, to clarify ideas that have arisen from your previous study, to obtain the opinion of the person interviewed, and to get suggestions for additional research. Arrange an appointment and explain the reason for the interview and the purpose that the information will serve. Properly planned and conducted, the interview may prove a valuable source of information.

Public addresses and programs

Valuable information may also be obtained by listening to lectures, discussions, and debates on the subject for debate. Chapter 2 discussed a planned program of lectures by a debate group as a cooperative method for preparation. Individual members of the debate squad may supplement this cooperative effort by seeking programs that bear on the subject. Other sources of information which may relate to phases of the subject or allied subjects are discussion programs on television, community lectures and discussions, and lecturers for local civic and study clubs.

Correspondence and questionnaires

Correspondence may be necessary to supplement materials found locally. The Library of Congress, Division of Bibliography, Washington, D. C., furnishes excellent bibliographies on many questions; selected bibliographies may be secured also from federal and state departments. For example, if the question deals with an educational program, the following departments and organizations in Washington, D. C., could supply bibliographies and other material: the United States Department of Health, Education, and Welfare; the National Education Association of the United States; and the National Advisory Committee on Education. The state educational association in almost any state would also furnish material upon request.

If the proposition pertains to some bill pending before Congress, copies of the bill may be secured from your congressman or senator. Many societies and leagues furnish partisan publications on questions affecting their causes. On socialized medicine, for example, write the American Medical Association or your state medical association. The cost of such material is small.

Many state university extension departments furnish material for the cost of return postage. This material may take the form of handbooks, clippings from newspapers, and long quotations from books. Some well-selected material is mimeographed or printed and sold to debaters at cost. It may be possible to obtain pertinent articles and pamphlets through correspondence with city librarians.

The questionnaire is useful in securing the latest information, and material thus secured has the advantage of originality. Suppose the proposition for debate contends that your state should adopt a retail sales tax. Information concerning the status of the sales tax may be obtained through questionnaires to the various departments of state. Such questions as the following would provide useful information:

1. When was the sales tax adopted in your state?
2. Has it been used continuously since its adoption?
3. What is the sales tax rate?
4. Has the rate been changed since its adoption?
5. Other than the sales tax, what are chief sources of tax income in your state?
6. Approximately what percentage of the revenue from the sales tax is required for its collection?
7. About what percentage of the revenue of your state is derived from the sales tax?
8. Compared to your state income tax, if any, what is your opinion of the extent of evasions of the sales tax? _____ greater than income tax; _____ about the same; _____ less than income tax.
9. Compared to your state income tax, if any, what is the public's attitude toward the sales tax? _____ more favorable toward the sales tax; _____ about the same; _____ less favorable toward the sales tax.
10. As a source for state taxation, rate the following types of taxes as first, second, third, and fourth: _____ income tax; _____ sales tax; _____ real property tax; _____ natural resource tax.

Know precisely the information needed before making out the questionnaire; otherwise the material secured may not be helpful. The value of the questionnaire depends on the percentage of returns, and short questions usually receive a higher percentage of replies than long and involved queries. The following suggestions should prove helpful:

1. Send a letter (typed, not mimeographed) with the questionnaire. State briefly the purpose and the importance of the information sought; express thanks for the courtesy of a reply; offer to send a compilation of your findings.
2. Type or mimeograph the questionnaire on paper size 8½ by 11 inches. Observe these rules:
   a. Use one side of the paper only; leave sufficient space for the answers.
   b. Make questions clear and to the point.
   c. Where exact information is not essential, ask for approximations. Avoid making it necessary to consult files, make telephone calls, or otherwise inconvenience the one who is asked for information.
   d. On matters of opinion use multiple choice questions. For example, instead of asking "What is your opinion of the sales tax?" use the check method; _____ for, _____ neutral, _____ against.
3. Send all letters and questionnaires first class mail.
4. Enclose a self-addressed and stamped envelope.
5. Send a second letter if no reply is received within ten days. A second follow-up letter may be sent.

Discussion

Discussion can become a major source of information through common efforts of a debate squad. The well-planned forensic program makes use of an exchange of ideas and serves as a method of pooling materials. Talking ideas over with others will help clarify your own thinking and improve your facility at expressing yourself on the subject. Discuss the subject with your roommate, your debate colleagues, and your professors. (Chapter 2 explained a program of formal and informal discussions.) Informal consideration of material and tentative plans of argument should be discussed first; these considerations lead naturally to the more formal discussion methods. Both formal and informal discussions help in cooperative preparation.

Research

Research constitutes the most important method of preparation. Consider the following sources:

Encyclopedias. As an initial step, consult a standard encyclopedia for a brief over-all view of the subject before making a detailed investigation from other sources. The general view derived from an encyclopedia helps acquaint you with the subject as a whole and indicates the direction for your research. Old editions are kept up-to-date by supplementary volumes; for example, *Encyclopedia Britannica* publishes its yearbook, *Britannica Book of the Year; The Encyclopedia Americana* issues the annual yearbook, *The Americana; The New International Encyclopedia* publishes *The New International Yearbook.* They treat economic, political, and social questions at length and include well-selected bibliographies. The references listed in the encyclopedias will lead to additional material which, in turn, will also contain bibliographies. With these aids, you can compile a working bibliography in short order. These sources plus those secured through correspondence and interviews will properly launch your study.

Source Books and Textbooks. Having gained an overall view of the subject, start your research in earnest by consulting source books and textbooks for basic knowledge.

In using a library, consult the card catalogue for bibliographical aids. All books in the library are listed alphabetically by author, title, and subject matter. Frequently you may have difficulty in finding articles or books that treat a given proposition directly. Suppose, for instance, the proposition is stated *Resolved, That the United Nations should be changed to a federal world government.* Most likely you will not find an article or book with this exact title, but you can select key words or associated terms and search for articles whose titles suggest other topics. Titles such as "United States Foreign Policy," "League of Nations," "Federation," or "Confederation" invite further study. To one who has an inquiring mind, the investigation of many topics will usually yield constructive material.

Since a thorough investigation must precede intelligent debating, concern yourself first with gaining background knowledge through source books. In the initial stages of research, give little attention to pro and con arguments. Do not restrict your investigation to the immediate question; give attention to related fields. For example, if the question relates to federal aid to education, study school administration, school finance, taxation for school purposes, and similar subjects.

Magazines and Newspapers. After gaining basic knowledge, give attention to dependable magazines and newspapers, such as those listed earlier in this chapter, for specific arguments. Evaluate all news stories cautiously; items disseminated by the news gathering agencies such as the Associated Press and the United Press International prove most reliable. Consult the *New York Times Index* for a complete listing of newspaper articles; most newspapers will carry similar news items on the same dates. Use the *Readers' Guide* and *Poole's Index* to find magazine articles. *Readers' Guide*, published monthly, is made into annual volumes by many libraries and into three-year volumes by others, and it lists magazine articles the same way as the card catalogue lists books—by author, title, and subject matter. Newspapers and magazines prove invaluable for keeping up to date on current questions, but be discriminating in your choice of articles.

Governmental and Private Documents. Use government publications to find authentic material and statistical information. The annual and monthly reports of state and federal departments provide reliable facts.

The *Congressional Record* may be invaluable as a source for current legislative debates on your subject. The official journal of Congress, it is published daily during congressional sessions and carries all congressional debates. Other pertinent articles and addresses are published in the appendixes.

The Library of Congress publishes governmental documents on almost all subjects. Many university libraries are depositories for such documents. Lists of references may be secured by writing the Division of Bibliography, Library of Congress, Washington, D. C. The *Catalogue of Public Documents* and the *Monthly Catalogue* will probably be available in your university library. Send orders for individual copies of governmental pamphlets to the Superintendent of Documents, Library of Congress, Washington, D. C.

Of special importance to college debaters is Public Law 88-246, passed by the Eighty-eighth Congress on December 30, 1963. This act provides for the "preparation and printing of compilations of materials relating to annual high school and college debate topics." House Document No. 363, dated September 1964, was the first publication issued under this act. It contains an excellent compilation of articles, analyses, and official statements on the national debate topic. Copies may be received free from your congressman and senator or from the United States Government Printing Office for one dollar.

Certain standard government documents prove helpful on almost all topics: The *Statistical Abstract of the United States* can be secured through the Government Printing Office, Washington, D. C., and the *Federal Reserve Bulletin* can be ordered from the Federal Reserve Board in Washington, D. C. In addition to official publications, many special pamphlets and books are issued by interested organizations and private research centers. The following publications provide needed factual data: *The World Almanac,* available through the *World-Telegram and Sun,* New York City; *The Statesman's Yearbook,* the Macmillan Company, New York City; *Information Please Almanac,* also by the Macmillan Company; the *Book of States* and various state almanacs. Other materials are readily available through public relations divisions of interested organizations. Some of these sources may show personal bias, but the serious student learns to study articles critically.

Handbooks. Several "debaters' handbooks" contain material and suggestions prepared especially for debaters. For example, the H. W. Wilson Company, New York City, publishes the *Reference Shelf Series;* J. Weston Walch, Publishers, Portland, Maine, issues a handbook series annually; The Congressional Digest Corporation of Washington, D. C., publishes the *Congressional Digest.* These publications contain selected articles, suggested interpretations, analyses, briefs, and bibliographies. Do not use the analyses contained in such handbooks as substitutes for independent research and analysis; use them as aids.

Attitudes in Research

Procedures and sources of research serve the debater well in thorough preparation, but the attitude he acquires toward research is also important.

The inquiring attitude

Develop an inquiring mind; unless you become a discoverer you will not get very far. Many false trails will be followed, for no one can tell beforehand exactly what articles will prove most helpful. In debate, as in almost all activities, persistency and consistency eventually prove effective. If you cultivate a real desire to find material, you will not lack opportunity.

Because you cannot incorporate in your arguments all the good material you find, some debaters may question the wisdom of collecting material not to be used in their debates. However, the information gained from investigation and the new outlook that comes from long hours of study are permanent assets—the tests applied to each argument make their contribution. Superficial indeed is the thinking that exhausts itself in the delivery of a few opinions or excerpts from digest materials prepared especially for debaters. Thorough investigation of national or international problems may lead to real contributions in later life. An interest in information comes through cultivating the inquiring mind.

The tentative attitude

Adopt a tentative rather than a fixed attitude toward questions during the early stages of investigation. The proposition should be approached with an open mind, not simply with the attitude of finding arguments to support preconceived ideas.

It may often prove difficult to distinguish between fact and opinion, especially when reading propaganda material. A good exercise is to read an article and classify each statement on the basis of fact or opinion; such classification will likely show a preponderance of the latter. Consider your own extreme views and ascertain if their source is fact or otherwise. If you are fully honest with yourself, you will find that often your views are prejudices rather than convictions.

Many matters once accepted as fact change. Nothing remains static. Note these common beliefs of the past which have been disproved: the world is flat; women are not physically able to use a typewriter for extended periods; air brakes cannot possibly stop a train; man will black out if he travels faster than sixty miles an hour. On the other hand, many theories or opinions of the past are demonstrable facts today, for example: germs cause communicable diseases; man's life expectancy can be extended; man can perfect a flying machine; a nuclear bomb capable of destroying an entire city is possible. In research, adopt the scientific attitude. The true scientist never works with a closed mind; he accepts certain hypotheses as true tentatively, but he depends upon further investigation to prove or disprove the hypotheses. Accept findings tentatively and alter your opinions if further investigation warrants change.

The discriminating attitude

Research calls for discrimination in reading. One of the common errors of immature debaters is that they believe everything they read. Some experienced debaters, on the other hand, acquire a propaganda neurosis—they do not believe anything they read. Alfred Korzybski [2] once said that "the two easiest ways to slide through life are (1) to believe everything and (2) to believe nothing." Either attitude relieves one of the necessity of thinking, of weighing arguments and evidence, of sifting opinions, and of coming to individual conclusions. Discriminating reading may take more energy, but it is necessary for any worthwhile research.

When a Senate committee was investigating activities of certain munition makers of World War I, a stinging denunciation of the committee appeared in an editorial of a popular magazine. This editorial gave statistics to prove its contentions of malpractices; these statistics contradicted the committee findings, based upon authoritative sources, before the committee published its conclusions. Upon investigation, it was discovered that the publishers of the magazine owned a large share of stock in a munitions factory. The opinion and the interpretation of purported facts by the magazine were based upon personal bias and selfish interests. The discriminating reader must weigh all statements carefully if he desires to find correct factual information.

Many of the tests of evidence and reasoning in succeeding chapters will help you distinguish between conflicting information encountered in research. It suffices here to caution you to cultivate the discriminating as well as the inquiring mind.

The weighing attitude

Recognize that facts and argument exist on both the affirmative and the negative sides of every debate proposition and issue in question. Often the evidence and reasoning may almost balance. Many debaters acquire the "all or none" attitude in their research, causing them to make dogmatic statements and sweeping conclu-

---

2 Irving J. Lee, *Language Habits in Human Affairs* (New York: Harper & Row, Publishers, 1941), p. xx.

sions. They think that an argument must be either 100 per cent true or 100 per cent false. The actual situation may be that it is 51 per cent true and 49 per cent false; it may even be 50-50. Associate Justice Robert Jackson once made a speech in which he discussed certain principles of education at length. At the conclusion of his talk, he expressed the belief that what he had said was about 51 per cent correct. He explained further that, since he had to act on the matter, he would act on his 51 per cent belief the same as if it were a 100 per cent belief. He recognized the close margin on which he had to base his decision.

The proposition *Resolved, That the federal government should adopt a retail sales tax* is illustrative. Fundamentally sound arguments and abundant evidence may be found on both sides of the proposition and on each argument for either side. One must make a decision on the matter, weighing advantage against disadvantage. Since equally intelligent people arrive at opposite conclusions through such a procedure, it becomes evident that the argument and evidence are not all on one side.

Recording Material

Wide reading on a subject is not enough. Through careful notes, you should make all worthwhile material available for future use. Of course, some materials may not be worth taking notes on because they reveal shallow thinking, false conclusions, and immature opinions; thus, the first problem in taking notes involves deciding what to record. You need not take full notes on everything when you begin your study because your first reading should be in source books for background understanding. When the general lines of the argument are clear in your mind, more copious notes will be in order. Naturally, more pages of notes than can be used will be made. Copious notes offer a wider choice of material when final arguments must be rounded into shape.

You must decide for yourself what method to use in making notes. Although no fixed rules prevail, you should adopt a definite plan and follow it rigorously in order to avoid wasted effort. You may find that cards offer the most convenient means for recording notes. There are cards three by five inches, four by six inches, or five by eight inches; the four-by-six size is large enough to contain ample material and is convenient to use. Jotting down scraps

of information on pieces of paper, envelopes, and margins of textbooks proves almost worthless.

Some debaters prefer to use a notebook instead of cards. The
notebook proves convenient for note taking, but it may be awkward
to use in a debate. If you choose a notebook, select the loose-leaf
variety so that the notes and arguments can be filed properly. Use
an alphabetical index or an index of your own devising; to be of
value the material must be easily located during a debate.

You may decide for yourself what notes to take and what form
to use, but there remains little choice on some matters—simple
honesty and efficiency demand that certain rules be followed.
Quotations must be accurate and should be acknowledged by use
of quotation marks. If you wish to record only the gist of the
writer's ideas and express them in your own words, do not juggle
the thought and the words of the author; give an accurate representation of his ideas. Never quote a few isolated sentences in a
paragraph or a few paragraphs at random unless the sentences and
paragraphs so selected represent accurately the conclusions of the
author. The omission of a word, a phrase, or a clause within the
sentence, or a sentence or two within the paragraph, may change
the writer's meaning. Misrepresentation through faulty quotation
is indefensible. It falsifies the author's purpose and adds the weight
of his name to an argument without his consent. A man's printed
opinion may be as dear a possession as a piece of material property.

The forms for card notes are shown on page 80. If the quotation
or note is too long for one card, use additional cards, lettered *a, b,*
and *c.* If you find opinions similar to one on a given card, indicate
such opinions by a cross reference. If the matter contained on the
card constitutes argument for the opponent, write down on the
same card a brief refutation of the argument or put such refutation
on a separate card with a cross reference on each card. Do not be
satisfied until you find refutation material on all possible points.
Dependence on your memory for refutation and sources of evidence
usually invites defeat—under stress of a closely contested point, a
lapse of memory may occur.

In recording notes, you should quote original sources rather
than books or articles based on them. If the debate concerns some
bill or similar document, secure an official copy of the matter;
instead of quoting from a book review, quote from the original
book. Certain publications that have established reputations for

6″

Author, Title, Magazine or Book, Page
Quotation or gist of article
Cross references

4″

or

6″

Topic
Quotation or gist of article
Cross references or refutation
Author, Title, Magazine or Book, Page

4″

accuracy of quotations and honesty in selecting representative parts may be accepted without question, but make it a rule to secure the original when possible. When quoting, be sure to give the source. To read from a work proves more effective than to read from a card, though a debater can hardly carry along all books used in his preparation.

Summary

Consider the many sources of debate material: (1) general knowledge, (2) conferences and interviews, (3) correspondence and questionnaires, (4) discussion, and (5) research. Adopt a systematic plan for research and include the following sources: (1) encyclopedias, (2) source books and current texts, (3) periodicals and newspapers, (4) governmental and private documents, and (5) handbooks.

Acquire an intelligent attitude toward research. The proper attitude includes: (1) an inquiring mind, (2) a tentative rather than a fixed attitude, (3) a discriminating mind, and (4) a weighing attitude.

The recording of materials to be used in the debate may take the form of: (1) cards of such size as desired, or (2) a notebook— preferably loose-leaf so that filing may be done conveniently. At all times remember to be fair in recording material. Whenever possible, make notes from original sources rather than from books or articles based on these sources.

Oral Assignment

Divide the class for another round of panel discussions on the subject "How can the problem best be solved?" on the topic chosen for classroom debates. Have each panel elect a chairman different from the chairmen of the first panel discussions. The chairman should give a five-minute report on the conclusion reached by his panel at the next class session.

Collateral Readings

Ehninger, Douglas, and Wayne Brockriede, *Decision by Debate,* Chs. 4, 5, 6. New York: Dodd, Mead & Co., 1963.

Freeley, Austin J., *Argumentation and Debate,* Ch. 4. Belmont, Calif.: Wadsworth Publishing Co., Inc., 1961.

Huber, Robert B., *Influencing Through Argument,* Ch. 4. New York: David McKay Co., Inc., 1963.

Kruger, Arthur N., *Modern Debate,* Ch. 6. New York: McGraw-Hill Book Co., Inc., 1960.

McBath, James H., ed., *Argumentation and Debate,* Ch. 5. New York: Holt, Rinehart & Winston, Inc., 1963.

Nichols, Alan, *Discussion and Debate,* Part I, Ch. 3. New York: Harcourt, Brace & World, Inc., 1941.

6
Analyzing the Proposition

Through analysis one considers a proposition in its various parts, determines its underlying philosophy, interprets its meaning, decides what should be excluded, and arrives at the main issues and subordinate points. The ultimate purpose of analysis is to discover the main issues—the basic points upon which the establishment or overthrow of the proposition depends. These main issues inhere in the proposition; they must be discovered through diligent study, reflective thinking, logical reasoning, and careful analysis, and they become the main divisions of the case. For example, the main issues of the proposition *Resolved, That the United States should join the European Common Market* may be stated as follows:

1. Do weaknesses in the United States foreign trade policy call for a change?
2. Would membership in the European Common Market remedy these weaknesses?
3. Would joining the European Common Market be a desirable policy for the United States?

When the affirmative side states these issues positively, they become the affirmative's main contentions. Each contention must be proved as a requirement to a prima-facie case. The negative side must then negate or concede each of the affirmative main contentions; when the negative side negates the main issues, they become the negative's main contentions in the debate. As explained in Chapter 3, the negative side will prevail if it can successfully defeat one or more of the affirmative main contentions. Discovering the main issues thus constitutes a prerequisite to intelligent argumentation.

Types of Issues

In determining the main issues, first consider the types: stock issues, potential issues, admitted issues, and real issues. The distinction among these types follows.

Stock issues

Stock issues are those principal points common to almost all topics for argumentation. When applied to a debate proposition, they help determine the real issues. They may be stated as follows:

1. Is a change needed?
2. Would the proposed policy meet the need?
3. Would the proposed policy be a desirable solution?

These questions apply to all propositions of policy. Relate them to the following national questions of recent years to see how readily they apply: *Resolved, That the federal government should guarantee an opportunity for higher education to all qualified high school graduates; Resolved, That the non-Communist nations of the world should establish an economic community; Resolved, That the United States should adopt a program of compulsory health insurance for all citizens; Resolved, That the federal government should establish a national program of public work for the unemployed.* Stock issues may not always be worded exactly the same way for all propositions, but they help determine the real issues—need, practicability, and desirability.

Standard questions may be applied in determining whether a stock issue will become a potential issue. Note how these questions apply to the proposition that the United States should adopt a policy of federal aid to education:

   I. Is a change in policy for financing education needed?
      A. Do evils in the present methods of financing education call for a change in policy?
         1. Do serious problems in financing education exist?
         2. Are the alleged problems really evils?
         3. Are the evils sufficiently serious to warrant a change?
         4. Are the evils inherent in the present policy?
      B. Does want for benefits other than the alleviation of financial problems make a change in policy desirable?
         1. Would benefits actually accrue?

2. Would these benefits be sufficient to justify a change in policy?
3. Could these benefits be secured without a change in the present policy?

II. Would the proposed policy of federal aid to education meet the need of the present system?
   A. Would the results justify a change in the present policy of financing education?
      1. Would it alleviate evils in financing education in sufficient degree to justify its adoption?
      2. Would it produce other benefits in a degree to justify its adoption?
   B. Would the attendant evils of the change make its adoption unwise?
      1. Would the proposed program be accompanied by new evils?
      2. Would the alleged evils produce harmful results?
      3. Would the alleged evils outweigh the advantages of the change?
      4. Would the policy of federal aid be inherently harmful?

III. Is the proposed policy of federal aid to education a desirable solution?
   A. Would it produce advantages other than the alleviation of evils?
   B. Would any other policy remedy the existing evils as effectively as the proposed policy?
   C. Would any alternate policy be as free from attendant evils as the proposed policy?
      1. Would it intensify the evils of the proposed policy?
      2. Would it have fewer evils than the proposed policy?
      3. Would it produce other evils?

These questions may be adapted to any proposition of policy to determine the potential issues. They serve as a starting point for complete analysis.

Potential issues

Potential issues must be proved to establish a case. They are the issues inherent in the proposition as distinguished from the issues of a particular debate. In Chapter 3, we learned that the affirmative side must present all potential issues even though one or more of them may be admitted. The proposition that the federal government should adopt a retail sales tax illustrates this point. The potential issues may be stated as follows:

1. Is there a need for additional revenue for the federal government?
2. Is the retail sales tax a practicable plan for securing the needed revenue?
3. Is the retail sales tax a desirable plan for securing the needed revenue?

The affirmative side must prove all three of these potential issues to establish a prima-facie case. Unless the need for revenue can be established, why proceed to the second issue? If the need is established, the affirmative case remains incomplete until the speakers can prove the other contentions—the plan will meet the need and it will be a desirable solution. Even if the affirmative could foresee the negative's concession of the "need for revenue," it would still have to present this contention because the issue of "need" is a requirement for a prima-facie case; all potential issues must be advanced to meet the requirements of an adequate case.

Admitted issues

The admitted issues consist of those main contentions advanced by the affirmative that the negative concedes without argument. When the negative concedes one or more of the potential issues, it implies that it does not care to contest such issues but will concentrate its attack on the remaining contentions. This concession does not mean that the affirmative has wasted time in presenting the conceded issues, because they constitute a necessary part of the prima-facie case. Neither does such an admission weaken the negative's case. The admission simply makes clear the negative's position and permits it more time to attack other issues. Negative concessions should always be made for cause, not mere preference; they should enable the negative to concentrate its attack on issues in which it has an advantage from the inherent nature of the issue.

The example cited in the proposition of federal retail taxation applies here. The negative may concede the first contention on "need for revenue" if it becomes apparent through study that the facts justify the concession. Such an admission would focus the argument on the second and third issues, one of which the negative must overthrow. Possibly the negative might concede both the first and second issues. In that event, it must either present a substitute tax program as preferable to the sales tax or show that the sales tax would cause more problems than it would remedy.

Real issues

The real issues consist of the potential minus the admitted issues. They become the decisive points of controversy in a debate, determining whether the case is sustained or defeated. Furthermore, the real issues in a proposition may vary from one debate to another. For example, on the federal retail sales tax proposition, if the negative contests all three of the potential issues, all become real issues in the debate. The potential and the real issues then coincide. On the other hand, should the negative concede the "need for revenue," this contention would be dropped from the debate; contentions two and three would then become the real issues. If the negative should admit the first two, the third would be the only real issue in the argument.

A debate may sometimes be narrowed to one real issue because of the importance of that issue. In debates on the national proposition that Congress should be given the power to reverse decisions of the Supreme Court, this condition frequently occurred. The argument that the proposal would destroy our system of checks and balances, making Congress not only the judge and jury but also a litigant, overshadowed all other arguments. When the negative side succeeded in making this argument the ultimate issue, it often won.

The argument over "will the plan work?" sometimes becomes the only real issue in a debate. This situation frequently occurred in debates on the proposition that nuclear power should be put under control of an international organization. The affirmative found it relatively easy to show a need for international control and that benefits would accrue from the plan. The negative team concentrated its attack on practicability, arguing that the plan would not work in view of conflicting ideologies in the world and that Russia could not be depended upon to keep her agreements.

Plan of Analysis

The following questions constitute a workable plan for analysis. Before attempting to read all available material on the subject for debate, think the question through and apply stock issues to the proposition. For example, in the proposition *Resolved, That the federal government should adopt a uniform retail sales tax,* the following analytical questions and subquestions apply.

    I. Is there a need for additional federal revenue?
        A. Is the present need for additional revenue imperative?
        B. Is this need permanent?
        C. Is the need a need for more revenue, or is it a need for the wiser expenditure of the revenue already available?

II. Will the proposed sales tax meet the need?
    A. Would it provide the needed revenue?
    B. Would it be a practical tax program?
    C. Would further taxation harm the consumer?
III. Is the proposed sales tax a desirable plan for raising the needed revenue?
    A. Would the sales tax result in more advantages than disadvantages?
    B. Is it more practical than to increase the tax on other sources of revenue?
    C. Is the sales tax superior to other forms of taxation not now utilized?

After thinking through the proposition and applying the stock issues, continue reading to correct and supplement original ideas. During research, keep lists of points pro and con on the question, recording these points at first without regard to organization. The following would likely find a place on the temporary list of affirmative arguments:

1. The sales tax is more likely to produce additional revenue than are other tax sources.
2. There is a need for additional federal revenue.
3. Present sources of taxation cannot raise additional revenue.
4. The national budget is not balanced.
5. Public welfare activities need additional funds.
6. National defense requires additional funds.
7. Many sources of revenue are overtaxed today.
8. Sales can bear additional tax.
9. Income is taxed too heavily.
10. Business is taxed too heavily.
11. Real property is primarily a source of revenue for state and local governments.
12. The sales tax is a desirable method for raising additional revenue.
13. Personal property is taxed heavily by state and local governments.
14. The federal government is more than 300 billion dollars in debt.
15. A uniform retail sales tax can provide additional revenue.
16. Agriculture needs further subsidies.
17. More funds are needed for developing nuclear power.
18. Tariffs keep out needed products.

This list is not exhaustive; it merely illustrates. In the final analysis all possible relevant points on both sides should be listed. A glance at the list shows that the arguments are not recorded in logical order; distinctions are not yet made between main points and subpoints.

Check the list and exclude irrelevant and unimportant points.

What should be excluded may not be evident at first, but a study of the proposition will add to your knowledge and develop your ability to distinguish the essential from the nonessential. For example, points 11 and 13 in the list should be excluded because they constitute sources for state revenue exclusively.

After irrelevant material has been excluded, all points may be organized into main contentions and subpoints. The tentative list of arguments may be arranged as follows:

I. There is a need for additional federal revenue. (point 2 on the list)
   A. The national budget is not balanced. (point 4)
   B. The federal debt is more than 300 billion dollars. (point 14)
   C. Public welfare activities need additional revenue. (point 5)
   D. National defense requires additional funds. (point 6)
   E. More funds are needed for developing nuclear power. (point 17)
   F. Agriculture needs further subsidies. (point 16)
II. The sales tax is more likely to produce additional revenue than are other tax sources. (point 1)
   A. Many sources of revenue are overtaxed today. (point 7)
      1. Income is taxed too heavily. (point 9)
      2. Business is taxed too heavily. (point 10)
      3. Tariffs keep out needed products. (point 18)
   B. Sales can bear additional tax. (point 8)
III. An increase of the sales tax is a desirable method for raising additional revenue. (point 12)
   A. Present sources of taxation cannot raise additional revenue. (point 3)
   B. A uniform retail sales tax can provide additional revenue. (point 15)

The preceding arrangement is only a skeleton brief; it shows the relationship between main issues and supporting points. The complete brief contains all possible subpoints and supporting evidence.

In short, a workable plan for analysis involves a fourfold procedure: (1) Think the proposition through. (2) During research keep a list of arguments and evidence found on both sides of the proposition. (3) Exclude the irrelevant arguments on the tentative list. (4) Arrange the remaining arguments into main contentions and supporting points.

Preliminary Steps in Analysis

The following preliminary steps will help you make a complete analysis. They serve as a necessary background for applying the plan of analysis explained in the foregoing section.

1. Determine the present significance or immediate reason for debating the subject.
2. Make a comprehensive study of the history of the question.
3. Dispose of extraneous matter.
4. Decide on a reasonable interpretation of the proposition.
5. Discover the underlying philosophy of the proposition.
6. Contrast affirmative and negative main contentions.

Give careful attention to these preliminary steps early in your preparation to insure a fundamental understanding of the question. During the actual debate, the first affirmative speaker gives a brief analysis of the proposition in his introduction, preliminary to the development of the affirmative case. He will not always give these steps one by one; he will, however, give all needed analysis with emphasis on the interpretation of the proposition. An explanation of the proposition as a whole must receive attention early in the debate. In the following discussion of the steps, segments of the introduction to a brief will be used to illustrate each step.

Determine the present significance of the subject

The immediate reasons for debating any proposition arise from the circumstances that give it current interest. An understanding of these circumstances makes clear what the proposition involves, how recent developments have changed its significance, and how the immediate attention of the audience can be secured.

On propositions dealing with recently developed principles, the present significance of the question becomes especially important. Such a question debated in recent years was that the non-Communist nations of the world should establish an economic community. The success of the European Common Market, established by treaties signed in 1957 among six European nations, gave rise to the concept of economic communities. The late President Kennedy's proposed Foreign Trade Expansion Act of 1962 gave the proposition further significance. These developments showed that the proposition dealt with a new concept in international relations.

For the proposition *Resolved, That the federal government should guarantee the opportunity for higher education to all qualified high school graduates,* the present significance of the subject may be briefed as follows:

I. Recent developments give the proposition present significance.
  A. The launching of the Russian sputnik in October, 1957, caused a re-examination of the United States school system.
    1. People began to ask "Why can't Johnny read?" "Why can't our schools keep pace with scientific development?"
    2. Students were urged to follow a college preparatory high school course, and high school curricula were strengthened.
    3. Colleges re-examined their curricula, eliminated "frill" courses, and adopted honors programs.
  B. The World War II "baby boom" is beginning to crowd our colleges today.
    1. Estimates are that college populations will likely double between 1960 and 1970.
    2. Crowded conditions have placed a financial burden on our colleges, increased the costs of attending college, and caused the colleges and students to seek new sources of funds.
  C. An increasing percentage of persons are attending high school and college.
    1. In 1920, 32.3 per cent of the 14-17 year group went to high school; in 1962, 87.3 per cent attended.[1]
    2. In 1920, 8.1 per cent of high school graduates went to college; in 1962, 37.2 per cent attended.[2]

Study the history of the question

Early in your preparation, study the origin and history of the question to insure a thorough knowledge of it. An understanding of the background clarifies the meanings involved and provides evidence for supporting arguments. You need not, however, give full details of the origin and history during the debate; give only as much of the history as necessary for explaining the background of the arguments.

For example, to get the full import of a proposal to strengthen the United Nations, you must know the previous efforts to secure world-wide cooperation. Become acquainted with the problems encountered in establishing the American Union, the League of Nations, the United Nations, the North Atlantic Treaty Organization, and the European Common Market. Only through an understanding of former efforts toward world organization can you understand fully a proposal for future world cooperation.

---

[1] Abraham Ribicoff, "The Battle for Better Schools," *Parent's Magazine* (February, 1962), p. 45.
[2] *Ibid.*, p. 45.

Note, as shown below, how the major events in history apply to the proposition that the federal government should guarantee an opportunity for higher education to all qualified high school graduates.

II. The relationship of the federal government to education in the United States has had an interesting history.
   A. It dates back to the Continental Congress, which in 1785 set aside land for educational use.
   B. The Federal Constitution of 1789 made no specific proposal about education.
      1. An examination of Madison's *Journal of the Constitutional Convention* shows that the question was considered extensively and was probably intended to be included under the general welfare clause.
      2. Beginning in 1802, the Congress of the United States has granted aid to education in general as well as to specific institutions.
   C. The Morrill Act of 1862 established the land-grant colleges.
      1. Conditions and requirements were set up for the expenditure of the funds.
      2. Prior to the Morrill Act, all federal grants were made unconditionally.
   D. The Marine School Act of 1911 marked a departure from previous grants.
      1. It was the first grant for special education.
      2. It was the first grant that required the states to match federal funds.
   E. The Smith-Hughes Act of 1917 was the first to give the federal government the right to administer the funds.
   F. During the depression of the 1930's, various measures to aid education were adopted by the federal government on a temporary basis.
      1. Economic conditions of the country were reflected in educational institutions, both public and private.
      2. Most of the federal aid took the form of direct grants.
   G. Various "G.I." bills were passed soon after World War II.
      1. The concept of federal aid was extended to include the financing of higher education to those who served during the war.
      2. The acts were motivated partly by the desire to raise the productive and social capacities of the American people and partly as recompense to soldiers for service to the country during the war.
   H. The National Defense Education Act of 1958 provided federally sponsored loans to needy and qualified students.
   I. Various acts in recent years have provided long-time loans for building dormitories and other revenue-producing buildings.

1. These funds were extended and enlarged in December, 1963.
2. Additional bills are now pending in Congress.

Dispose of extraneous matter

All points in a proposition cannot be argued; the disputable and the indisputable must be separated. Do not think that you should contest every statement made by the opposition, for no argument is possible without an admitted basis of fact. Concessions of irrelevant matters are necessary for orderly debate—the disposal of irrelevant matter limits the question to the main contentions and centers interest on the basic issues. For example, on the question of whether or not the federal government should guarantee the opportunity for higher education to all qualified high school graduates, the following arguments may be excluded, as shown below.

III. As a basis for argument, certain matters should be admitted or declared irrelevant.
   A. The constitutionality of the proposal should be waived.
      1. The proposition pertains to the desirability of the proposal, not its legality.
      2. The argument concerning separation of church and state does not apply.
         a. The aid would go to students, not colleges.
         b. The aid would be available to students of all faiths and would be voluntary, not compulsory.
   B. Whether or not the framers of the constitution established the principle of federal aid to education is irrelevant.
      1. No specific provision was made for federal aid.
      2. Whether or not federal aid was implied cannot be ascertained with certainty.
   C. That the cost of the program might exceed the national debt ceiling is immaterial.
      1. The ceiling of the national debt can be raised.
      2. The national debt should be considered relative to the gross national product and national wealth.
   D. Whether or not the federal government can actually "guarantee" all students an opportunity for higher education should not render the proposition void.
      1. Making higher education financially possible for qualified students meets the intent of the proposition.
      2. Financial aid would be made on application only; the extent of the grant would depend on financial need.
   E. That education faces other financial problems more serious than those involved in the proposition is irrelevant.

1. This proposition relates to one facet of the problem, not to all the financial problems of higher education.
2. Other propositions could be debated within the framework of education.

In disposing of extraneous matter, consider the various types. Of the several classifications of this type of matter, the following predominate: (1) irrelevant matter, (2) waived matter, (3) omitted matter, (4) conceded matter, and (5) admitted matter.

Irrelevant matter does not pertain directly to the subject under discussion; waived matter consists of those points that both sides agree not to discuss although they may relate to the subject. Usually constitutionality is waived because many things may be desirable, yet not constitutional; furthermore, the constitutionality of an act cannot be determined except by court action. Omitted matter is that left out of the discussion by design although it may be pertinent to the question. Conceded matter consists of those points brought forward by one side and granted by the opposition. Admitted matter is matter well known to all and hence not subject to argument. For instance, in the proposition concerning trial by jury, it would probably be admitted that certain evils exist under the present method of administering justice. Under some conditions, classification of these matters may be changed; for example, instead of waiving the constitutionality of a given question, it could be considered irrelevant.

Decide on a reasonable interpretation

Decisions on the meaning of a proposition must be made before there can be an effective debate, and they constitute a fundamental part of preparation and analysis. Definitions may be tentative early in your study, subject to final decision after additional study and analysis. The interpretation of the proposition, however, should come early in a debate in order to avoid confusion and to insure a debate on the issues rather than an argument over the meaning of the proposition.

As pointed out in Chapter 3, the affirmative has the right to interpret the proposition as well as the obligation to be fair and objective. The best safeguard against disagreement over the meaning is a logical interpretation in the introductory speech. Remember that every good question has a principle involved. For example, on the question of increasing the federal income tax the affirmative is not prohibited from favoring other tax measures, but it must uphold the principle of income taxation as its primary contention.

On the other hand, the negative may favor any number of tax reforms, but it should not incorporate the basic principles of federal income taxation. Interpret the proposition so as to bring out the basic philosophy underlying it.

Terms and words must be defined before a clear interpretation can be made. Dictionary definitions are not always satisfactory, because the dictionary defines words as a collective process; defining words for the purpose of debate is a selective process. Also, terms used in debate questions take on new meaning under changing conditions.

Definitions of specific words in a proposition or terms that arise in the course of a debate may be arrived at by the following methods: (1) etymology, (2) authority, (3) exemplification, (4) explication, and (5) negation.

Etymology deals with the origin and history of words. Since meanings of words change, a consideration of origin alone may be insufficient and the etymology of a word may not help distinguish a general from a specific meaning. The study of origins of words, however, may lead to working definitions.

The citation of an authority applies only to the extent that you can find an acceptable expert. For example, if the term "nuclear weapons" should appear in a proposition, Edward Teller would be an acceptable authority because of his expert training in the field of nuclear power. George Romney would be helpful in defining terms pertaining to industrial management. An acceptable authority must be qualified in the field in which you quote him; accomplishment in one field of endeavor does not imply knowledge of other fields.

Definition by exemplification means selecting an individual case to represent the whole. This method is valuable when a typical example can be found. The word "quadruped," for instance, is defined in *Webster's New International Dictionary* as "an animal having four feet, as most mammals and many reptiles. . . ." The horse or the cow exemplifies. The term "economic community" could probably best be explained by citing an example of the plan in action, for example, the European Economic Community.

Explication enlarges upon bare statements to make clear what may be involved or implied. The value of explication depends upon the soundness of the reasoning behind the explanation. In the proposition *Resolved, That labor should have a direct share in the management of industry*, the term "direct share" must mean more than the right to make suggestions, because labor has that privilege now. Any share less than an equal share, however, would be ineffective. More than an equal share would give too much power to labor. Thus, by explication, a definition of "direct share" indicates that capital and labor should have equal shares in management.

Negation defines by explaining what a term does not mean. To illustrate, restate the explanation above as follows: "direct share" does not mean the right of labor to make suggestions to management because labor already has that right; it does not mean that labor should be given advisory powers only because in essence this power would mean little more than the right of suggestion; it does not mean a majority control by labor on industrial management boards because this plan would put the final control of industry into the hands of labor. Thus, through a process of elimination, an acceptable definition may be arrived at. Definition by negation rarely suffices within itself, but it may be valuable when used in conjunction with other methods.

Definitions should be fair, clearly stated, and concise. They must be based upon reason, not mere preference. Never define terms in an unusual way in order to take the opposition by surprise; such interpretations may give you a temporary advantage when debating inexperienced opponents, but they will lead to a poor debate. Formerly, teams often agreed on terms prior to the debate to prevent wasted time and to insure a debate on issues; now, definition of terms is considered to constitute an essential part of analysis. Definition in the first affirmative speech increases spontaneity and reserves for the affirmative one of its basic rights to offset the burden of proof. Failure to agree on the meaning of terms early in a debate may prevent a clash of arguments; unless a direct clash occurs, there will be no intelligent debate. If definitions given by the first affirmative speaker are not acceptable, objection and clarification should be given by the first negative speaker immediately upon securing the floor.

The following section IV of a brief defines necessary terms of the proposition *Resolved, That the federal government should guaran-*

tee the opportunity for higher education to all qualified high school graduates.

IV. For a mutual understanding, the following terms should be defined.
  A. "Federal government" means the United States government acting through legally elected representatives to Congress.
    1. The federal grants shall be made directly to the student or college.
    2. The federal government shall not make the grants to the various states for distribution.
  B. "Should" means that the affirmative must advocate adopting the proposal.
    1. The affirmative does not have to show that the proposal will be adopted.
    2. The proposal means immediate adoption, not some plan for the future.
  C. "Guarantee the opportunity" means that the federal government shall make it financially possible for qualified high school graduates to attend college.
    1. The federal aid should be in the form of money grants to the student to finance college attendance.
    2. Whether or not the federal government makes additional grants to the college is optional.
  D. "Higher education" means education beyond the high school level.
    1. It may include junior college, senior college, professional school, or graduate school according to the qualifications of students.
    2. It does not include trade schools.
  E. "Qualified high school graduates" means those students who meet the reasonable requirements of the program.
    1. The financial needs of the student should be based on family income and other finances available.
    2. The academic qualifications of the student should be determined by (a) a national testing program, and (b) the student's high school record.

Discover the underlying philosophy

The underlying philosophy means the implications of the proposition that go beyond the arguments for or against its adoption; it means a change in basic concepts. Almost all policy propositions involve a fundamental change in a principle or a basic economic, political, or social philosophy. For example, the proposition that the non-Communist nations of the world should establish an economic community involves a fundamental change in international trade relationships, based not upon individual nations but on a combination of nations. It calls for a combination of nations to act as a unit in competing with individual nations or with another combination of nations. The community adopts trade restrictions against outside nations but maintains free trade among member nations. In short, the proposition embodies a relatively new trade concept in international relations, the community-of-interests concept. This change in fundamental policy constitutes the underlying philosophy of the resolution.

What underlying philosophy applies to the proposition that the federal government should guarantee the opportunity for higher education to all qualified high school graduates? As you learned from the brief history of the proposition, higher education has not until recently been considered as a necessary part of one's schooling. Now, however, technological progress, increasing specialization, higher standards of living, and greater responsibility of the individual citizen in world affairs call for a re-examination of our concept of higher education. All of these variables interact to demand an educated public. Never before has economic progress been so dependent on an educated populace; never before have the demands of individual jobs been as high; never before have all income levels, especially the relatively lower levels, been so high as they are now, demanding capable judgment in their expenditure; and never before have the decisions of the American voters been so far-reaching in their effect. In brief, changed conditions have given rise to a new concept regarding the responsibility of the federal government toward the education of its citizens.

The two basic questions that involve a change in underlying philosophy are:

1. Are the demands of present-day society such that we should change our concept of higher education to include public responsibility for educating qualified students?
2. Should the federal government execute this change by a program of grants to qualified students to insure their higher education?

What does the concept of higher education actually involve? Do present conditions demand acceptance of the creed that "every qualified individual has a right to a higher education"? This philosophy has never been accepted in the past, but it must be considered under the proposition. In a political period of taking for granted one's rights, we often forget such underlying assumptions. The affirmative must prove by a logical sequence of contentions that this particular philosophy of higher education financed by the federal government should be adopted. This philosophy probably will never be explicitly stated, but it should be understood by all who debate the question. It inheres in a basic understanding of the new problem of education, and the basic philosophical concepts inherent in all propositions of policy must be discovered as a part of proper analysis.

Contrast affirmative and negative main contentions

The last step in analysis is illustrated by the following contrast of the affirmative and negative contentions on the issues of guaranteeing an opportunity for higher education to all qualified high school graduates.

Affirmative Contentions

I. There is a need for federal assistance to qualified students who cannot afford higher education.
  A. Because of high costs of attending college, an increasing number of potential students have become financially unable to attend.
      1. The average annual family income in the United States is $5,700; the annual cost of education has risen to approximately $1,500 in public schools and $2,200 in private schools.
      2. Private sources of assistance, although helpful, are not sufficient for children of low-income groups.
          a. Present scholarship programs are designed primarily to attract superior students.
          b. Loan programs involve too great a risk for students from low-income families.
          c. Student work is insufficient to meet the high costs of attending college.
  B. The public as a whole loses by failure to educate all qualified students.
      1. It fails to realize the full productive capacities of all citizens.
      2. It fails to realize the full capacities of all citizens for informed judgment in national and international affairs.
II. The policy of federal aid to qualified students is a practical plan.
  A. The federal government is the only agency with a national taxing ability; it can obtain the money to finance the program on a more equitable basis than can the individual states.
  B. Private contributions and endowments, although helpful, have failed to keep pace with the need.

C. The various veterans' bills have given the federal government a precedent for administering such a program.

D. The plan will enlarge the concept of federal relationship to education by removing the financial barrier to equality of opportunity.

III. The policy of federal aid to qualified students is a desirable plan.

A. Cultural benefits would accrue from an educated populace.

B. It would place the responsibility of financing education on society in general, which ultimately receives the benefits.

C. It would result in a better informed electorate.

Negative Contentions

I. There is no need to guarantee a higher education to all qualified high school students.

A. There is not a serious need for an increase in the number of college trained personnel because the United States has the highest percentage of college graduates in the world.

1. The need for the future is for more laborers, not executives.

2. The nation's colleges are taxed to the limit today to care for present enrollments.

B. The motivational factor in nonattendance in most cases is something other than inability to pay the costs.

1. Many children of low-income groups would not attend if they had the money.

2. The need is for better guidance and greater motivation, not for more finances.

C. Students who have both the capacity and the desire to attend college can do so at the present.

1. More than thirty million dollars in scholarships go unused every year.

2. Loan programs are available to meet the needs of almost all students from states, industry, and colleges.

3. Industry is supplying more and more funds to students in the form of both scholarships and loans.

4. A college scholarship service has been set up to help those who need aid; many colleges give attractive scholarships from current funds.

5. Needy students can work part-time at campus jobs and during summer months.

6. The federal government has already established large loan funds by the National Defense Act of 1958 and by supplements in 1963.

II. A policy of federal grants to qualified high school graduates is impractical.

A. The administration of such a program would be difficult.

1. The cost would add to an already large national debt.

　　2. It would create a still larger federal bureaucracy.

　B. Experience with the veterans' programs will not help much because they were limited programs conducted through the Veterans Administration.

　C. To extend the concept of federal activity in higher education to include grants to all qualified students would not assure equality of opportunity. Many students could not attend because they must work to supplement family income.

　D. Federal aid would lessen local interest in education.

III. A policy of federal grants to qualified high school graduates would be undesirable.

　A. The standards of education are lowered when it is extended to the masses.

　B. The federal government would have another program, difficult to administer, to add to its already large number of enterprises in the educational field.

　C. There would be an increasing dependence on the federal government for financing all education; thus private sources of loans and scholarships would disappear.

　D. The federal government could eventually usurp control of the schools and establish a standardized plan.

　E. Federal aid would cause an increase in the costs of attending college and thus increase the number of students who would need federal aid.

The affirmative and negative contentions may vary in different debates. Normally, affirmative teams would contend for all three issues; the negative could admit the need for additional funds for qualified students but contend that the funds are rapidly becoming available through private sources. The negative might argue that federal aid is neither a practical nor desirable means of financing the education of qualified high school students. Although procedure may vary, the principles of contrasting main contentions exemplified here are common to all propositions and constitute an essential part of analysis.

Summary

Analysis is the process of breaking down a debate proposition into its parts or of discovering the main issues. There are four types of issues: stock, which are questions common to all policy propositions; potential, which are basic points that inhere in the proposition; admitted, which are those issues excluded from the debate by the negative through concessions; and real, which are the ultimate issues in a particular debate. You discover issues by logical reasoning and research.

A workable plan of analysis calls for a fourfold procedure: (1) Think the proposition through. (2) During research, list arguments pro and con on the proposition. (3) Exclude irrelevant arguments from the list. (4) Arrange the remaining arguments into main contentions and supporting points.

The preliminary steps in analysis consist of six steps: (1) Determine the present significance or immediate reason for debating the subject. (2) Make a comprehensive study of the history of the question. (3) Dispose of extraneous matter. (4) Decide on a reasonable interpretation of the proposition. (5) Discover the underlying philosophy of the proposition. (6) Contrast affirmative and negative main contentions.

Oral Assignment

The chairmen of the panel discussions of the last class period should report on the conclusions reached by their panels—time limit, five minutes. Class members should take notes. An open forum should follow the reports.

Collateral Readings

Baird, A. Craig, *Argumentation, Discussion and Debate,* Ch. 6. New York: McGraw-Hill Book Co., Inc., 1950.

Crocker, Lionel, *Argumentation and Debate,* Ch. 3. New York: American Institute of Banking, 1962.

Ehninger, Douglas, and Wayne Brockriede, *Decision by Debate,* Ch. 14. New York: Dodd, Mead & Co., 1963.

Freeley, Austin J., *Argumentation and Debate,* Ch. 3. Belmont, Calif.: Wadsworth Publishing Co., Inc., 1961.

Huber, Robert B., *Influencing Through Argument,* Ch. 3. New York: David McKay Co., Inc., 1963.

Kruger, Arthur N., *Modern Debate,* Chs. 4, 5. New York: McGraw-Hill Book Co., Inc., 1960.

7
Applying and Evaluating Evidence

Chapters 5 and 6 developed research and analysis as simultaneous rather than independent processes. As you study a subject, apply the principles of analysis so that you may understand the proposition thoroughly. In preparation and analysis, seek the best arguments to develop your case and the most valid evidence to support your arguments. Keep in mind your ultimate purpose—to develop the most logical case possible for or against the proposition. Proof is a result of all your allegations, reasons, appeals, and forms of support. You must convince your listeners of the truth and reasonableness of your case.

In his writings on rhetoric, Aristotle discussed three forms of proof: (1) ethos—the ethical factors that reside in the speaker, or the impressions that listeners form of the integrity, attitude, ability, and knowledge of the speaker; (2) pathos—the appeal to the basic drives, motives, and desires of man, or the emotional appeal; (3) argument proper—the appeal to reason and evidence, or the logical appeal.[1] As a debater, use all three forms of proof to gain acceptance for your contentions, but stress logical proof. Evidence, as a part of logical proof, receives detailed treatment in this chapter. The following chart shows how evidence relates to proof and how it applies to the subordinate points, the issues, the case, and the proposition.

The Divisional Processes of Debate

I. *The Proposition:* the resolution that the affirmative side affirms and the negative side negates—each team attempts to prove its side.

---

[1] The discussion of evidence and reasoning in this text follows Aristotle's *Rhetoric,* which differentiates among the forms of proof above. For a treatment that considers them together, see Stephen E. Toulmin, *The Uses of Argument* (Cambridge, Eng.: Cambridge University Press, 1958).

A. *The case:* the total of all the contentions and proofs presented for a side of the proposition—the case must be prima facie, sufficient to win as originally presented.

1. *The issues:* the inherent main divisions or points of the proposition that, when proved, constitute a prima-facie case.

   a. *The subordinate points:* all the subpoints used to prove an issue.

      (1) *Ethical proof:* the factors of integrity, ability, attitude, and knowledge displayed by the debater that help him gain acceptance of his arguments.

      (2) *Emotional proof:* the appeals to the basic drives, motives, and desires of man that help the debater persuade his listeners.

      (3) *Logical proof:* the argument itself, based on the reasons and evidence that help the debater convince an audience.

         (a) *Evidence:* the facts and opinions used to support an argument.

         (b) *Reason:* the inferences drawn from the evidence.

Evidence Explained

Evidence consists of any factual material or opinion used to prove a contention. It gives support to arguments and serves as a basis for inferences, which relate to the issue through reasoning. The facts and circumstances per se constitute evidence; inferences drawn from the facts and circumstances constitute reasoning. Logical proof, the result of both evidence and reasoning, serves as the foundation upon which the agreement to a proposition rests; it is the conclusion established through evidence and reasoning.

Unrelated evidence has little value. A fact must be related properly to an argument before it can contribute to proof. For example, the facts that ignorant and prejudiced men exist and that miscarriages of justice often occur prove nothing about trial by jury. But if it can be shown that whenever ignorant and prejudiced men sit on juries, miscarriages of justice result, the reasoning demonstrates the logical relationship between the two statements. Further, if the proposition involves the question of needed changes in trial by jury because of injustices, the relation established above would then constitute proof of the need for changes. To be sure, the existence of other weaknesses in our system must be shown, but this reasoning establishes one phase of the proposition, that ignorant and prejudiced men cause miscarriages of justice.

Evidence has its origin in the law of evidence in our courts. The rules of evidence are more voluminous and complicated in law than in educational debate, but the same principles apply. In courts of law the following constitute evidence: physical objects such as a lethal weapon, fingerprints, handwriting, and stolen property; the circumstances surrounding the commission of the act; statements made by persons concerning the defendant; statements made by the defendant to persons testifying at the trial. Statements by experts may, under certain circumstances, be admitted as evidence although the person testifying does not have first-hand information about the facts of the case; for example, the ballistics expert may testify that a bullet came from a certain gun or the psychiatrist may state that certain acts constitute insanity. Briefly, in courts, evidence consists of objects or things, statements of fact, and statements of opinion.

To protect the defendant, a large body of rules has grown up concerning what constitutes evidence and what evidence becomes admissible. The *hearsay* rule, for example, states that a person cannot testify as to what a person says about another. *A* cannot testify what *B* told him about *C*, except under well-defined conditions. The best evidence consists of *B*'s own testimony. Exceptions exist, however, to the hearsay rule; for example, *A* would be permitted to testify under the circumstances above if *B*'s statements were a dying declaration. Through legal rules, the courts seek the best evidence. The hearsay rule affords a working example of how evidence in law protects the individual.

In educational debate, an economic, social, or political principle is on trial rather than a person. There is no occasion for the testimony of persons on the witness stand or for the introduction of objects; no need exists for strict rules on the admissibility of evidence such as prevail in law.

Evidence in debate can be explained best by example. The affirmative on the proposition of federal aid to education alleges an unequal distribution of educational facilities among the various states. The questions arise: What evidence may be submitted to prove this allegation and where can such evidence be found? The debater may cite reports of governmental agencies and of educational surveys or quote informed persons. He can establish, for comparative purposes, that states with long school terms spend more money on education than do states with short terms. Evidence for use in debates may be found in statistical tables and in statements of facts and opinions gathered from many sources—books, magazines, newspapers, government reports, and research publications. All arguments must be supported with evidence sufficient for proof conforming to the tests for authenticity.

Types and Characteristics of Evidence

There are two kinds of evidence in educational debate, as there are in courts of law: *facts* and *opinions*. Facts consist of statistics, circumstances surrounding examples and analogies, and other tangible evidence, whereas opinions are statements of belief concerning the proposition. A statement, based upon a government report, that the national debt is 309 billion dollars constitutes factual evidence; a statement that we must increase our payments on the national debt to avoid inflation exemplifies opinion evidence. Each type applies in developing an argument.

Facts

Statistics and the circumstances of examples and analogies should be applied accurately and effectively in developing each argument. Consider the following explanations and precautions for each type.

Statistics. Statistics consist of compilations of numerical facts on the basis of relative numbers of occurrences. They show the proportion of instances of a specific kind and serve as a basis for inference. For example, on the issue of the increasing cost of state government, a debater cited statistics covering a ten-year period as follows: "In 1954, the total cost of the state government was $126,498,724.83; in 1959, it was $406,672,473.30; in 1964, it was $648,323,499.81. These statistics show an increase of more than 500 per cent over ten years." The matter was thus presented graphically and concisely.

Statistics mean more than a collection of figures. Figures become statistics when they represent a situation or condition. Unless comparative statistics use the same definition of the unit of measurement, they have no common meaning. That 30 million mentally disturbed people live in the United States means nothing until we define "mentally disturbed." One cannot show that more juvenile crimes occurred in X state than in Y state in 1964 simply by citing figures released by the attorneys general of the two states; first it must be determined if each state used the same definition of "juvenile." Suppose that X state defines a juvenile as a person under 18 years of age and Y state defines him as under 21? Furthermore, the term "crime" may not have been defined the same in the two states. To compare the two sets of statistics would be misleading.

Statistical information may be obtained from government reports, publications of economic research organizations, statistical abstracts, authoritative almanacs, industrial guides, or other authentic sources. Statistical information released by propaganda agencies, public-relations departments, and other organizations hired for creating good will often proves misleading, since propaganda organizations usually disseminate only those facts favorable to their cause.

Consider the following suggestions for presenting statistics: (1) Cite the exact source; avoid overworked phrases like "statistics gathered with great care show," "reliable figures show," "the undeniable facts prove." Say instead, "these statistics were published by the United States Department of State in January, 1964"; "according to the American Medical Association report 'Socialized Medicine,' page 171, the facts . . .'"; "these figures were taken from the book *Schools in America* by John Doe, a 1964 publication, page 816." (2) Present statistics in round numbers when using large figures where exactness is not important; they are more easily understood and applied, and they also save time. Instead of stating that foreign aid appropriations in 1964 were $3,167,894,342.75, say that the appropriations were approximately three billion dollars. (3) Make statistical information vivid and graphic by relating it to matters familiar to the audience. The statement that foreign aid appropriations total three billion dollars makes small impression upon the average citizen; but when it can be shown that this appropriation costs each man, woman, and child approximately twenty dollars as his proportionate share, the statement takes on added meaning. The assertion that the national debt is 309 billion dollars means less to many people than does the statement that every individual's share of the national debt approximates 2,000 dollars. (4) Check statistics against other sources of information in order to test their authenticity. If statistics arouse doubts, check them against information released from official sources.

Usually propaganda agencies do not fabricate figures; rather, they place misleading interpretations on figures, make incomplete surveys, or carefully select only favorable statistics. They sometimes compare releases based upon different units of measurement and thus distort facts. The responsibility rests upon the debater to distinguish between reliable and unreliable sources.

   Examples. An example for argumentation is a specific instance, a past happening, or a hypothetical situation from which one infers that a similar condition prevails in the instance at issue. Suppose you want to show the cumulative effect of strikes in industry, that not only the industry in which the strike occurs is affected but that allied industries also become involved. You cite the coal strikes as an example; they shut down production of coal, then the steel mills cut down production for lack of coal, the automobile manufacturers curtail production for lack of steel, and other industries become affected because they cannot buy automobiles. The facts and circumstances of this example constitute evidence; such facts per se contribute to conviction. You go beyond the evidence and infer that since this strike affected other industries, the same condition will result in the future from other strikes. Inference from facts of an observed situation to the conclusion that the same circumstances will prevail in an unobserved situation is known as generalization—the process of reasoning from example.

   Observe these suggestions in presenting examples: (1) Cite examples representative of their class, not exceptions to the general rule. The evidence derived from an example serves as a basis for inferences on similar cases; to draw an inference from an extreme example leads to a false conclusion. Suppose you contend that prices did not increase after the war, and base your contention on examples of the rubber industry, public utilities, and the postal system? Do these examples represent industry in general? Examination shows they do not: development of synthetic rubber tended to keep prices down; public utilities are quasi-public industries; and the postal system is governmentally owned. More representative industries would be steel, automobiles, building, clothing, and food. (2) Present the example fairly and accurately; do not omit unfavorable parts of the circumstances; consider all pertinent details. To illustrate, it would be unfair to use the postal system as an example of government efficiency in business if the deficit in our postal system were omitted. (3) Point out examples that make clear the point to be gained and give the circumstances in sufficient detail to make the conclusion evident. Bear in mind that the audience may not be familiar with the details of the illustration. A simple reference to an example without giving details to make it understandable lessens its value. (4) See that the example is vivid and timely. Present the details clearly and interestingly. Whenever practical, choose examples within the immediate interest range of an audience. In a debate on the strike problem where other teams had invariably referred to larger strikes in distant cities, one visiting team emphasized two strikes then in progress in the locality. The cases with the local setting were more effective because the audience had a personal interest in them.

The Analogy. An analogy for argumentation consists of a comparison of certain known features of two things in order to draw inferences concerning unknown features. By analogy we contend that if two things are alike in many known respects, they will probably be alike in unknown respects. For instance, we may argue that a common market of the Western Hemisphere would be successful because the European Common Market has been successful. Numerous points of likeness among the nations of Europe and those of the Western Hemisphere would have to be shown. Then the analogy would state that since the nations of Europe and the Western Hemisphere are alike in respects affecting economic problems, and since the common market has been successful in Europe, a common market would likewise be successful in the Western Hemisphere. The similarities cited constitute the evidence; the inference that a common market in the Western Hemisphere would be successful constitutes the reasoning.

The following suggestions apply to the analogy: (1) The points of likeness should outweigh the points of difference. In the example of the common market, the evidence must show that the nations of the Western Hemisphere and Europe are more alike than different in matters concerning the success of international trade. If the contrary were true, the inference from the comparison would not hold. (2) The points of comparison must be true; that is, the points of likeness in an analogy must actually exist. (3) The objects compared must be representative of their class. In the example of the common market, let us suppose that Europe and the Western Hemisphere are unlike other communities of the world. In such event, the inference made concerning the Western Hemisphere would be justified, but a generalization including other communities of that class would not be justified. In many instances, the analogy serves as a basis for generalization concerning all objects or things in the class of those compared, and the things chosen for comparison must be representative of their class.

Opinions

Opinions as evidence consist of statements of what people think about a proposition. In essence, opinion statements are simply conjectures or beliefs. For argumentation we infer that because qualified experts support our inferences, their opinions add probative force to our conclusions.

Consider the following precautions when quoting an opinion: (1) Quote experts only. To be of value, the opinions must come from a person qualified through experience and training to give expert opinion on the proposition. The writers of textbooks, of articles in recognized professional journals, and of reports in other objective sources usually fulfill this requirement. (2) Do not rely exclusively on opinion statements. Quotations from authorities are more persuasive than logical and cannot be conclusive proof within themselves, although they lend prestige and dignity to conclusions based on careful reasoning and adequate evidence. Since the experts disagree on almost all questions of policy, however, opinion statements should be used only to corroborate conclusions. (3) Quote men in the field of their competence only. The fact that a person qualifies as an expert in one field does not within itself qualify him in other fields. The opinion of a member of the United States Supreme Court on a question of law would carry more weight than would his opinion on federal aid to education; the fact that a person is a well-known athlete does not qualify him to give expert opinion on the nutritional effects of certain foods; and the popularity of a person does not necessarily indicate his degree of competence. (4) Quote authorities accurately and do not take statements out of their context. Make sure the quotation reflects accurately the expert's beliefs. Do not omit essential parts of a quotation so that you distort the author's meaning.

Classification of Evidence

Classification of evidence follows legal usage closely although the classification is more rigid for law than for educational debate. Evidence, as used in law and applied to debate, may be testimonial or circumstantial, spoken or written, expert or ordinary, original or hearsay, positive or negative, real or personal, deliberate or casual. Evidence used in establishing proof must be properly related to the proposed issue. This relationship can be better understood after consideration of the different classes of evidence in legal usage.

Testimonial or circumstantial

Testimonial evidence arises from statements of individuals about observed happenings made for the purpose of establishing the truth or falsity of an allegation. In law, the person giving the testimonial evidence is one who witnessed the happening about which he reports or who speaks from recognized knowledge of admittedly original documents. The one who gives direct evidence bases his statements upon his own personal knowledge and observation rather than upon hearsay or inference. He may not offer as direct testimony what someone else has sworn he witnessed except under clearly defined circumstances; such evidence is often ruled inadmissible.

Circumstantial evidence is based upon inference or presumption, conclusions that go beyond the observed facts. Inference may be the result of associating certain facts and showing that a known conclusion could be inferred from the facts. These types of evidence may be illustrated as follows:

> Tom and John are members of the same class in college. Tom has established an excellent academic record; John has recently been placed on academic probation. John and Tom take the same difficult examination, resulting in papers strikingly similar despite the fact that John attended a ball game during the afternoon preceding the examination and later attended a dance, whereas Tom attended neither, but spent the afternoon preparing for the test. John sat by Tom on the morning of the examination. When one testifies to these situations, he gives circumstantial evidence that establishes probability that John copied from Tom's paper.

> Smith sees Brown hit Jones with a club; later Jones dies from the effects of the blow. The testimony of Smith would be direct evidence or testimony in the case. On the other hand, suppose that Smith sees Brown furtively leave a house; later, Jones is found in the house suffering from knife wounds. A knife recognized as Brown's is found near the body of the wounded man. Upon investigation it is learned that Brown hurriedly left town. These facts would constitute circumstantial evidence that Brown was guilty of assault upon Jones.

Circumstantial evidence is of greater value when there are several phases to the circumstance. Ordinarily one circumstance alone has little weight in establishing a case. For instance, if a calling card engraved "John Smith" is found in a man's pocket, that circumstance alone would be insufficient for making a conclusion concerning his name. If, in addition to the card, there are found in the man's possession a billfold, a brief case, and articles of clothing all inscribed "John Smith," the cumulation of evidence would lead to a high degree of probability that the man is John Smith.

Testimonial evidence in law has close parallels in educational debate. In both law and debate, evidence includes factual material and opinion; both make use of statistics, example, analogy, and quotation from authority. Circumstantial evidence in law is analogous to reasoning in debate. The conclusion must be inferred; the bases for inference are the facts and circumstances thereof.

Spoken or written

Spoken evidence consists of the words of a person repeating what he has heard or describing what he has observed and is the type of evidence most widely used in courts of law. Oral testimony is brought into the law case when witnesses are questioned. Written evidence may be an original document—a will, a resolution, an official set of minutes; or it may be an opinion based on such original document. For debate purposes, written evidence may be found in books, magazines, governmental pamphlets, and other writings, and is more widely used than spoken evidence since the procedures allow little opportunity for oral testimony.

Expert or ordinary

If an opinion comes from a recognized authority, the evidence is expert; otherwise it is ordinary. The doctor who testifies concerning the cause of a man's death gives expert testimony; if the same doctor expresses his opinion on socialized medicine, he gives ordinary testimony. A lawyer gives an expert opinion on a question of legal procedure; his opinion concerning the value of nuclear power or the economic soundness of income tax reduction would be ordinary testimony.

This distinction often becomes important in debate. A large automobile manufacturer may warrant public acclaim, but his industrial genius does not justify the acceptance of his opinion on the European Common Market. An individual must be qualified to give expert information on the point at issue before his opinion can count heavily as evidence.

Original or hearsay

Original evidence originates with the one presenting it. For instance, witness *A* testifies concerning what he saw at the scene of a crime; correspondent *A* writes about what he observed in Russia. Hearsay evidence consists of evidence that one receives from another. For example, witness *B* testifies as to what *A* told him that he saw at the scene of the crime; correspondent *B* writes about what he heard and read about Russia. Although often pertinent, hearsay evidence is inadmissible in law as a general rule, although exceptions to the hearsay rule exist. If Smith's word carries force as evidence in law, he should be called to testify himself.

Strict compliance with the hearsay rule cannot be enforced in an educational debate. If an authority is quoted as having made a statement and such statement is not offered in writing, it would not be possible to prove its authenticity by direct testimony. Usually the evidence used by debaters comes from books, pamphlets, and other documentary sources; if possible, this evidence should be quoted from original sources. If secondary sources must be used, it must be determined if the evidence has passed through reliable hands or if it has been altered. The tests of evidence in the final section of this chapter will help in determining these matters.

Evidence from original sources has more probative force than does material from secondary sources, but this does not rule out evidence that originates with the debater—for example, materials derived from an interview or from a personal survey. It does emphasize the importance, however, of showing how original evidence was derived from an objective study.

Positive or negative

Negative evidence differs from positive evidence in that the former is noticeable by its absence. The absence of filling stations and garages in an isolated community indicates that few of the inhabit-

ants own automobiles; the absence of liquor houses in a city constitutes evidence that the city is in "dry" territory. Positive evidence
consists of any existing facts or opinion statements relative to a
proposition. The presence of many filling stations and garages in
a community would be positive evidence that automobiles are used
there; the presence of numerous liquor houses in a city would be
positive indication that the city is in "wet" territory. Because most
evidence is positive, one seldom hears the terms positive and negative differentiated.

Negative evidence is more important in law than in debate. A
lack of evidence where one would reasonably expect to find it may
be convincing in itself. A debater depends largely on positive evidence.

Real or personal

At a court trial, real evidence consists of objects such as a gun, an
official document, or a will. Personal evidence consists of statements
of people expressing their own opinions or describing the circumstances of a situation. The introduction of a weapon used in a crime
exemplifies real evidence; a description of the weapon by a witness
is personal or verbal evidence. In debate, the submission of an actual contract agreement between employer and employees constitutes real evidence; an explanation of the agreement constitutes
personal evidence.

Real evidence plays a more important part in court trials than
in educational debate. Objects introduced in a court trial are subject
to inspection by the opposing counsel, judge, or members of the
jury. The procedures in college debate prevent extended use of real
evidence, but they admit use of personal evidence.

Deliberate or casual

Deliberate evidence is given with the knowledge or intent that
it may be used at a later date, whereas casual evidence is given without such knowledge or intent. If a person expresses his opinion for
publication, such a statement would be deliberate evidence. If the
same person expressed an offhand opinion in conversation with a
group of friends, such a statement would be casual evidence. Casual
evidence usually has the advantage of being free from bias and from

the effect of public opinion. The increasing use of brainstorming sessions by industry is based on this principle. Deliberate evidence has the advantage of prior thought and investigation. Although both types apply in educational debate, deliberate evidence predominates.

Use of classification

In educational debate, the strict rules of evidence of our courts of law do not apply, but from the law of evidence in the courts come many of the accepted procedures for presenting evidence in educational debate. The admissibility of evidence in debates is determined by relevancy in the absence of strict rules of procedure. Rarely does a debater have occasion to make fine distinctions among the kinds of evidence, but he should know the differences in order to understand fully the place of evidence in argumentation.

In using any kind of evidence, be sure to advance arguments and not mere assertions. Assertion consists of statements unsupported by convincing evidence; argument carries weight because inferences drawn from the evidence follow logically. Anyone who, without further efforts to establish his contention, becomes satisfied with the validity of a statement because "it is generally understood to be true" is guilty of using assertion for argument. It may be true that a certain investment in stock is safe, but the assertion that a prominent rich man recently became an officer in the company does not make the investment safe, for that assertion offers little proof. Do not be satisfied, therefore, until you find reliable evidence to corroborate each contention.

Tests of Evidence

The tests of evidence may be summed up under three heads—source, quality, and quantity.

If the source of evidence warrants the belief in its validity, then proceed to apply tests of probability and consistency to determine its quality. These tests apply to the evidence as well as to the person giving it. If the evidence meets the requirements of quality, next test its sufficiency; determine if enough evidence has been presented to establish probability. If the source of the evidence proves to be untrustworthy, there is little need for refuting the evidence itself.

Likewise, few reasons exist for applying the tests of quantity to evidence that lacks quality. Strong evidence may come from unexpected sources; poor evidence may have its origin in what appears to be an acceptable source.

As a debater you have a twofold responsibility: to challenge all evidence not likely to stand up under attack; to present only the type of evidence that can be successfully sustained under attack. By applying the following tests we may determine what constitutes reliable evidence.

Source

The following questions test the validity of the sources of fact and opinion evidence:

Is the Authority Prejudiced? It matters little why an authority becomes prejudiced, because he usually has a distorted view; he seeks evidence that will support his preconceived ideas and overlooks the rest. Some of the syndicated writers in our daily newspapers are pro-administration and others are anti-administration, so the reader who knows the topic and the writer of a given article can often anticipate its general trend. Since some men become prejudiced because of the positions they hold, the testimony of a high official in either a labor union or an industrial organization would likely be objectionable in a dispute between labor and capital. In a proposition advocating the outlawing of strikes, the testimony of such men would probably be biased.

We distrust statements issued by propaganda agencies and many public relations departments because prejudices stem from the very nature of their organizations. Any person less interested in discovering the total facts of a situation than in finding only those facts favorable to his own cause shows prejudice. Whatever the cause of the prejudices, the testimony from these sources carries little weight.

Is the Authority Mentally Qualified? An authority must be mentally qualified to render a mature judgment. The fact that a man has attained a prominent position does not qualify him per se as an authority. He may have been elected senator because he was a good showman—a master at hoodwinking people rather than at enlightening them. He may have bought his position as mayor of the city or inherited his position as vice-president of the company. You can determine the caliber of a writer by studying the reasons he gives for his opinions. Be less interested in what a purported authority says than in why he says it. A quotation from an article used in support of a contention should be considered in relationship to its context. Ask yourself if the article as a whole gives evidence of the author's qualifications as an authority.

Is the Authority Morally Qualified? Next, the moral qualification of the authority must be tested. What is his general reputation for truth and honesty? Judge the moral qualifications of an authority in part by his special interests in the issue. If it can be shown that he will gain undue wealth or prominence from his testimony, a motive for possible dishonesty may be established. In a debate on price fixing, the negative team quoted extensively from the findings of an economic research organization; later the affirmative side presented evidence to show that the research organization was maintained by an industrial concern opposed to price fixing. This information largely nullified the negative's evidence, for most people distrust a person whose opinions are patently influenced.

Is the Authority Qualified by Training and Experience? A witness may stand the tests concerning prejudice and mental and moral qualification, and yet fail as a competent authority because he lacks training and experience. An authority must be in a position to know the facts and to interpret them properly; he should speak from first-hand knowledge, not from shallow investigations. Above all, he ought to be well informed concerning the matters about which he writes.

The question arises, "What special opportunities has the witness had that enable him to speak with authority?" Too often greatness is only relative. For example, the opinion on an interpretation of the Constitution by a district judge would hardly offset the opinion of a recognized author on constitutional law; the word of an employee in a department of our national government would not carry the weight of the secretary of that department. A statement from an editor of a college newspaper would scarcely be worth as much as a statement from a nationally-known columnist.

Quality

After testing the source of evidence, next inquire into its quality. The fact that an authority meets all the tests of source does not guarantee that his statements constitute the best evidence. Investigation must determine the probability and the consistency of the evidence. Apply the following test questions:

Is the Evidence Probable? Regardless of how logical and valid a piece of evidence may appear, it must harmonize with general knowledge and human experience. Human beings will react to a given situation much as they have done in the past. Evidence that a prominent politician refused to take office after winning his campaign for governor will hardly be accepted without question; incongruous behavior must be explained and justified.

In a debate about strikes, one speaker presented evidence to prove that only one-tenth of one per cent of the workers were ever involved in strikes at the same time. The implication was that only a few people are affected by strikes; hence strikes could not be so bad as claimed. But at that time the locality was experiencing a bus strike, and the audience indicated by their reactions that they did not accept such evidence; they knew that a majority of the local workers were adversely affected by the tie-up of transportation. As a matter of fact, the evidence as presented about the number of workers on strike was valid, but the implication that the debaters inferred was not accepted because the evidence was not probable in the light of human experience.

Is the Evidence Consistent? Determine if the evidence is internally and externally consistent. Evidence becomes inconsistent internally when it presents contradictory material to prove an argument or to prove different contentions in the same case. For example, in a debate on increasing natural-resource taxes, one speaker gave evidence to prove that the producers of natural resources would be driven out of business by an increase in taxes. Later in the same speech, he showed that the natural resource producers would pass the tax on to the consumer by higher process costs. These contentions contradict each other. In another case, a debate on socialized medicine, the first negative speaker contended that the evils of the present system did not warrant a change. His colleague presented a counter-proposition, thus admitting the need for a change and substantially contradicting the first contention.

External inconsistencies result when evidence from one source contradicts that from another. Such inconsistency often occurs in the presentation of statistical information. In one debate tournament, students presented evidence to show that the cost of living had increased during the preceding five years. Some teams cited evidence that the increases were as little as 29 per cent; others gave evidence that the increases were as high as 175 per cent. These extremes constitute an inconsistency; both claims could not be correct. No doubt the inconsistency could be explained by an examination of how the groups of statistics were derived. Since few debaters bother to give details about statistical material, listeners become confused when such discrepancies arise.

The tests of probability and consistency may be made clearer by an illustration applied to legal usage. A witness testified to the identity of people who had been involved in a gunfight. The witness stated that he recognized certain persons during the disturbance, and as proof he submitted a piece of paper naming several persons allegedly involved. Upon inquiry he said that he had written the names during the disturbance, and that he recognized the persons by the flashes of gunfire. The paper was not soiled; the names were written evenly; and there was no evidence of nervousness on the part of the witness. Naturally the testimony was challenged. First, general experience suggests that men are hardly so thoughtful under such circumstances; second, men seldom show such calmness under fire; and finally, the neatness and orderliness of the sheet contradicted the statements of the witness. Despite the fact that the case is exceptional, it remains true that frequently evidence fails to meet the various tests. The alert debater will scrutinze evidence presented by his opponent as well as test his own evidence before presenting it.

Quantity

After applying the tests of source and quality, next determine if sufficient evidence has been given to justify your conclusions. There can be no "one and only" answer to how much evidence is necessary to prove an argument—much depends upon the nature of the argument and the beliefs of the audience. Obviously, quoting one authority or presenting one or two examples or giving statistics that cover a limited phase of the subject does not provide sufficient evidence to establish proof. For example, in proving that the evils of the present system of medical service warrant a change, considerable evidence will be necessary. No one evil warrants a change of the entire system. Therefore, cite several evils and support each by an abundance of evidence. On the other hand, to prove that there is an unequal distribution of medical facilities requires little evidence, for disparity in facilities is recognized by most people.

Do not waste time citing extensive evidence on points on which there will be little likelihood of disagreement. It requires more evidence to establish vital issues than it does to establish inconsequential points. Be sure, however, to offer sufficient evidence to prove the contention advanced. Do not draw conclusions that go beyond the evidence.

The beliefs of the audience help determine the sufficiency of evidence; evidence accepted as sufficient by one audience might be inadequate for another. The following questions should help determine audience acceptability:

1. What are the attitudes of the audience toward the argument?
   a. Does the audience favor the point of contention?
   b. Are the members of the audience on the whole neutral?
   c. Would the audience likely oppose the point of contention?
2. What is the background of the training and experience of the audience?
   a. Is the audience highly or poorly trained?
   b. Is there disparity in training?
3. What is the social and cultural background of the audience?
   a. Are personal desires of the audience much the same?
   b. What is the general social opinion of the group?
4. What is the approximate age level of the audience?
   a. Are the majority young?
   b. Are there disparities in age?

The existing beliefs of the audience help determine the extent of evidence required. Obviously if members of the audience already believe the contention, less evidence will be needed. The attitude of the audience may be gauged by political affiliation, geographical location, economic status, social and cultural attainment, religious beliefs, and current importance of the problem. Attitudes vary on public questions from time to time and from locality to locality. Before World War II, the subject of isolation was debated frequently. At that time the Middle West favored isolation more than did the Southwest and Far West. Since the war, the general attitude in almost all localities favors international cooperation. Whenever possible, get information concerning beliefs of the listeners before the debate.

Consider the intellectual level of the audience in determining the sufficiency of the evidence. Ascertain the general background of training and experience of the listeners in relation to the proposition for debate. The higher the critical ability, the greater will be the need for supporting material. Similarly, informed people are less likely than the poorly informed to accept a speaker as an authority.

People usually interpret what a speaker says in relationship to their own desires, and these desires often result from social and cultural standing. For instance, on the proposition of a minimum salary for public school teachers, less evidence would usually be needed to convince the college graduate than the nongraduate. On propositions for public improvements—such as new roads, schools, and hospitals—more evidence and different types would ordinarily be needed to convince persons with lower-class social and cultural backgrounds than for others. In testing the sufficiency of evidence, therefore, consider the interests and attitudes of different social groups.

Attention to the age level of the audience may also help determine the sufficiency of evidence. Since young people lack wide experience and knowledge, they are usually less critical and take suggestions more readily than do mature people. Likewise, older people are less likely to consider a speaker an expert than are younger persons.

Finally, corroborate one type of evidence by other types. Rarely should one type alone be used to support an argument. This principle applies especially to expert opinions, because for each authority cited an equally distinguished authority who holds a contrary view can usually be found. Since opinions held in common by many carry more weight than does the opinion of one person, do not rely on one or two authorities. Corroborate opinions by evidence such as statistics, examples, and analogies. Variety in both types and sources of evidence shows breadth of understanding and tends to support one's contentions.

Summary

Ethical, emotional, and logical proofs apply to educational debate, but logical proof forms the basic appeal. Evidence and reasoning constitute logical proof. Evidence consists of factual material and opinion; reasoning consists of inferences from the evidence. Evidence for debate closely parallels the law of evidence in our judicial system. The two general types of evidence are *fact* and *opinion*. Facts come from statistics, examples, and analogies; opinions grow out of beliefs. Statistics consist of compilations of facts on the basis of relative numbers of occurrences; examples are specific instances; analogies are comparisons.

Evidence may be classified as follows: (1) testimonial or circumstantial, (2) spoken or written, (3) expert or ordinary, (4) original or hearsay, (5) positive or negative, (6) real or personal, and (7) deliberate or casual. The tests of evidence come under three classifications: (1) tests of source, (2) tests of quality, and (3) tests of quantity. In testing the source of evidence, ascertain if the authority is prejudiced, mentally qualified, morally qualified, and qualified by training and experience to render acceptable testimony. The probability and consistency of evidence determine its quality. Quantity is determined by the nature of the argument, audience beliefs, and by the corroboration of evidence.

Oral Assignment

The oral assignment shall be in the form of a restricted symposium.
1. Each member of the class should prepare a list of seven topics on the subject chosen for classroom debates suitable for a symposium.
2. The best program, as determined by the instructor, should be selected for presentation.
3. The instructor should select a chairman and speakers for each topic.
4. The time limits for each speech should be five minutes.
5. An open forum should follow the discussion.

Collateral Readings

Abernathy, Elton, *The Advocate: A Manual of Persuasion,* Ch. 3. New York: David McKay Co., Inc., 1964.

Freeley, Austin J., *Argumentation and Debate,* Chs. 5, 6. Belmont, Calif.: Wadsworth Publishing Co., Inc., 1961.

Huber, Robert B., *Influencing Through Argument,* Ch. 5. New York: David McKay Co., Inc., 1963.

Kruger, Arthur N., *Modern Debate,* Ch. 10. New York: McGraw-Hill Book Co., Inc., 1960.

McBath, James H., ed., *Argumentation and Debate,* Ch. 9. New York: Holt, Rinehart & Winston, Inc., 1963.

McBurney, James H., and Glen E. Mills, *Argumentation and Debate: Techniques of a Free Society,* Ch. 7. New York: The Macmillan Company, 1964.

8
Reasoning Logically

Chapter 7 developed evidence as a part of logical proof. Reasoning, the other component of argument, receives detailed development in this and the following chapter.

Reasoning Explained

Argumentation is an appeal to the understanding for the purpose of influencing belief. Conviction results in part from logical reasoning. Logic, the process of distinguishing between good and bad reasoning, tests the thinking process to determine if the inferences drawn from evidence conform to the established rules of reasoning.

Evidence alone is not sufficient to establish logical proof. There must be a means of relating the evidence to the proposition, and this relationship must be established through reasoning—the process by which we infer a conclusion from premises. By diligent effort, we can secure abundant evidence; changing the evidence into argument requires mature thinking and reasoning. Certain inferences must be made from the evidence at hand; these inferences must be set forth so that others may understand the relationship. Careful thinking and communicative presentation are both necessary for effective oral argument. From the study of logic one learns how to interpret evidence; from the study of rhetoric one learns how to communicate the interpretation to others. The importance of reasoning, therefore, becomes readily seen.

Deduction and Induction Distinguished

The methods of reasoning differ according to the character of the inference. As explained in Chapter 1, reasoning may be classified broadly into induction and deduction. Inductive reasoning proceeds from the particular to the general; deductive reasoning proceeds from the general to the particular. Through the deductive process we go from a general statement in the premise to a particular statement in the conclusion; in inductive reasoning we go from a number of particular premises to a general conclusion. For example, suppose the proposition concerns inflation. You could establish a general statement concerning price increases through induction. By examining conditions in several representative states, and finding that prices have increased in these states since the Korean war, you could infer that prices have increased in the United States since the Korean war. Having established this general statement, you could then through deduction apply a particular situation to the general statement and infer a particular conclusion. The process is represented as follows:

Induction

> Prices have increased in New York since the Korean war.
> Prices have increased in Michigan since the Korean war.
> Prices have increased in California since the Korean war.
> Therefore, prices have increased in the United States since the Korean war.

Deduction

> Prices have increased in the United States since the Korean war.
> Illinois is a state of the United States.
> Therefore, prices have increased in Illinois since the Korean war.

The same process may be applied to almost any situation; for example, by examining unemployment problems in several representative industries, you may draw the general conclusion that there has been unemployment in the major industries. The general conclusion thus derived may serve as the basis of a deduction to a particular case.

Although the method of reasoning differs in induction and deduction, they are not antagonistic types of reasoning. The one supplements the other. Some deduction is present in induction, since induction must proceed from assumptions, and the inductive method for establishing a general premise serves as the starting point for deduction.

Induction Explained

In induction, the truth concerning a general class results from an examination of its parts. Individual instances constitute representative examples of the entire class, and from these known instances a conclusion can be drawn relating to the whole class. The conclusions arrived at by induction cannot be conclusive because they are based on approximations. Inductive reasoning should be looked upon as scientific investigation—a process of investigating, analyzing, and explaining individual cases in an attempt to establish a general rule.

There are two kinds of induction, *perfect* and *imperfect*. Perfect induction results when all parts of a class are examined and found to have certain characteristics in common. To understand perfect induction, consider the well-known example: All the planets revolve on their axes, since Mercury, Venus, Earth, Mars, Jupiter, Saturn, Uranus, Neptune, and Pluto revolve on their axes. The general conclusion, that all planets revolve on their axes, comes after the discovery that each individual planet revolves on its axis. The perfect induction, in reality, does not require an inference since the conclusion is based on established facts. There is no going from a known to an unknown; it is all known. As various logicians point out when considering similar cases, there is no reasoning in the true sense because a conclusion can be reached without an inference.

Imperfect induction differs from perfect induction in that only a part of the class is examined and from this examination a general conclusion is drawn. For instance, one may conclude that the planets revolve on their axes from an examination of only three representative planets—Mars, Mercury, and Earth.

Generalization

The process of generalization calls for the examination of several representative cases or examples. If certain factors appear in each example of the same class, you may conclude that the same factors prevail in those cases or examples not examined. In short, certain known instances may be examined and a conclusion drawn regarding a whole class without an examination of each instance in the class.

Suppose the conclusion to be drawn states that the work of Congress was commendable last session. Individual cases may be given of the work of Congress relative to taxation, labor, civil rights, foreign aid, and control of nuclear power. If you find that the work of Congress was commendable in these legislative acts, you may conclude that the work of Congress as a whole was commendable.

Note the following illustration:

> *Example 1:* Debaters make superior academic records at Stanford University.
> *Example 2:* Debaters make superior academic records at Northwestern University.
> *Example 3:* Debaters make superior academic records at Harvard University.
> *Example 4:* Debaters make superior academic records at Michigan State University.
> *Conclusion:* Therefore, debaters make superior academic records.

Let us assume that these universities constitute representative institutions and that the facts are as stated. This generalization proceeds on the basis that what is true concerning the academic records of debaters at these four universities is universally true. Thus a general conclusion results from an examination of particular instances.

In generalization you do not examine all cases; to do so would be complete or perfect induction. Many propositions, however, cannot be established short of complete induction. For example, to prove that all senators are over 50 years of age, nothing short of a consideration of all 100 senators would suffice. Even one exception would disprove the conclusion. However, to prove that senators past 50 years of age make greater contributions to the country than do those under 50 is possible without an examination of the record of every senator.

To avoid fallacies, consider the following questions.

Have you given a sufficient number of examples?

The answer to this question depends upon an examination of all the facts of the generalization. No set formula for measuring the number of instances necessary to warrant a generalization can be stated because the number varies with each proposition. Using the states of California, Texas, and Florida as examples would hardly be sufficient to generalize that agricultural production increased in the United States in 1964. In measuring general agricultural production, a variety of products must be considered, some of which are not produced by these states. Furthermore, agricultural production depends upon such factors as rainfall and other climatic conditions, which differ considerably over wide areas. To warrant the generalization, it would be necessary to select several representative states from different sections of the country.

On the other hand, the examples of California, Texas, and Florida probably constitute a sufficient number to generalize that the production of oranges increased, since these three states are the principal producers of oranges, and other states that produce small quantities have climatic conditions similar to those of the states mentioned. Thus it becomes evident that the number of examples needed for a generalization depends largely upon the nature of the proposition. One must apply thought and reasoning in determining whether or not the number of examples given justify the stated conclusion.

The type of resolution also determines whether or not all the instances of a proposition must be examined. That all members of the Supreme Court are college graduates must be established in this manner. As explained earlier in this chapter, this procedure is known as complete or perfect induction and involves no inference or reasoning; in generalization, a few examples represent all examples of a class. Usually the greater the number of examples cited, the stronger the argument becomes.

Are your examples representative of their class?

The examples chosen must not be exceptions to the general rule. Nonrepresentative instances may be found under almost all propositions, and you must avoid the common error of choosing them. For example, you can find some citizens in the United States who do not believe in free enterprise. If you take these exceptions and generalize that the United States is becoming communistic, you are likely to misrepresent actual conditions. In the same manner, you might argue that business is bad by citing the railroad industry, the carriage industry, and other industries adversely affected by scientific and technological advances. To ascertain the condition of business today, you must consider representative business concerns, such as construction, steel, and clothing.

The human tendency to choose extreme examples for making one's contentions convincing applies especially to debate. In debating government control of industries with war contracts, for instance, you might use extreme examples disclosed in sensational articles or books to show the malpractices of some manufacturers who had war contracts. In fact, the majority of wartime contract industries produce peacetime commodities except during war. A few sensational examples of how unscrupulous manufacturers abused their war contracts hardly represent these industries as a whole. Examples should be chosen that fairly represent the examples not chosen; the parts should represent the whole.

Can you account for negative examples?

Negative examples are exceptions to those chosen for generalization. A generalization need not be invalidated by negative instances, but such examples must be accounted for if the generalization is to stand; otherwise the way is open for opposing speakers to call attention to them and thus weaken or destroy the argument. Account for negative instances by showing them to be exceptional cases. For example, by reviewing the record of the production of wheat in the state of Kansas over a fifteen-year period, you may generalize that Kansas is an excellent state for growing wheat. Records that reveal poor production for some one year may be cited, but this negative instance will be explained if you can show that the poor yield resulted from hurricanes, hailstorms, or other unusual circumstances.

If negative examples exist in an appreciable number, the generalization will be weakened or possibly destroyed; to what extent it is weakened depends upon the number of negative instances not proved to be exceptional. Beware of assuming that negative examples do not exist because they are unknown, for negative examples have been found where they seemed not to exist. A well-known instance is the old belief that all swans were white—black swans have been found. In choosing examples for a generalization, assure yourself that either no negative examples exist or those that do exist can be satisfactorily explained.

*Is your conclusion corroborated by other known
facts and arguments?*

If the argument meets the requirements of the foregoing tests,
determine whether or not any causal connection exists between the
conclusions and other known facts. The ultimate test of any conclusion depends upon whether or not it follows logically. For example, a person notices several college graduates who fail in
business and concludes that a college education causes failure in
the business world. How does this conclusion harmonize with other
known facts? Records of our colleges and universities show that
enrollments in their business schools have progressively increased
during the last decade. Big business is increasing its demand for
college graduates. Surveys show that college graduates, as a class,
advance more rapidly in business than nongraduates. The conclusion from the generalization is contrary to other known facts; the
causal connection between education and failure in business has
not been established even though several examples may be found
as an apparent basis for the generalization.

If the examples from which the generalizations come are representative, if a sufficient number are given, and if negative instances
can be accounted for, a probable truth relative to the whole class
may be reached. Remember that such a conclusion cannot be considered conclusive without an examination of all possible cases. It
must be corroborated by other facts and reasons. When a probable
universal law has been reached by induction, the conclusion may
then become the basis for deductive reasoning. In fact, if either
premise of the syllogism is not accepted as true, the premise under
question must be established by induction. These two processes
must go hand in hand; one must serve to substantiate the conclusions drawn from the other.

Analogy

Analogy is reasoning based on the assumption that if two things
are alike in several important known respects, they will probably
be alike in other respects not known or investigated. This form of
reasoning can best be understood when differentiated from deductive reasoning and inductive reasoning by generalization. Deductive

reasoning is inference from a general statement to specific instances; generalization is inference from specific instances to a general statement; analogy is inference from one specific instance to another specific instance. As such, analogy does not lead to a conclusion regarding a specific case, but rather to a resemblance of relationships between the compared objects. For instance, having observed that university X and university Y have an equal number of students and are alike in make-up of student bodies, school curricula, and student interests, the reasoner infers that because a system of student government has been successful at university X, it would also be successful at university Y. From this point the reasoner may extend the inference and contend that student government would be successful in all American universities similar in size and characteristics to X university. Thus we see that analogy deals with a resemblance of relationships and consists in comparing things alike in the relation they bear to other things.

Analogy is divided into two classes, *literal* and *figurative*. Literal analogy is based upon similarity of two objects of the same class. It is inferred that the objects resemble each other in points not known because they resemble each other in known respects. To illustrate, two men came from the same community, attended the same public school, later attended the same college, and held common membership in clubs and churches. Because of the similarity in social, religious, and educational background, we infer that the two men belong to the same political party. Of course, the inference may be wrong, but a degree of probability has been established. The inference that other planets are inhabited because they resemble the earth in many respects necessary for human habitation may likewise be wrong, but the comparison helps establish probability. The tests that follow in this section help determine the validity of the conclusion arrived at through analogy.

A common analogy heard in debates on world federation was that a federation of the United Nations would be successful because the federation of the fifty American states has been successful. The analogy was based on the arguments that conditions facing the original states in colonial times were analogous to the conditions facing the United Nations. The inference is made from a preponderance of resemblances between two situations within a class—we infer that the resemblances in known particulars extend to unknown particulars.

Figurative analogy carries the comparison to objects in different classes. The parables in the teachings of Christ are good illustrations of this form of analogy—for example, the parable of the seeds falling onto different kinds of soil. Another example is found in the parable "cast your bread upon the waters and it will not return unto you void," where the bread represents good deeds and the waters represent life. Milton, in *Lycidas,* gives an excellent analogy in his comparison of unworthy bishops and faithless shepherds. He says a bishop should foresee dangers and supply spiritual food for his church or parish just as a shepherd should guard his flock against the ravages of wild beasts and lead it into good grazing places. The effectiveness of argument based on figurative analogy depends upon the strength of the resemblance that has been pointed out.

Strictly speaking, analogy is not an identity of one thing with another, but an identity of relationships. Clear-cut relations, pertinent to conclusions reached, must actually exist and be shown in the comparison. Even when similarities appear to exist, the conclusions from analogy cannot offer absolute proof, for there may be only apparent similarity. The analogy, therefore, should be used in conjunction with other forms of proof.

In using the analogy, determine if it meets the following tests for this type of reasoning.

Are the similarities more important than the known differences?

That many points of similarity exist between two things does not always warrant an inference that the things are fundamentally similar. The number of similarities may be of less value than their weight or strength. Irrelevant details, regardless of number, cannot serve as the basis for a valid analogy. For instance, a common analogy used in debates on the proposition that the United States join the World Court was a comparison of the World Court to the system of courts in the United States. The similarities pointed out were as follows:

> Both had a permanent bench of jurists.
> Both met regularly at an appointed time and place.
> Both employed strict legal procedure.
> Both had a definite body of law upon which to base their decisions.

One important point of difference, however, outweighed these points of likeness. The United States provided an enforcement agent for the decisions of the Supreme Court; the nations comprising the World Court provided no such enforcement agency. Although the points of likeness were many, their importance was not so great. In using analogy, therefore, check carefully both the number and importance of the points of similarity.

Can the differences be accounted for?

Differences will not necessarily invalidate the conclusion from an analogy if you can explain them or demonstrate that they are nonessential. Similarities in the cases compared need exist only in matters relative to the point at issue. To illustrate: in the analogy that a certain type of student government would succeed at university Y because it had succeeded at university X, suppose it could be shown that the two schools differed greatly in endowment. Would this difference be a factor in the success or failure of student government at either of the institutions? No—the difference is not material to the point at issue.

Conversely, suppose we know that Y has fraternities and sororities, whereas X forbids such organizations. This difference applies specifically to the issue—fraternities and sororities, with their inter-club councils, may well provide the principal functions that a student government provides in universities without such organizations. It would be difficult to minimize this important difference. In reasoning by analogy, you must show either that no differences exist between the cases compared or that the existing differences are not important.

Is the conclusion corroborated by other known facts and arguments?

The probative force of an argument by analogy is less than that of some other types of reasoning, because analogy leads to a conclusion concerning the relationships of the two cases involved, not to a conclusion relative to a general class. For this reason, do not use the argument from analogy as the only form of support; supplement it by other types of argument.

Causal Relation

All reasoning from causal relation arises from the belief that a cause exists for every effect and every cause will produce its effect. The acts of nature are uniform and consistent—the same cause will produce the same effect, and the same effect will result from the same cause, as long as natural law is not interfered with by extraneous factors. We read that hailstorms have hit the Oklahoma grain fields; we infer that the grain crop from this section will be short. We note a large cotton crop; we infer that the price of cotton will decrease. We observe a high divorce rate; we attribute the cause to hasty or ill-advised marriages. We read that many former school teachers are returning to the profession; we infer increased salary scales.

Reasoning by causal relation results in a particular conclusion and is largely inductive in form. Our acceptance of the conclusion depends upon the observance of numerous similar instances. We assume that an economic recession will follow a period of inflation and speculation because recessions have always followed periods of inflation. Since prices have decreased in former recessions, we assume that prices will decrease in any recession.

The principal types of reasoning from causal relation are from effect to cause and from cause to effect.

Reasoning from effect to cause

In argument from effect to cause, you observe a known effect and try to determine the cause. You attempt to prove the observed effect can result from no other cause or causes than those suggested. The argument is from what comes after to what has gone before. For example, statistics show an increasing crime rate in the United States. This increase may be traced to an aspect of war that has fostered a spirit of disregard for law. Again, we note that the birth rate of the nation increases noticeably during war; the cause we attribute to this known effect is that war brings about many hasty marriages. In each instance, we start with a known effect and attribute the effect to a specified cause or causes. Apply the following tests.

Is the Alleged Cause Adequate to Produce the Known Effect? The strength of the argument from effect to cause depends on the extent to which the cause can be established. If the cause is merely a possible one, the argument is weak; if it is probable, the argument may still be inconclusive; if the cause is absolute, the argument is conclusive. In some instances, the alleged cause may not be sufficiently strong to create the known effect. In a debate on government ownership of industry during periods of war, one speaker argued that the desire for wartime profits by private industry caused the war. Few people would agree that this factor alone could cause war. Philosophers, theologians, political scientists, sociologists, economists, and others have considered without unanimity of agreement many causes that may lead to war. One historian points out more than a hundred contributing factors. It becomes apparent that no single cause for war can be established definitely—although the desire for financial gain may be a powerful human motive, it can hardly be powerful enough to create war. We must weigh carefully the adequacy of the alleged cause for producing the known effect.

Could Other Causes Produce the Known Effect? The argument from effect to cause may be weakened by establishing a more probable cause or causes than those alleged. For example, hasty war marriages may be alleged as the cause for our increasing divorce rate, but among other causes are inadequate divorce laws, laxness of our courts in upholding existing laws, and the effect of the movies, television, and modern literature in glamorizing divorce. Any of these causes may be as important as the alleged cause. The soundness of the argument depends largely on the strength of the probability that no other cause or causes than those alleged could produce the known effect. This factor does not prevent the possibility of attributing more than one cause for an effect; the multiplicity of causes for most effects, however, gives warning not to omit a cause greater than those advanced.

Reasoning from cause to effect

In argument from cause to effect, you reason that a certain happening is probable in that the assigned causes are sufficient to bring it about. You start with the circumstances sufficient for a cause and attempt to establish what the effect will be. For example, you observe that the nation's wheat supply is diminishing rapidly. What will be the effect of this scarcity of wheat? Rationing will be instituted throughout the nation as a means of controlling the consumption of wheat. Again, it may be noted that in spite of attempts to bolster the economy, unemployment persists. What effect will this decrease in employment have? More drastic measures will have to be taken to encourage employment. Will decreased income taxation, more liberal interest notes, or a combination of several measures be effective? Argument from cause to effect attempts to establish the most probable effect of a given circumstance.

The following tests apply.

Is the Cause Sufficient to Produce the Alleged Effect? The strength of the argument from cause to effect depends upon the adequacy of the cause. In some instances a cause may tend toward a certain effect without having sufficient force to produce the alleged effect. For example, the voluntary purchase of government bonds tends to absorb excess purchasing power, but that plan alone would hardly prevent inflation. To contend that a program of government bond purchasing will prevent inflation attaches undue strength to a cause.

In a debate on state medicine, the affirmative contended that the high cost of medicine caused a lack of practice of preventive medicine. The debaters reasoned in part: "The high cost of medicine discourages use of preventive remedies. Because of the high fees charged by doctors, many people refrain from using such facilities until they become absolutely necessary. . . . Such individuals postpone consulting a doctor, hoping that it will not be necessary and that they may save the fee." In this instance the contention was that the cause "high fees" produced the effect "failure to practice preventive medicine." The opposing speakers reasoned that the suggested cause was insufficient to produce the alleged effect: "These facts indicate that the present system of medicine makes every effort to encourage preventive medicine even to the point of furnishing such service free of charge to those who cannot pay and charging others according to their ability. The cause of the failure to use preventive remedies is more fundamental than the high cost of medical care. A better explanation for this condition is that the people have not been taught the value of preventive medicine."

Is the Cause Prevented from Producing the Alleged Effect? If other forces sufficient to prevent the given cause from producing the alleged effect can be shown, the argument from cause to effect will be weakened or destroyed. The owner of an automobile might reason that his car radiator froze during the night since the temperature fell below the freezing point—until he learns that his chauffeur had put an antifreeze solution in the radiator. The antifreeze solution prevented the original cause from producing the assumed effect. Similarly, a farmer might reason that the sugar-beet crop of a given section will be curtailed by an extended drought until he learns that the beet producers use irrigation. In these instances, the causes are sufficient to produce the alleged effects, but intervening conditions prevent the causes from operating in the usual manner.

In a debate on state medicine, one speaker attempted to show how a cause would be prevented from producing an alleged effect as follows:

> The gentlemen of the negative contend that state medicine will destroy the incentive of the doctor to do his best work since he will be under state control. They reason that state control means a fixed salary and standardized methods of treatment and that both factors are destructive of incentive. We do not deny that the doctor's remuneration and freedom of procedure affect his initiative; we do deny that these factors will operate to cause the effect alleged by the opposition. The doctor will still control the medical profession under state medicine. The state will be responsible only for providing the general organization of the plan and for raising the necessary funds. Instead of being paid a fee for each service rendered, the doctor will be paid a salary. His salary will depend upon his ability and experience. The better the service, the higher his salary will be under state medicine. This plan will provide a strong incentive for the doctor to do his best work. State medicine will relieve the doctor of tedious business details, and will thus give him more time to practice his profession. . . . Certainly there will be every incentive for the physician to excel under state medicine because the greater his accomplishments, the better his position with the state.[1]

Summary

Evidence and reasoning constitute the components of logical proof. Reasoning, the process of inferring conclusions from premises, may be classified as inductive and deductive. Induction proceeds from a specific instance to a general conclusion; deduction proceeds from a general premise to a conclusion about a particular case.

There are two types of induction: (1) complete or perfect and (2)

---

[1] Taken from a class debate.

incomplete or imperfect. Perfect induction consists of an examination of all the specific instances of a general class; imperfect induction consists of an examination of representative examples within the class. Inductive reasoning by example, or generalization, is the process of reaching a conclusion from an examination of representative instances. Suggested tests for generalization are as follows: (1) Have you given a sufficient number of examples? (2) Are the examples you gave representative of their class? (3) Can you account for negative examples? (4) Is your conclusion from the generalization corroborated by other known facts and arguments?

Argument by analogy consists of a comparison between two things; it is based upon the belief that if two things are alike in certain known respects they will also be alike in those respects not known. Analogy is divided into two classes: (1) literal analogy—similarity of two objects of the same class; (2) figurative analogy—similarity of two objects of different classes. Tests for the argument by analogy are: (1) Is the comparison based upon a greater number of important similarities than there are known differences? (2) Can the differences in the cases compared be accounted for? (3) Is the conclusion from the analogy corroborated by other known facts and arguments?

The method of causal relation is based upon the universal belief that nothing happens without cause. Two forms of argument from causal relations are (1) argument from effect to cause—the effect is observed and one attempts to determine the cause; (2) argument from cause to effect—the circumstances are known and one attempts to establish the probable effect. The following tests apply to argument from effect to cause: (1) Is the alleged cause adequate to produce the known effect? (2) Could other causes produce the known effect? Argument from cause to effect should be subjected to the following tests: (1) Is the cause adequate to produce the alleged effect? (2) Is the cause prevented from producing the alleged effect? Knowledge of the methods of argument give proper order and arrangement to reasoning.

Oral Assignment

Prepare the following assignment in the form of an unrestricted symposium:

1. Each member of the class should prepare a program for an unrestricted symposium discussion on the subject chosen for classroom debates.

2. The best program should be chosen by the instructor for presentation before the class.
3. The instructor should select a chairman and speakers for each topic. The discussion members should not be the same as chosen for the restricted symposium in the last assignment.
4. The time limit for each member should be five minutes.
5. An open forum should follow the discussion.

Collateral Readings

Braden, Waldo W., and Earnest Brandenburg, *Oral Decision Making*, Ch. 6. New York: Harper & Row, Publishers, 1955.

Crocker, Lionel, *Argumentation and Debate*, Ch. 8. New York: American Institute of Banking, 1962.

Ehninger, Douglas, and Wayne Brockriede, *Decision by Debate*, Ch. 10. New York: Dodd, Mead & Co., 1963.

Huber, Robert B., *Influencing Through Argument*, Ch. 6. New York: David McKay Co., Inc., 1963.

McBath, James H., ed., *Argumentation and Debate*, Ch. 10. New York: Holt, Rinehart & Winston, Inc., 1963.

McBurney, James H., and Glen E. Mills, *Argumentation and Debate: Techniques of a Free Society*, Ch. 8. New York: The Macmillan Company, 1964.

9
Applying Deductive Forms

Deduction should be looked upon as a form rather than a type of reasoning. Given a general premise accepted as true, you can bring a specific case under the general premise and draw a conclusion about the particular instance. The *syllogism* constitutes the principal form for deduction; the *enthymeme* and *sorites* are other forms.

The Syllogism

The syllogism consists of the logical arrangement of three statements or propositions so related as to warrant the inference of the last statement from the first two. The two statements from which the inference is drawn constitute the major premise and the minor premise. The third statement forms the conclusion.

The major premise consists of a general rule or statement from which the deduction arises. The minor premise consists of a particular instance or statement that falls within the class of the major premise. The conclusion follows from the two premises relative to the particular instance contained in the minor premise. The following syllogism illustrates these principles:

> *Major premise:* All speech courses have practical value.
> *Minor premise:* Argumentation is a speech course.
> *Conclusion:* Therefore, argumentation has practical value.

The first two statements must be true and properly related before a factual conclusion can be reached. The form of the syllogism may be correct, however, whether or not the premises are in fact true. Before we can determine whether the conclusion follows logically, we must subject the three parts of the syllogism to certain tests.

The syllogism should not be considered as an end within itself but rather as a form in which reasoning may be expressed. It may serve a useful purpose in examining and testing reasoning as well as expressing the results of reasoning. Putting arguments into syllogistic form stimulates the ability to think reflectively, to express relationships logically, and to test the reasoning of others. The examples of syllogisms used throughout this chapter are for illustrative purposes only—the premises may not in fact be true. In debates the premise must be proved true as a basis for syllogistic reasoning.

There are three principal types of syllogisms: (1) complete or categorical, (2) conditional or hypothetical, and (3) alternative or disjunctive. These terms may be found in textbooks on logic and under various names in textbooks on argumentation and debate. No attempt will be made here to go into an exhaustive study of these forms; only such discussion as will be helpful in actual debate work will be developed.

Categorical

In the categorical syllogism, the major premise consists of a categorical or unqualified statement in which no exceptions exist. It concerns the classifying of things.

> *Major premise:* All speech courses have value.
> *Minor premise:* Acting is a speech course.
> *Conclusion:* Acting has value.

or

> *Major premise:* Every speech course is beneficial.
> *Minor premise:* Debate is a speech course.
> *Conclusion:* Debate is beneficial.

In these examples, the terms "all speech courses" and "every speech course" are unqualified statements. If the terms "some speech courses" or "a few speech courses" are substituted, the conclusions do not follow. Further, note that "acting" and "debate" are classifications of "speech courses." The categorical syllogism must conform not only to general rules but to the specific rules for this type of syllogism.

There Must Be Only Three Terms. The terms are known as major, middle, and minor. Each term should be used twice in the syllogism. The major term may be recognized as the predicate of both the major premise and the conclusion. The middle term is the subject of the major premise and the predicate of the minor premise. The minor term is the subject of both the minor premise and the conclusion.

	Middle term		Major term
Major premise:	All art	is	cultural.
Minor premise:	Minor term		Middle term
	Singing	is	an art.
Conclusion:	Minor term		Major term
	Singing	is	cultural.

For illustrative purposes, consider the following syllogism:

Major premise: All men are mortal.
Minor premise: Rover is mortal.
Conclusion: Rover is a man.

Immediately we sense that something is wrong; the conclusion does not necessarily follow from the two premises. The fault lies in the failure to include the middle term in the minor premise. If the major premise had been "All mortals are men," the form would be correct. If the minor premise had been "Rover is a man," the conclusion, "Rover is mortal," would follow logically.

The Middle Term Must Be Distributed in at Least One of the Premises. A distributed term is universal; it relates to a class of things in its entirety or all the parts of a whole. The terms "all" and "every" signify universality. Such terms as "all art" and "every course" are distributed terms, whereas such terms as "some art" and "many courses" are undistributed.

Major premise: All effective debaters study logic.
Minor premise: Joe Doe is an effective debater.
Conclusion: John Doe studies logic.

or

Major premise: Many effective debaters study logic.
Minor premise: John Doe is an effective debater.
Conclusion: John Doe studies logic.

In the first syllogism, the term "all effective debaters" is distributed because it includes the entire classification. The form of the syllogism is therefore correct whether or not the conclusion be true. The second syllogism contains the middle term "many effective debaters," which is undistributed. Although the conclusion may be true, it does not follow logically because of the undistributed middle term—John Doe may be one of the few effective debaters who has not studied logic.

If a Term Is Distributed in the Conclusion, It Must Be Distributed in One of the Premises. This rule is based upon the principle that a term in the conclusion cannot have a more all-inclusive meaning than it has in the premises. The rule applies only to the major and minor terms since the middle term never appears in the conclusion. The following example illustrates the illicit major (major term has a more restricted meaning in premise than in conclusion):

> *Major premise:* Debaters are students of logic.
> *Minor premise:* Actors are not debaters.
> *Conclusion:* Actors are not students of logic.

The major term "students of logic" is undistributed in the major premise. The premise does not state that debaters constitute all of the students of logic; only some students of logic are debaters. The major term, used in a distributed sense in the conclusion, excludes actors. The conclusion does not follow; actors may be students of logic the same as debaters.

The following example illustrates the illicit minor (minor term has a more restricted meaning in the premise than in the conclusion):

> *Major premise:* All debaters are students of logic.
> *Minor premise:* Some effective speakers are debaters.
> *Conclusion:* All effective speakers are students of logic.

The minor term "some effective speakers" is undistributed in the minor premise because it does not include all effective speakers. Debaters may be effective speakers without comprising all the group so classified. The minor term is distributed in the conclusion since it includes "all effective speakers." Thus the minor term says more about effective speakers in the conclusion than it says in the minor premise.

No Conclusion Can Be Drawn from Two Negative Premises. Reference to the first rule of the categorical syllogism shows the reasonableness of this rule. Negative premises tend to invalidate the arrangement of major, middle, and minor terms; the major and minor term cannot be located in relation to each other;

in essence, no middle term exists. Note the lack of connection among the major, middle, and minor terms in the following example:

Major premise: No actors are debaters at X University.
Minor premise: John Doe is not an actor at X University.
Conclusion: John Doe is a debater at X University.

The conclusion is not valid, nor would any other conclusion follow from these negative premises. John Doe may be neither an actor nor a debater at X University.

If One Premise Is Negative, the Conclusion Must Be Negative. An affirmative conclusion is impossible where negative premises occur. The conclusion should be negative with either a negative major or minor premise. Note the negative in the major premise of the following illustration:

Major premise: No actors are debaters at X University.
Minor premise: John Doe is an actor at X University.
Conclusion: John Doe is not a debater at X University.

If no actors are debaters and John Doe is an actor, we know that he cannot be a debater.

The following illustration contains a negative in the minor premise:

Major premise: Only "A" students are debaters.
Minor premise: John Doe is not an "A" student.
Conclusion: John Doe is not a debater.

If only "A" students are debaters and John Doe is not an "A" student, he cannot be a debater.

No Conclusion Can Be Drawn from Two Particular Premises. A particular premise includes only part of a class, whereas a universal premise contains all the class.

Major premise: Some debaters are "A" students
Minor premise: Some law students are debaters.
Conclusion: Some law students are "A" students.

The conclusion does not follow from the two particular premises —all law students who are debaters may be included in that group of debaters who do not make "A" grades.

The Conclusion Must Be Particular if One of the Premises Is Particular. This rule is deducible from a general understanding of deductive reasoning; deduction proceeds from a general principle to a particular instance. In the following illustration of the rule, the major premise is universal, the minor premise and the conclusion particular.

Major premise: All debaters are "A" students.
Minor premise: Some law students are debaters.
Conclusion: Some law students are "A" students.

The particular conclusion follows logically from the universal major premise and the particular minor premise.

Conditional or hypothetical

The hypothetical syllogism is based upon probability; that is, it has in its premises a condition. In essence, this form states: "If one proposition is true, then another follows." Note the condition expressed in the following propositions: (1) If world peace is to be achieved, world government must be perfected. (2) If Congress decreases taxes, inflation will ensue. (3) If taxes are increased, industry will curtail investment. (4) If prices continue to soar, a recession will result. In the hypothetical syllogism, the major premise contains a condition. The minor premise comes within the class of the hypothesis expressed in the major premise. The conclusion shows that what is true of the generalization in the major premise must also be true of the particular instance expressed in the minor premise. The "if" or conditional clause of the major premise constitutes the antecedent, and the clause to which the condition applies is the consequent. In the following example, "if Congress decreases the income tax" is the antecedent; "purchasing power will increase" is the consequent.

Major premise: If Congress decreases the income tax, purchasing power will increase.
Minor premise: Congress did decrease the income tax.
Conclusion: Purchasing power will increase.

The rules for testing the hypothetical syllogism follow:

If the Minor Premise Affirms the Antecedent, the Conclusion Must Affirm the Consequent. This form is the most common of the hypothetical syllogisms. It is expressed in the preceding example and in the following:

Major premise: If Congress decreases taxes, inflation will increase.
Minor premise: Congress will decrease taxes.
Conclusion: Inflation will increase.

The minor premise affirms the antecedent—"if Congress decreases taxes"; the conclusion affirms the consequent—"inflation will increase."

For practical purposes, let us examine the following statement made by a debater: "If the present method of trial by jury secures incompetent jurors, we should have a substitute for our present method of trial by jury. All men will recognize the fact that many incompetent men serve on our juries today. Then, gentlemen, we should have a substitute for trial by jury." Did the debater affirm the consequent in the minor premise of his argument? The minor premise affirms that incompetent men serve on juries, but it does not affirm that the present method of trial by jury secures incompetent men. Were all the possible conditions considered? There might have been flaws in the machinery instead of in the method of trial by jury. The conclusion, therefore, is fallacious.

If the Minor Premise Denies the Consequent, the Conclusion Must Deny the Antecedent. The minor premise of the example above may be changed to illustrate this rule:

> *Major premise:* If Congress decreases taxes, inflation will increase.
> *Minor premise:* Inflation will not increase.
> *Conclusion:* Congress will not decrease taxes.

If we assume the major premise to be true, the conclusion follows logically. The major premise makes inflation an absolute consequent of a decrease in taxes. If inflation does not increase, taxes will not be decreased. The minor premise denies the consequent— "inflation will not increase"; the conclusion denies the antecedent —"Congress will not decrease taxes."

If the Minor Premise Affirms the Consequent, No Valid Conclusion May Be Made. Arranged in this order, the example used above appears as follows:

> *Major premise:* If Congress decreases taxes, inflation will increase.
> *Minor premise:* Inflation will increase.
> *Conclusion:* Congress will decrease taxes.

The conclusion does not necessarily follow from the condition stated in the major premise. Although further inflation is an absolute consequent of a decrease in taxes, inflation may result from other causes. The major premise does not state that inflation will increase only upon the condition of a decrease in taxes. The conclusion could easily be true, but it does not necessarily follow logically from the premises.

If the Minor Premise Denies the Antecedent, No Valid Conclusion May Be Made. Let us consider the same syllogism arranged in this order:

> *Major premise:* If Congress decreases taxes, inflation will increase.
> *Minor premise:* Congress will not decrease taxes.
> *Conclusion:* Inflation will not increase.

Again, the conclusion does not necessarily follow from the condition stated in the major premise. Although the premise states that inflation will increase if Congress decreases taxes, it fails to make any statement about the conditions that prompted no decrease in taxes. Even though Congress does not decrease taxes, increased inflation could result from numerous other causes, such as increased government spending, payment of bonus to soldiers, cashing of savings bonds, or any measure that greatly increases buying power without a corresponding increase in production. The conclusion is therefore invalid.

Alternative or disjunctive

A third form of syllogism is the alternative or disjunctive. In this form, the words "either . . . or" occur and present alternative possibilities. The major premise states the alternative possibilities; the minor premise either affirms or negates one of the alternatives; the conclusion negates the alternative not affirmed or affirms the alternative not negated in the minor premise.

> *Major premise:* The student is either a graduate or an undergraduate.
> *Minor premise:* The student is an undergraduate.
> *Conclusion:* He is not a graduate.

or

> *Major premise:* The student is either a graduate or an undergraduate.
> *Minor premise:* The student is not an undergraduate.
> *Conclusion:* He is a graduate.

The following rules govern the disjunctive syllogism:

The Possibilities Enumerated in the Major Premise Must Be All-Inclusive. Rarely can problems be resolved into either-or statements since most problems have more than two alternatives. Failure to include all possible alternatives in the major premise of a disjunctive syllogism renders it invalid.

> *Major premise:* To prevent inflation, either taxes must be increased or wages must be decreased.
> *Minor premise:* Wages cannot be decreased.
> *Conclusion:* Taxes must be increased.

In this example, the major premise overlooks other preventives for inflation—increased production, an expanded program of savings, widespread purchase of government bonds, and other methods designed to take surplus purchasing power out of circulation. Thus inflation could be prevented without either increasing taxes or decreasing wages.

The Possibilities Enumerated in the Major Premise Must Be Mutually Exclusive. The alternative possibilities of the major premise should not overlap because the destruction of one alternative would weaken or destroy the other. Note this error in the following example:

> *Major premise:* To prevent inflation, either purchasing power or wages must be decreased.
> *Minor premise:* Wages cannot be decreased.
> *Conclusion:* Purchasing power must be decreased.

Decreasing wages is one of the principal methods for decreasing purchasing power. If wages cannot be decreased, purchasing power cannot be decreased. The alternatives are not mutually exclusive.

When the Minor Premise Affirms One of the Alternatives of the Major Premise, the Conclusion Must Deny the Other.

> *Major premise:* To prevent inflation, either purchasing power must be decreased or production must be increased.
> *Minor premise:* Purchasing power can be decreased.
> *Conclusion:* Production need not be increased.

When the Minor Premise Denies One of the Alternatives of the Major Premise, the Conclusion Must Affirm the Other.

> *Major premise:* To prevent inflation, either purchasing power must be decreased or production must be increased.
> *Minor premise:* Production cannot be increased.
> *Conclusion:* Purchasing power must be decreased.

The Enthymeme

The enthymeme, for the purpose of this discussion, is an incomplete syllogism with either one of the premises or the conclusion missing.[1] When the missing part is supplied, the enthymeme be-

---

[1] There are other interpretations of the enthymeme, but the explanation here applies specifically to college debate. For a discussion of the enthymeme as a chain of reasoning leading toward probability, see James H. McBurney and Glen E. Mills, *Argumentation and Debate: Techniques of a Free Society* (New York: The Macmillan Company, 1964), pp. 145-51.

comes a complete syllogism. The rules for the syllogism then apply. An enthymeme may take the following form:

> *Major premise:* All lawyers are good debaters.
> *Conclusion:* John Doe is a good debater.

The minor premise "John Doe is a lawyer" is supplied by implication. In its complete syllogistic form, the argument appears as follows:

> *Major premise:* All lawyers are good debaters.
> *Minor premise:* John Doe is a lawyer.
> *Conclusion:* John Doe is a good debater.

In this form the enthymeme may be classified as a categorical, hypothetical, or disjunctive syllogism.

Rarely do we present an argument in debate as a formal syllogism. Either one of the premises or the conclusion is assumed; the missing part is implied. Without the enthymeme, deductive argument would be too stilted and formal for debate.

Types

The three types of enthymemes differ according to the part omitted from the complete syllogistic form. These types are termed enthymemes of the first, second, and third orders.

The enthymeme of the first order has the major premise omitted.

> *Minor premise:* Russia is a major nation.
> *Conclusion:* Russia must cooperate to attain a world nuclear control program.

The major premise is supplied by implication—"all major nations must cooperate to attain a world nuclear control program." If the major premise is not apparent, it may be reasoned out by principles already discussed. In the categorical syllogism, the middle term is the subject and the major term is the predicate of the major premise. These terms become apparent from the enthymeme as stated since the middle term is the predicate of the minor premise and the major term is the predicate of the conclusion.

The enthymeme of the second order has the minor premise omitted.

> *Major premise:* If the United Nations is given sufficient powers, it can control nuclear warfare.
> *Conclusion:* It will control nuclear warfare.

The implied minor premise is "the United Nations will be given sufficient powers." This premise becomes apparent when we consider the rule for the hypothetical syllogism that "if the minor premise affirms the antecedent, the conclusion must affirm the consequent."

The enthymeme of the third order has the conclusion omitted.

Major premise: The principles of the atomic bomb must either be kept secret or be shared with other nations.

Minor premise: The principles of the atomic bomb were not kept secret.

The conclusion that "the principles of the atomic bomb were shared with other nations" is implied. This conclusion is substantiated by the rule for the disjunctive syllogism, "when the minor premise denies one of the alternatives of the major premise, the conclusion must affirm the other."

Weaknesses

Weaknesses in use of the enthymeme may be illustrated by the following examples:

All men are liars.
John James asserts that he is a man.

Here the conclusion that John James is a liar follows if the two premises are admitted. In fact, this form is more effective than the form of the categorical syllogism because the conclusion appears obvious. Examine this statement: He is a university man, for he swaggers. Here it is suggested that all university men swagger.

The weakness of the two examples may readily be seen. The statement "all men are liars" does not mean that men always lie, that they never tell the truth. It does mean that at times or upon occasions men do depart from the absolute truth. When one forces a general statement into a particular instance, as in the case here, the result or conclusion may be erroneous. The same may be said in reference to swaggering university men, for this does not apply to all university men.

In some instances the enthymeme is substituted for careful thinking; in others it may be expanded into a valid syllogism.

All means for decreasing purchasing power will help prevent inflation.
The purchasing of government bonds will help decrease purchasing
power.

Here the conclusion "the purchase of government bonds will help
prevent inflation" is implied.

All means for decreasing purchasing power will help prevent inflation.
A higher income tax will help prevent inflation.

In this example, "a higher income tax is a means for decreasing
purchasing power" is the implied minor premise.

Sorites

A third form of deductive reasoning is the sorites—a chain of
reasoning. This form consists of a succession of syllogisms or
enthymemes with all but the last conclusion suppressed.

Disarmament causes suspicion.
Suspicion causes fear.
Fear leads to alliances.
Alliances lead to war.
∴ Disarmament leads to war.

A slightly different form of the sorites is illustrated in the following example:

Whiskers is a cat.
A cat is an animal.
∴ Whiskers is an animal.
An animal is a living thing.
∴ Whiskers is a living thing.

In the last example, the conclusion of the first group serves as a
basis for the major premise of the second group. To test the validity
of the chain of reasoning, start with the first statement in the chain
and express each separate link in a complete syllogism. The validity
of each link should be tested. Analyze the following chain of
reasoning by this procedure:

Inflation is caused by high wages.
High wages are caused by increased business activities.
Increased business activities are caused by increased demands for goods
   and services.
War causes increased demands for goods and services.
∴ War causes inflation.

Summary

Deduction proceeds from a general proposition or law to a particular application of it. The syllogism is the principal form for deductive reasoning. The syllogism has three parts: (1) major premise—general or all-inclusive statement, (2) minor premise—particular or subordinate statement, and (3) conclusion—result of inference from relationship of premises.

There are three types of syllogism: (1) categorical, (2) hypothetical, and (3) disjunctive. In the categorical syllogism, the major premise consists of an unqualified statement without exceptions. The hypothetical syllogism has in its major premise a condition or an "if" clause. The disjunctive syllogism presents alternative possibilities in its major premise and affirms or negates one of the alternatives in its minor premise. Each of these types has tests to determine the validity of the reasoning.

The enthymeme is an incomplete syllogism with either one of its premises or the conclusion omitted. Most reasoning for debate takes the form of the enthymeme since the syllogism often proves too formal and stilted. When the enthymeme is expanded into a complete syllogism, the rules for the syllogism apply to it.

Sorites is a chain of reasoning, consisting of a succession of syllogisms or enthymemes with all but the last conclusion suppressed. To test the chain, expand each link of the chain into a complete syllogism.

Oral Assignment

1. Each member of the class should nominate one person in the community qualified to participate in a lecture forum on the subject selected for the classroom debates.
2. The class should discuss the nominees and select one person and two alternates by majority vote.
3. A committee from the class should invite the person chosen to lecture to the class.
4. The lecture should be followed by an open forum in which the class members participate.

Collateral Readings

Abernathy, Elton, *The Advocate: A Manual Of Persuasion,* Ch. 5. New York: David McKay Co., Inc., 1964.

Crocker, Lionel, *Argumentation and Debate,* Ch. 8. New York: American Book Co., 1944.

Freeley, Austin J., *Argumentation and Debate,* Ch. 8. Belmont, Calif.: Wadsworth Publishing Co., 1961.

Huber, Robert B., *Influencing Through Argument,* Ch. 7. New York: David McKay Co., Inc., 1963.

Kruger, Arthur N., *Modern Debate,* Ch. 15. New York: McGraw-Hill Book Co., Inc., 1960.

McBurney, James H., and Glen E. Mills, *Argumentation and Debate: Techniques of a Free Society,* Ch. 9. New York: The Macmillan Company, 1964.

10
Briefing the Debate Case

Chapter 3 and much of Part III have pointed toward the building of the debate case. A case encompasses all the reasons, evidence, ethical factors, and psychological appeals that you employ to convince others of the reasonableness of your side of the proposition. We are now prepared to outline the cases for and against the proposition into the form of a debate brief.

Nature and Purpose of a Brief

The brief consists of the logically arranged arguments on both sides of a proposition. Each side of the proposition may be briefed separately, but the complete brief includes the steps of analysis and a thorough marshaling of arguments on both the affirmative and negative sides. A properly prepared brief contains all the valid arguments on the proposition and consequently includes more arguments than can be presented in a single debate. Thus, after preparing a brief, you choose certain sections of it to constitute your arguments for a particular debate. The brief encompasses a complete plan or over-all view of the entire case; it shows the relationship of issues one to another and of the subpoints and evidence used to support them.

The brief performs the same function for the debater that the blueprint does for the building contractor. The contractor would not start the construction of a building without a finished plan of the various parts of the building; neither should you attempt to debate until you have a complete, over-all understanding of the proposition. The brief helps furnish this understanding. By means of the brief, you can test the logical arrangement of your arguments; it thus serves you as an invaluable guide and helps you organize a clear and concise case.

Do not attempt to construct a brief before making a thorough study of the question. Whenever possible, delay preparing the final brief until after a series of discussions and practice debates so that you can be sure of the proper divisions of the case and the arguments that should be included under each division. Make the brief the final step in, as well as a test of, the preparation. If you plan to debate the proposition in a series of debates, let the brief remain open for additions and changes. Under no circumstances should you let the case become crystallized during the debate season.

Adopt a definite plan for briefing the proposition. Find the main issues; arrange the arguments and evidence under the general headings of these issues; and then brief them into final form according to rules for briefing.[1]

The Brief and Outline Distinguished

Consider the brief as an objective arrangement of arguments of the proposition and the outline as an arrangement of arguments for a particular debate speech. The brief should be more thorough and exact than the outline. In some respects they reverse the process of construction. The brief states the conclusion and then shows why the conclusion logically results from the statements that follow; the outline may use generally accepted statements in order to reach the conclusion as a climax. The outline may consist of a few sentences, phrases, clauses, or even words in the subordinate parts; the brief uses only closely related sentences without dependent clauses. The properly prepared brief is intelligible to anyone, even by sections; the outline is frequently understood only by the compiler. An outline may be made early in your preparation; not so the brief. The following form illustrates some of these differences:

Outline

I. World government practical
   A. Eliminates causes of war
      1. Provides reconciliation
      2. Substitute for war
      3. Enforces peace
   B. Solves economic problems
      1. Removes trade barriers
      2. Competitive practices

---

[1] See pages 154-64.

Brief

I. World government is a practical method of solving international problems, for
    A. World government solves the problem of war, for
      1. It provides for the reconciliation of the causes of war.
      2. It provides a substitute to perform the functions of war.
      3. It provides adequate means of enforcing peace, for
        a. It provides for changing conditions.
        b. It provides the necessary elements of force.
    B. World government will solve the problems of international economic relations, for
      1. It is a practical means of removing trade barriers.
      2. It substitutes orderly regulations for competitive practices.

Rules for Constructing the Brief

The following rules for briefing come largely from legal usage. Although some of the rules may appear technical, they are far less rigid than the rules for legal briefing. Compliance with them is necessary for a properly constructed debate case.

General rules

Divide the Brief into Three Sections: (1) an introduction to the proposition, (2) a development of affirmative arguments with a conclusion, and (3) a development of negative arguments with a conclusion.

The first section of the brief introduces both the affirmative and negative divisions and contains all the exposition necessary to an understanding of the proposition. The introduction should be unbiased in its treatment and should not contain arguments. In a formal debate, the first affirmative speaker presents the part of the analysis contained in the introduction that he deems advisable for an understanding of his case.

The section "affirmative proof" contains the main contentions supporting the proposition as developed by subpoints. The main divisions of the brief include all the arguments on the proposition. This section is concluded by a restatement of the affirmative main contentions.

The section "negative proof" develops the arguments opposed to the proposition in the same manner and form as the affirmative proof. The general outline of the brief appears graphically as follows:

Brief

STATEMENT OF THE PROPOSITION

  I. Introduction: Analysis and exposition of the proposition, including the six steps discussed in Chapter 6
  II. Affirmative Proof
    A. Statements of main contentions; subpoints—supported by reasoning and evidence
    B. Conclusion; restatement of main contentions
  III. Negative Proof
    A. Statements of main contentions; subpoints—supported by reasoning and evidence
    B. Conclusion; restatement of main contentions

Make Each Statement in the Form of a Complete Sentence. Words and phrases instead of complete sentences may be used in an outline, but complete sentences for each division and each subhead are necessary in a brief. The complete sentence states a point precisely and indicates clearly the relationships between points and subpoints. The following form illustrates this rule:

Wrong

I. Powers of World Federation
  A. Required powers
    1. Declare and wage war
    2. International commerce
    3. Taxation
  B. Optional powers
    1. Financial matters
    2. Postal systems
    3. Communications

Right

I. A world federation must be given definite powers to insure effectiveness, for
  A. Certain powers are obligatory, for
    1. The power to maintain armies is necessary as an enforcement agency.
    2. The power to regulate international commerce is necessary for healthy economics.

3. The power of taxation is necessary to finance the plan.
B. Some powers are optional, for
1. Power to regulate financial matters would be advantageous.
2. The power to provide a common postal system would strengthen the ties among the various nations.
3. The power to regulate international communication would help remove international barriers.

Make Each Statement Single in Form. The brief requires that each head or subhead be a single statement; compound and complex sentences should be avoided. Confusion results from an attempt to support a dual statement by subheads.

Wrong

I. War causes political and economic upheavals in the world, for
  A. War causes immediate and long-range problems, for
    1. In the economic field the immediate problems are to alleviate widespread suffering and to transform the war economy into a peacetime economy.
    2. The long-range economic policy includes problems of absorbing the military personnel into peacetime employment, the serious effect on monetary and credit systems caused by large war debts, and the replenishment of large stocks of goods.
    3. The immediate political problems include controlling conquered countries and writing the terms of the peace.
    4. The long-range political problem involves working out difficulties in political systems.

Right

I. War causes economic upheavals in the world, for
  A. War causes immediate problems, for
    1. It becomes necessary to alleviate worldwide suffering.
    2. It becomes necessary to transform the war economy into a peacetime economy.
  B. War causes many long range problems, for
    1. It becomes necessary to absorb military personnel into peacetime employment.
    2. It becomes necessary to rebuild disrupted monetary and credit systems occasioned by the war debts.
    3. It becomes necessary to replenish the supply of goods depleted by the war.
II. War causes political upheavals in the world, for
  A. War causes immediate political problems, for
    1. It becomes necessary to establish governments in conquered countries.

    2. It becomes necessary to write the peace terms.
  B. War causes long-range political problems, for
    1. Difficulties arising from defunct political systems have to be solved.
    2. Problems of keeping the peace need major attention.

Use a Consistent System of Symbols Throughout the Brief. The system of symbols used may vary according to individual desires, but one system should be used consistently throughout the brief. To change the system of symbols within a brief destroys the relationships between points and subpoints. The following form is recommended:

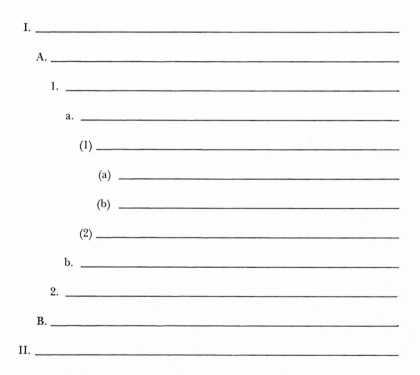

I. _____

  A. _____

    1. _____

      a. _____

        (1) _____

          (a) _____

          (b) _____

        (2) _____

      b. _____

    2. _____

  B. _____

II. _____

Arrange Each Division into Heads and Subheads. Each subordinate idea should be indicated by a proper symbol and correct indentation so that the relationships between points and subpoints can be easily recognized. Failure to subdivide arguments obscures the logical sequence of ideas.

Wrong

There is a need for a change in the present policy of international relations. Under the present system, wars occur frequently. The causes of war are traceable to dissimilar ideologies among nations. Furthermore, the present system offers nothing to replace war. It cannot enforce a desirable peace because it does not provide for changing conditions and there is no element of force in the present system.

Right

I. There is a need for a change in the present policy of international relations, for
   A. Under the present system wars recur frequently, for
      1. The causes of war are traceable to conflicting ideologies among nations.
      2. The present system offers nothing to replace war.
      3. The present policy cannot enforce a desirable peace, for
         a. It does not provide for changing conditions.
         b. It has no power to enforce international policies.

Mark Each Statement with One Symbol Only. To mark one statement with two symbols destroys the logical relationship between points and subpoints.

Wrong

I. Federation is a practical plan for solving international problems, for
   A. 1. Federation supplies positive elements of solution.
      2. Federation is an international approach to an international problem.
   B. Federation provides united action, for
      1. a. It will bring military competition to an end.
         b. It will do away with the treachery and intrigue practiced in present diplomatic negotiations.
         c. It will permit trade to conform to the pattern that will best satisfy international economic demand.

Right

I. Federation is a practical plan for solving international problems, for
   A. Federation supplies positive elements of solution.
   B. Federation is an international approach to an international problem.
   C. Federation provides united action, for
      1. It will bring military competition to an end.

2. It will do away with the treachery and intrigue possible under present diplomatic negotiations.

3. It will permit trade to conform to the pattern approved by international economic demand.

Make All Statements Impersonal. Such statements as "we contend," "I believe," and "we propose" have no place in a brief. Make the brief an impersonal statement of all factors involved. Do not include illogical statements or special pleading in any form.

Wrong

I. There is a need for world federation, for
  A. There are many causes for war, for
    1. There are economic causes.
    2. There are political causes.
    3. I believe the social causes are strongest; war is a curse to mankind.
  B. World federation will decrease the causes for war.
    1. I am fully convinced that economic problems can be settled around conference tables.
    2. Problems in politics could be discussed under conditions conducive to peace.
    3. I contend fervently that the federal council would disapprove war.

Right

I. There is a need for world federation, for
  A. There are many causes for war, for
    1. There are economic causes.
    2. There are political causes.
    3. There are social causes.
  B. World federation will decrease the causes for war, for
    1. Economic problems can be settled around conference tables.
    2. Problems in politics could be discussed under conditions conducive to peace.
    3. On general principles the federation council would disapprove war.

Rules for the introduction

Include the Steps in Analysis. The steps in analysis, as discussed in Chapter 6, consist of the following:

1. the present significance or immediate reason for discussing the problem,
2. comprehensive history of the question,

3. the disposal of admitted and irrelevant matter,
4. interpretation and definition of the proposition,
5. the underlying philosophy of the proposition,
6. statement of the main issues of the proposition.

Include All Necessary Exposition of the Proposition.
Much of the material included in the introduction need not be presented in a debate, but the information proves valuable for achieving background understanding of the proposition. The following specimen introduction of a brief illustrates how to present exposition in the introduction:

Brief

Resolved, That a federal world government should be established.

INTRODUCTION

I. It is important that this question be discussed.
  A. The increasing destructiveness of war emphasizes the need for seeking a method for the peaceful settlement of disputes between nations.
  B. Our increasing mastery of time, space, and human conditions makes us more and more dependent upon each other (James T. Shotwell, *The Great Decision,* p. 15).
  C. It is important that individuals acquaint themselves with world conditions.
    1. In democratic states, the perpetuation of foreign policies rests ultimately with the electorate.
    2. A better understanding of world problems is conducive to rational behavior (Caesar Saerchinger, *The Way Out of War,* p. 87).
    3. An appreciation of the other person's point of view is a prerequisite to a sensible foreign policy.
  D. The economic interdependence of nations reflects itself in the establishment of regional economic communities.

II. History shows that the consideration of a world government is not new in the minds of men.
  A. In 1899, at the suggestion of the Czar of Russia, twenty-six powers met in the First Hague Conference for the purpose of promoting universal amity.
  B. In 1907, at the prompting of Theodore Roosevelt, forty-four nations met in the Second Hague Conference for the purpose of mitigating the horrors of war.
  C. In 1919, the League of Nations was formed for the promotion and maintenance of world peace.

D. In June, 1945, the representatives of fifty-one nations signed the charter that brought into being the United Nations, the purpose of which is to promote peace and economic betterment.

E. Establishment of the North Atlantic Treaty Organization, the European Common Market, and other regional organizations indicate a trend toward international cooperation.

III. The following matters should be agreed upon as a common basis for argument:

A. No specific time limit should be imposed for the establishment of a federal world government; however, it should be established in the reasonably near future.

B. A detailed plan for the proposed organization need not be presented.

IV. The interpretation of the following terms is necessary for an understanding of the question:

A. Federal government means a government to which the member states relinquish certain powers, among them being the power to act upon the individual citizen as well as upon the member state.

1. The federal world government should have power to maintain a world army.

2. It should have power to wage war.

3. It should have authority over world trade.

4. It should have authority to levy taxes.

B. World government means a government that exercises authority over all the inhabitants of the member states.

V. The underlying philosophy of the proposition involves two major concepts.

A. The principle of nationalism is outmoded; the only way to international peace and economic well-being is through international cooperation.

B. Any international organization with power to affect military and economic peace must be federal in scope.

VI. The main issues are:

A. Is there a need for some type of world organization other than the present system?

B. Is federal world government a practical means of world organization?

C. Would a federal world government prove advantageous?

Do Not Include Argument. Since the introductory section introduces both the affirmative and negative sections of proof, only expository statements should be included. This principle is exemplified in the introduction of the brief in the preceding section. You will note that all statements are objective and nonargumentative.

Rules for the proof

Make the Main Contentions in the Proof Correspond to the Statement of Issues Listed in the Introduction. The main issues of the proposition should be listed in question form as the final section of the introduction. When the issues are affirmed or denied, they become the main contentions in the affirmative and negative sections of the proof. These differences are illustrated as follows for the proposition that a federal world government should be established:

Main Issues of the Proposition

I. Is there a need for some type of world organization other than the present system?
II. Is federal world government a practical means of world organization?
III. Would federal world government prove advantageous?

Main Contentions of the Affirmative

A federal world government should be established, for,
I. There is a need for a stronger world government.
II. A federal world government is a practical means of world organization.
III. A federal world government would be desirable.

Main Contentions of the Negative

A federal world government should not be established, for,
I. There is no need for a federal world government.
II. A federal world government would prove impracticable.
III. A federal world government would be undesirable.

Make Each Main Contention Read as a Reason for the Truth or Falsity of the Proposition. This rule was illustrated in the preceding section. Each main contention relates directly to the proposition. Note that the main issues, as listed in the introduction, are affirmed in the affirmative proof and are denied in the negative.

Make All the Main Contentions Combined Prove the Proposition. The probative force of contentions I, II, and III, properly developed, must prove the proposition. Unless the main contentions combined prove the proposition, the brief does not present a prima-facie case.[2]

Make Each Subpoint of a Main Contention Help Prove the Main Contention. Unless a subpoint reads directly as a reason for the contention under which it appears, it has no bearing on the case. Furthermore, in order to have probative force in a brief, all the reasoning given in a subpoint must be sufficient to prove the subpoint when supported by evidence. This rule is illustrated by subpoint *A* under the first main contention that follows:

A federal world government should be established, for,
I. There is a need for some type of world organization other than the present system, for
  A. A system of independent sovereign states has not proved successful in preventing war, for
    1. The areas of peace have been widened only if or where sovereignty has been abandoned or shared (Caesar Saerchinger, *The Way Out of War,* p. 124).
    2. Sovereignty must sooner or later make way for the principle of the greatest good for the greatest number.
    3. Two major world wars have been fought in the past fifty years.
    4. The cold war since World War II has kept the nations in a state of unrest.
    5. Nations have devised weapons capable of destroying the world.

Make the Combined Subpoints of a Main Contention Prove the Main Contention. For the same reasons that the cumulative effect of the main contentions of a brief must be sufficient to prove the proposition, so must all the subpoints of a main contention, when combined, prove that contention. The weakness of a main contention may be exposed by attacking either the main contention itself or any of its subdivisions.

Put the Source of Evidence, If Included, in Parentheses at the Close of the Statement in Which It Appears. If this rule is observed, it gives authority to the brief. It also provides useful information that will be readily accessible during a debate. The rule may be illustrated as follows:

  A. The United Nations is incapable of meeting the need, for
    1. It cannot take decisive action, for
      a. The General Assembly has only the power to discuss and recommend solutions.

---

[2] The effect of the failure to present a prima-facie case was discussed in detail in Chapter 3.

    b. The Security Council is unable to take action, for
       (1) The presence of two conflicting ideologies on the coun-
          cil makes unanimous agreement virtually impossible
          (Joseph H. Ball, *America and the New World,* p. 146).
       (2) By exercising the veto, any of the Big Five can prevent
          any important decision (*ibid.,* p. 147).

    In Briefing Points of Refutation, State Clearly the Argument to Be Answered. In constructing a brief, it sometimes becomes necessary to answer arguments that favor the opposition, preliminary to advancing your own arguments. Let the point answered be so stated that it becomes positive argument for the side of the proposition briefed. Include points of refutation in the body of the brief where the point arises. The following section of a brief illustrates this rule:

II. A federal world government would not be practicable, for
  A. There is not a sufficient basis for organization, for
    1. There is no common political philosophy around which the or-
      ganization could be built (Joseph H. Ball, *America and the New World,* p. 145), for
      a. Russia is dedicated to the retention and extension of the communistic theory of government.
      b. The United States supports the democratic theory.
      c. Neutral nations differ in their beliefs.
    2. There are no common ties of religion between the peoples of the world.

Rule for the conclusion

    Make the Conclusion a Restatement of the Main Contentions and an Affirmation or Denial of the Proposition. The affirmative and negative sections contain separate conclusions; a detailed summary is not necessary. The usual procedure consists of a restatement of the main contentions followed by an affirmation or denial of the proposition. The following form illustrates this rule as applied to the affirmative.

Conclusion

Since:
  I. There is a need for some type of world organization other than the present system, and
  II. Federal world government is a practical world organization, and

III. A federal world government would prove advantageous,
Therefore:
A federal world government should be established.

Summary

The debate brief may be defined as a logically arranged compilation of the arguments on both sides of a proposition. The brief is an arrangement of all arguments, as distinguished from an outline of certain arguments for a particular debate. The brief includes a complete plan for an entire case. Observe the following rules when drawing up a brief:

1. Divide the brief into three sections: (1) an introduction to the proposition, (2) a development of affirmative arguments with a conclusion, and (3) a development of negative arguments with a conclusion.
2. Make each statement in the form of a complete sentence.
3. Make each statement single in form.
4. Use a consistent system of symbols throughout the brief.
5. Arrange each division of the brief into heads and subheads.
6. Mark each statement with one symbol only.
7. Make all statements impersonal.
8. Include in the introduction the steps in analysis.
9. Include in the introduction all exposition necessary for an understanding of the proposition.
10. Do not include argument in the introduction.
11. Make the main contentions in the proof correspond to the statement of issues listed in the introduction.
12. Make each main contention read as a reason for the truth or falsity of the proposition.
13. Make all the main contentions combined prove the proposition.
14. Make each subpoint of a main contention help prove the contention under which it appears.
15. Make the combined subpoints of a main contention prove the main contention.
16. If you indicate the source of evidence, put it in parentheses at the close of the statement in which it appears.
17. In briefing points of refutation, state clearly the argument to be answered.

18. Make the conclusion a restatement of the main contentions and affirmation or denial of the proposition.

Oral Assignment

1. The class should be divided into panel groups with no more than seven students on a panel.
2. Each student should prepare an outline for a panel discussion on the subject "The Affirmative Case" on the proposition selected for class debates.
3. The panel discussions may be held in various sections of the lecture room or in small rooms or offices.
4. Each student should hand in a summary of the discussion in which he participates.

Collateral Readings

Crocker, Lionel, *Argumentation and Debate,* Ch. 11. New York: American Institute of Banking, 1962.

Freeley, Austin J., *Argumentation and Debate,* Ch. 12. Belmont, Calif.: Wadsworth Publishing Co., 1961.

Huber, Robert B., *Influencing Through Argument,* Ch. 12. New York: David McKay Co., Inc., 1963.

McBath, James H., ed., *Argumentation and Debate,* Ch. 6. New York: Holt, Rinehart & Winston, Inc., 1963.

McBurney, James H., and Glen E. Mills, *Argumentation and Debate: Techniques of a Free Society,* Ch. 13. New York: The Macmillan Company, 1964.

Reeves, J. Walter, and Hoyt H. Hudson, *Principles of Argument and Debate,* Ch. 5. Boston: D. C. Heath & Company, 1941.

11
Preparing for Rebuttal and Refutation

Rebuttal Explained

Rebuttal is the process of destroying opposing arguments and re-establishing your own constructive arguments. Almost all types of formal college debate provide for both constructive and rebuttal speeches. In the constructive speech you present a positive case in support of one side of the proposition. This constructive case, as originally planned, should be completed in the constructive speeches; no essential issue should be left to the rebuttals. After the constructive arguments, each side has rebuttal speeches in which it attempts to weaken or destroy the opposing case and rebuild its own. Look upon the rebuttal as argument against argument or strengthening what has been said. The nature of the rebuttal speeches makes them extemporaneous, for they must be organized during the debate to adapt to the opponent's arguments.

Refutation and Rebuttal Distinguished

Debaters sometime use refutation and rebuttal synonymously. One distinction, however, should be understood. Refutation consists of destroying opposing arguments, a tearing-down process, whereas rebuttal includes both destructive and reconstructive methods, attacking your opponents' arguments and rebuilding your own. Refutation is usually used throughout the debate. After the first affirmative speech, refutation becomes necessary in each succeeding constructive speech to clear the way for additional constructive arguments. The first negative speaker should not begin his constructive speech until he has refuted essential parts of the first affirmative speaker's argument.[1] Likewise the second affirmative must not ignore what the first negative has said and start with his own constructive speech—he must first attack the principal arguments advanced by the negative.

A speaker may use refutation to advantage if he can anticipate a particularly strong argument. Refutation of an argument in advance of its presentation weakens that argument when it does come. Refutation becomes, therefore, a part of both the constructive and the rebuttal speeches. Rebuttal is a broader process that includes refutation.

Types of Rebuttal and Refutation

The tearing-down and building-up processes in debate are threefold, including (1) attacks on opposing arguments, (2) defense of own arguments, and (3) attacks on minor points.

Attacks on opposing arguments

In most instances, you should attack your opponent's arguments before rebuilding your own. This method helps keep the opposition on the defense and leaves the opposition less time to destroy your arguments. It frequently becomes necessary to clear away the beliefs advanced by opponents before you can hope for acceptance of constructive arguments that you present. This destructive phase of argument is illustrated in the final debate of the 1962 National West Point Tournament when Miss Sarah Benson of Ohio State University began the second negative constructive speech as follows:

> I'd like to go right to that affirmative plan and consider it in relationship to each of the need areas which we heard. First of all, remember we're told that unions can restrict production through makework practices. Well now, remember, at the opening of this debate the affirmative team told us there was a legal inconsistency between what labor unions can do and what business could do; therefore, we need antitrust applied to labor organizations. Well, I'm going to submit that, first of all, the affirmative need area here is not compatible with the philosophy of antitrust legislation. Now remember, we've never been told that business can't restrict production. I point out to you that business certainly does restrict production. We know that steel mills only operate 9 or 10 months out of the year. Certainly there is no legal in-

---

[1] For an effective instance of this method, see how Milton has Belial open his argument in *Paradise Lost*, Bk. II, ll. 120ff.

consistency here. This doesn't fit in with the philosophy of the affirmative team. It doesn't fit in with the philosophy of antitrust legislation.[2]

Defense of own arguments

When you face arguments that tend to tear down your side, you must strengthen your original arguments. This type of rebuttal seeks to offset the attacks of your opponents and thus enables you to re-establish your constructive case. In the following illustration, note how Calvin Kent of Baylor University sought to re-establish his case from the attack presented by Miss Benson in the example above.

> First of all, they tell us this: well, we don't think that you're complying with the principle of antitrust. Because why? The steel mills aren't forced to operate all the time. Well, this doesn't have any relevance to our case at all. I think we pointed out to you that we were within the philosophy because the court had clearly decided in the case of *U.S. v. Brims* that makework and featherbedding were restraints of trade. And this point they never dealt with. Why? Because they raised prices and pinched productivity. And antitrust, as they themselves admit, is intended to do away with this particular problem. So I think we are complying with the antitrust principle.[3]

Attacks on minor points

Minor points may be attacked for several purposes: to introduce a speech, to gain favor with the audience, to weaken the authenticity of a particular argument, or to lessen the prestige of the opposing speakers. In the final debate of a national Pi Kappa Delta tournament, one speaker began as follows:

> Ladies and gentlemen: The last speaker for the affirmative opened his address by saying that he had never debated before a more intelligent audience. I assume that, since we are on the negative, it is our burden to claim that we have. However, we will shift this burden for the moment.[4]

This opening was an amusing diversion from the main argument and brought a favorable reaction from the audience.

---

2 James H. McBurney and Glen E. Mills, *Argumentation and Debate: Techniques of a Free Society* (New York: The Macmillan Company, 1964), p. 436.
3 McBurney and Mills, *op. cit.,* p. 444.
4 George W. Finley, *Winning Debates, Orations, Speeches* (New York: Noble & Noble, Publishers, Inc., 1936), VI, 30.

Later in the same debate, an opponent opened his rebuttal with this refutation:

> We cannot let one statement pass without correcting it. My colleague offered five cases in which we would prophesy, if we were forced by the gentlemen to take the role of prophet, that the Congress of the United States would have passed the law a second time by a two-thirds vote. Those five cases were: the Minimum Wage Law, the Child Labor Law, the Triple A, the Hot Oil provisions of the NRA, and the Legal Tender Act. The first speaker for the negative came back and said that only one of those laws got a two-thirds majority vote. Gentlemen, we respectfully submit to you that you are mistaken and I offer to you on the basis of the Congressional Record that all five of them got a two-thirds majority vote.[5]

The probative effect of this point of controversy was not so important as was the loss of prestige and ethical appeal occasioned by the preceding speaker's lack of knowledge of the facts.

General Methods of Refutation

Opposing arguments may be destroyed by either one of two methods or a combination of both. The first method consists of showing an error in the reasoning process; the second consists of questioning the validity of the evidence or showing that the evidence does not support the conclusion. If you can show errors in reasoning as well as inadequacies of evidence, your refutation will be all the more convincing.

Methods of attacking reasoning—fallacies

A fallacy consists of an error in the reasoning process. A complete classification of fallacies is perhaps impossible, since it is not possible to perceive exactly what takes place in the mind of the reasoner, but four types of fallacies are of primary concern to debaters. Fallacies of inductive reasoning have already been covered in Chapter 8; fallacies of deductive reasoning were discussed in Chapter 9. Such fallacies occur when one violates the rules for these types of reasoning as explained in the chapters cited. In addition to these formal or logical fallacies, there are two common fallacies of presumption: ignoring the question and begging the question.

---

5 Finley, *op. cit.*, p. 51.

Ignoring the Question. The fallacy of ignoring the question consists of arguments irrelevant to the point in controversy. The most common forms follow.

ATTACKING PERSONALITIES. Evading the issue by attacking a person connected with it ignores the question. An example is seen in the classic advice of an old lawyer to a young one, "If your argument is weak, abuse the opposing lawyers." The following examples illustrate: (1) A student advances a plan for settling labor-capital difficulties; the opponent, instead of giving valid objections to the plan, infers that college students are incapable of devising a workable plan for capital-labor difficulties. (2) A student presents an argument, based upon sound reasoning and supported by adequate evidence, for the proposal that the United States should join the European Common Market; the opponent disregards the soundness of the argument and launches an attack on the personal characteristics of a prominent politician who favors the proposal. (3) A debater quotes the reasoning of a prominent authority supporting a proposal for changes in succession to the presidency following President Kennedy's assassination; the opponent evades the argument by stating that the authority held an opposite view twenty years ago. All these responses have one point in common—they attempt to evade arguments by an attack on personalities.

APPEALING TO PREJUDICES. This fallacy occurs when the speaker makes use of prejudices rather than logical reasoning. Note the following refutation of an argument that the unicameral system of legislation should be adopted:

> The affirmative offers nothing distinctively unicameral. They put forward only those reforms which we can secure and still keep our American system. Let us not destroy this time-tried plan of legislation, but rather let us allow it to rise to its full vigor, unhampered by ills that encumber it—ills which are strictly extraneous in nature. A system which has stood the test of years of troublous times in the formation of a new and mighty nation could not have inherent evils. . . .[6]

Examples of appeals to prejudice are common among special-interest groups and in political campaigns. "Alcoholism is a sin" is no answer to the arguments against prohibition, nor is "in America all men are still free" refutation to arguments for prohibition. Likewise, "the constitution does not forbid it" is no answer to the argu-

---

[6] Classroom debate recorded and transcribed for study.

ment against capital punishment. Such reasoning may be effective, but it ignores the basic argument by appealing to prejudice.

APPEALING TO TRADITION AND CUSTOM. A fallacy similar to the one above consists of an appeal to tradition and custom as a substitute for reasoning; it ignores the point at issue. The following point illustrates:

> The opposition claims that government control of railroads will give us a more efficient transportation system. Do the gentlemen realize the full impact of their proposal? It involves increased regimentation of private business. It drives us one step nearer to socialism and one step farther away from the time-honored American free enterprise. Let us keep America free of all foreign "isms." [7]

The tendency to preserve the status quo gives impetus to committing this fallacy. It may be easier to reply to an argument favoring a plan for world peace by the phrase "war is inevitable" than to meet it with counterreasoning and evidence. Such refutation may be effective, but it is nonetheless deficient in logic because it evades the basic argument.

APPEALING TO IGNORANCE. Assuming that because the facts may not be known, they do not exist, or that a contention must be assumed true because it cannot be disproved, appeals to ignorance. Lack of knowledge is substituted for logical reasoning and evidence. Affirmative teams sometimes commit this fallacy in an endeavor to avoid discussing the practicability of their proposal. Pressed for a definite proposal for solving labor-capital problems, the affirmative responds that a specific program is beyond the ability of college students—that the details of the plan must be left to Congress and the experts. Affirmative teams are seldom required to present detailed plans, yet they should give the general principles upon which a plan could be devised and should not avoid this responsibility by pleading ignorance of the problem. Negative teams sometimes commit this fallacy when they contend that the affirmative cannot prove its plan practicable because the plan has never been tried. Such a conclusion relies upon the assumption that because facts are lacking, there can be no proof. Many sound reasons may favor the practicability of a plan that has never been tried.

ATTEMPTING DIVISION. This error arises when one attempts a division or classification of an argument and omits an essential

---

[7] Classroom debate recorded and transcribed for study.

part of the problem. An affirmative speaker argues that the nations must either adopt an economic community or follow a plan of isolation. This division fails to consider the possibility of favored-nation agreements. In a debate on the adoption of a sales tax, the affirmative contended that there are four basic and accepted types of taxation: property, business, income, and consumption. The speakers attempted to demonstrate that the first three of these could not be utilized for obtaining additional funds, and they concluded that only the consumption tax could produce additional revenue without hardships. In refutation, the negative speakers proposed that natural resources could well stand additional taxation sufficient to meet the demand for needed revenue. The affirmative had overlooked an essential part of the question.

SHIFTING GROUND. A debater shifts ground when he deserts the point of contention. He abandons a point without proof, but leaves the impression of supporting it by giving arguments on an allied point.

> The third evil submitted by the affirmative is that the present system discourages preventive medicine. The gentlemen have contended that they desire to encourage preventive medicine under their program of compulsory health insurance. The negative has cited the example of sulfapyridine as a preventive medicine that hastens the cure of pneumonia. The gentlemen say that this program started in England. That is exactly where it started, but England does not have a program of compulsory health insurance. It has a program of government medicine, a program that would be totally unacceptable to the American people. Let us avoid this Socialistic scheme.[8]

Begging the Question. This type of fallacy occurs when one assumes the truth of a point that is the same or equivalent to the point in question. The principal forms of this fallacy follow.

REASONING IN A CIRCLE. This reasoning uses two or more unproved propositions in turn to prove another. A student who said that his colleague was a poor debater because he did not reason well, and that he did not reason well because he was a poor debater, was reasoning in a circle. The same error occurs in the following argument concerning strikes: "The cost of living has increased because many strikes have occurred in American industries, and many strikes have occurred in American industries because the cost of living has increased."

---

[8] Adapted from a classroom debate.

USING A NONEVIDENT PREMISE. The nonevident premise assumes the truth of a premise that still requires proof. The unproved premise then serves as the basis for drawing another conclusion, which in turn serves as the premise from which another conclusion may be made. In the inductive-deductive processes of reasoning, each conclusion serves as a premise for another deduction. Thus a statement may be both a conclusion and a premise —a conclusion from evidence and reasoning given in its support, and a premise serving as the basis for drawing another conclusion. For example, consider the following chain of syllogisms:

> *Major premise:* All industries have experienced price increases.
> *Minor premise:* The soft drink business is an industry.
> *Conclusion:* The soft drink business has experienced price increases.
> *Major premise:* The soft drink business has experienced price increases.
> *Minor premise:* The Coca-Cola Company is a soft drink business.
> *Conclusion:* The Coca-Cola Company has experienced price increases.

The major premise "all industries have experienced price increases" requires proof. To use the statement as a major premise without proof exemplifies the fallacy of nonevident premise. The conclusion of the syllogism, "the soft drink business has experienced price increases," may not be in fact true. This statement in turn may serve as the major premise of another syllogism, and all succeeding conclusions in the chain of reasoning may also be fallacious since they are drawn from a statement that required proof. To avoid this fallacy, prove the premises in the chain by inductive reasoning. For example:

> The steel industry has experienced price increases.
> The housing industry has experienced price increases.
> The clothing industry has experienced price increases.
> The farm implement industry has experienced price increases.
> *Conclusion:* All essential industries have experienced price increases.

The conclusion from this generalization may then serve as the premise for the first of a chain of syllogisms.

Methods of attacking evidence

Although the reasoning of an argument may be sound, the evidence used in support of such reasoning may not be valid. In addition to the methods of attacking the reasoning process of arguments, at least four methods may be used to test the validity of the evidence.

Insufficient Evidence. Probably the most common error made in the presentation of evidence arises from failure to give sufficient evidence to establish the contention. The amount of evidence necessary depends upon the nature of the argument. Unless one kind of evidence appears unusually convincing or the point to be proved requires little support, use two or more kinds of evidence to support an argument. Use corroborating statistics from two or more sources to strengthen the contention, or cite several examples that conform to the general class exemplified. Base analogy upon something more familiar to the audience than the argument at issue. Seek the opinions of several authorities to show agreement. Each argument advanced does not have to be supported in a formal way by several kinds of evidence, but take care to give sufficient evidence to justify the conclusion. In actual practice, too many debaters draw conclusions that are not convincing because the evidence does not warrant such conclusions. In the following argument, a speaker points out the insufficiency of the evidence in a debate on state medicine:

> The ladies of the opposition have just two things to say in regard to our preventive medicine argument. First, they say that the present system encourages preventive medicine; they cited only one example, that of sulfapyridine's cutting down the death rate of pneumonia. . . . Then the ladies say that preventive medicine is only a matter of educating the people to its use. We say that we should first make such services available to the people before trying to educate them to its use. The ladies have not given sufficient evidence that the present system encourages preventive medicine nor have they been able to justify its failure to do so.[9]

Misapplied Evidence. Evidence advanced to prove a point may warrant an entirely different conclusion; such evidence should be attacked by showing that it is misapplied. In an attempt to show a need for change from the present system of medical service, evidence may be given that tends to prove only the need for modification; to prove that the evils mentioned warrant a change to state medicine, one must show that such evils are inherent in the present system. If the negative can show how the evils pointed out by the affirmative can be corrected without a change in the princi-

---

9 Adapted from a classroom debate.

ples of private medicine, the negative justifies its contention that the evidence used by the opposition does not prove the conclusion drawn. A fundamental principle in debate demands that the evidence presented must prove the conclusion.

> The affirmative speakers have given us evidence which they say shows four evils of bicameralism, which evils prove a need for the one-house legislature. These evils are not necessarily a part of the system itself. They are but the result of subsequent development and would exist in any form of government unless precautions were taken against them. . . . They have put major emphasis upon two charges against the bicameral system. First, that much of the legislation is unsatisfactory; second, that there is no fixing of responsibility. As to the first charge, it is not a result of the two-house system. We find most unsatisfactory legislation on the statute books because of two real reasons. There is a lack of scientific knowledge and skill in the drafting of bills. There is also insufficient time for deliberation. Shall we supply this needed skill, shall we provide for more time for deliberation of bills, or shall we destroy the whole system in favor of a system that has met with failure in every trial in history? As to the charge of failure to fix responsibility, we also say that it is in no way directly chargeable to the bicameral system. This failure to fix responsibility is due to the unlimited number of bills which a representative may introduce or sponsor, and to the operation of the committee system. We agree that too many bills are introduced, but we oppose destroying the whole system of the government just to weed out these ancillary evils. It is like killing a man to cure a cold. The affirmative cannot lay either of these two charges upon the bicameral system. . . . They have failed to prove a need for change even if we accept their evidence of these evils.[10]

Inaccurate Evidence. In some instances the evidence presented may be sufficient and apply specifically to the point and yet be distorted or inaccurate. Types of inaccurate evidence follow: (1) Quotations may not be complete. (2) Statistics gathered from different sources may not be based upon the same unit of comparison. (3) Only extreme examples that are not representative may be given. (4) Alleged points of likeness in analogies may not be true.

Misleading quotations of expert opinion may result from quoting an incidental or isolated statement that the authority made in reaching his final conclusion. To take a statement out of the context of an academic discussion and quote it as a conclusion leaves an impression not intended by the authority. A similar situation results when a set of statistics from one source is compared to a set from

---

[10] Classroom debate recorded and transcribed for study.

another source based upon entirely different units. Misrepresentation of evidence is inexcusable. As a debater, you must accept the responsibility of determining the accuracy of your evidence.

In an intercollegiate debate, one speaker attempted to show the inaccuracy of evidence as follows:

> The lady who just spoke made no attempt to refute our arguments that the advantages she claimed for unicameralism could not be had by our proposals. She restricted her entire rebuttal to pointing out that the two advantages we claim for bicameralism would not be obtained. Let me consider her arguments on these points. First, as to the diversity of representation she quoted a statement from Professor Senning to the effect that the argument that a two-house legislature permits representation of areas as well as population has become obsolete. In making this statement, Professor Senning was speaking generally of the several states. We too have his book, and if you will read further on in his discussion you will find that he stated that in some states a real conflict does exist between the rural and urban sections. Such a condition exists in this state.[11]

Unreliable Sources. Evidence may be objectionable because it comes from a prejudiced source. Constantly bear in mind that many organizations have personal interests in certain questions of public policy and maintain propaganda agencies for the purpose of distributing information favorable to their particular activities. Other sources may be unreliable because of inadequate investigation or incompetence of the author. Check carefully the truthworthiness of evidence, for personal bias or incompetence will invalidate it.

Dr. Morris Fishbein uses this method of attacking evidence as follows:

> The report of the committee on the costs of medical care which is kept alive only by the propaganda which is financially sustained by the Milbank and Rosenwald funds would remove from physicians the right to say how medicine shall be practiced and put it into the hands of nonmedical directors.[12]

Mr. Ellis Storey of the University of Alabama exemplified this method in the final debate at the West Point National Tournament in 1955 when he argued against recognizing Communist China.

> The members of the opposition quoted us *The London Mirror*, a British newspaper, in an editorial criticizing America's policy. I would

---

[11] Intercollegiate debate recorded and transcribed for study.
[12] Morris Fishbein, "Doctor and the State," *American Medical Journal* (March 3, 1934), p. 701 (reprint of speech).

like to point out to you *The Mirror* does not express the views of the British Government. However, we do find an Associated Press dispatch from John Hightower in London, February 18, that Sir Anthony Eden had said, with British support the United States has established a firm policy in the defense of Formosa. That's Eden speaking at the present time for the British Government.[13]

Special Methods of Refutation

In addition to the foregoing general methods of refutation, there are six special methods for showing the weaknesses of opposing arguments.

Reductio ad absurdum

Reductio ad absurdum means the process of reducing an argument to an absurdity. By this process you assume, for the sake of argument, the truth of your opponent's statement. You then carry the same line of reasoning to its ultimate conclusion and show the absurdity of it. For example, the negative advances the objection that state medicine would subject the medical profession to political influence and would, therefore, be a source of political graft and corruption. The affirmative accepts the argument and uses it as a basis to extend the reasoning. The public school system, today under state control, is also subject to political influence and domination. By the same process of reasoning advanced by the negative, the affirmative argues that state education be abolished. Carrying this same reasoning further, the affirmative concludes that all activities controlled by the state should be abolished because they are all subject to political influence. The absurdity of the argument appears when the negative's reasoning is forced to a logical conclusion.

This type of reasoning may be overcome by showing how clearly it applies to the issue under consideration. If it can be demonstrated that state medicine would more likely be subjected to political graft and domination than other forms of governmental activities—education, for example—the reduction to absurdity would not stand.

---

[13] Russel R. Windes and Arthur N. Kruger, *Championship Debating* (Portland, Me.: J. Weston Walch, Publishers, 1961), p. 190.

Method of residues

Reducing an argument to a definite number of possible conclusions and showing all conclusions but one impracticable constitutes the method of residues. For example, the affirmative may present three possible methods for providing medical service: (1) a continuation of the present system, (2) a modification of the present system, and (3) a plan of state medicine. By a process of logical reasoning, the affirmative then shows the impracticability of the first two methods. The conclusion leaves state medicine as the only remaining plan.

This method of refutation includes a twofold weakness: first, all possible alternatives may not be presented; second, all alternatives except one may not be destroyed. Either error weakens the argument.

The dilemma

The dilemma consists of showing that an argument leads logically to only two conclusions—both untenable. These alternatives become the horns of the dilemma. To illustrate, the negative offers the objection that state medicine would reduce the remuneration received by the surgeon or physician. In attempting to get the negative into a dilemma, the affirmative raises the question of whether the doctor practices for his own financial gain or because of a desire to render needed medical service. If the doctor desires merely to make money, he should have his income curtailed; if he is primarily concerned with rendering needed service, he will not object to government control. In either event, the argument that state medicine will reduce the remuneration received by the doctor loses its force as an objection to state medicine.

The soundness of a dilemma depends upon two conditions: first, it must present all the alternatives; second, it must destroy all the alternatives. In the use of the dilemma, danger lies in the fallacy of division—the opposition may refuse to accept either of the alternatives offered and establish itself safely in a third position that the dilemma overlooked. For example, the doctor may be motivated by both the desire for financial profit and the desire to render service; the alternatives need not be mutually exclusive.

Inconsistencies

Inconsistencies are exposed when one points out contradictory contentions in the opposing argument. Contradictions may be made in either the reasoning process or the presentation of evidence. The negative on the question of state medicine might contend that the evils of the present system do not warrant a change, and then present a counterproposition such as compulsory health insurance. The counterproposition, virtually admitting the need for a change, contradicts the contention that the present system is satisfactory. Although easily made, contradictions may be difficult to reconcile. Make a careful check of your entire case to avoid inconsistencies.

The tables turned

To turn the tables in an argument, you interpret the evidence or the reasoning of your opponent in a manner to prove your own contention. For example, the negative team proposes voluntary health insurance as a better means of distributing medical costs over a larger group of people than the present system. It contends that this proposal answers the affirmative's objection to the unequal distribution of medical costs. Under health insurance a few unfortunate people would no longer have to pay the high costs of medical service occasioned by expensive operations or prolonged illness, for the cost would be borne by the insurance program. The affirmative accepts this line of reasoning and shows that the same principle applies to state medicine—which spreads the cost among all the people instead of only those who take out health insurance. The ability to pay taxes offers a more accurate standard for assessing the costs of catastrophic illnesses than does the ability to purchase health insurance. Thus state medicine incorporates the same principle as health insurance and furthermore spreads the risk over a greater number of people. The practice of appropriating opposing arguments to prove one's own case proves especially effective when skillfully done.

Irrelevant arguments

You expose irrelevancy when you show that an argument advanced by the opposition does not materially help prove its case.

Exposing irrelevancy is sometimes called the "so what" method. To illustrate, a popular argument of the affirmative for state medicine charges the present system with unequal distribution of doctors throughout the state. The facts show a lower proportion of doctors in relation to population in rural than in urban sections. The negative should deny that this argument opposes the present system—so few people live in rural districts that it would be an economic waste to have more doctors in these areas; modern systems of communication, improved highways, and automobiles make complete medical facilities unnecessary in every village and rural section. Also, it may be more satisfactory as well as more economical to have medical facilities concentrated in urban districts, for people in rural districts prefer the complete medical facilities found in cities. Thus, the argument of unequal distribution of doctors and medical facilities favors rather than opposes the present system of medical care. Exposure of irrelevancy constitutes one of the most effective methods of refutation.

Preparation for Rebuttal

Two prerequisites to successful rebuttal are: (1) reasoning ability and (2) a fundamental knowledge of both sides of the question. Do not seek short cuts to these prerequisites, for they may be met only by continuous practice and diligent research.

Constructive cases may be worked out well in advance; final organization for rebuttal must be made during the debate. This statement does not mean that the general plan of refutation cannot be worked out in advance. An experienced debater can anticipate almost all opposing arguments and plan his refutation prior to the debate. For such preparation, the following suggestions may prove helpful:

1. Plan the general method of attack on each argument that you anticipate your opponents may advance.
2. Assemble evidence needed to develop your rebuttal on each anticipated argument.
3. Decide on methods of attacking specific items of evidence that your opponents may be expected to advance.

Your general plan of attack to meet opponents' arguments must at all times remain adaptable to the specific way your opponent presents an argument. Never memorize a set of rebuttal points on anticipated arguments, because rarely do opponents present an argument in exactly the same way. With an understanding of the methods of attack and an abundance of evidence at hand, final organization of your rebuttals should not be a difficult task.

Organization of Rebuttal Points

Although preparation for rebuttal should be made in advance, the final organization of your points must be made as the debate progresses. Organize rebuttal arguments as clearly as you do the constructive speeches; during the debate, continuously exclude unimportant arguments and arrange the important arguments into effective form. A strong rebuttal cannot be made if you take notes on your opponents' arguments in a haphazard manner without separating the important from the unimportant. When attacking an argument, present sufficient evidence to answer each point fully before taking up a new point. Rebuttal speeches are ineffective unless you proceed in a logical and orderly manner.

Consider the following three steps in each main rebuttal argument: (1) In the introduction, make clear exactly what you propose to refute. This clarification should be as brief and clear as possible. (2) Refute your opponent's arguments and rebuild your own arguments where necessary. (3) Show clearly wherein your refutation has destroyed or weakened your opponent's argument and explain the status of the debate as a result of your refutation.

Note how a rebuttal speech on the proposition of unicameral legislation follows these three steps.

> The second advantage claimed by the negative for bicameralism is that it provides a check on hasty legislation—one house checks on the other, thus preventing ill-considered legislation. I shall show that this check is both unnecessary and undesirable. It is unnecessary because legislation is sufficiently checked where it originates. There now exist three effective checks to hasty and unwise legislation; an effective additional check would be introduced by a plan of unicameralism. The first check is that of the initiative and referendum whereby the electorate assumes direct participation in the process of lawmaking. According to Mr. W. F. Dodd in *State Government,* twenty-one states made direct legislation a part of their state constitutions in the twenty year period from 1899 to 1918; he states that it proved an effective check. By means of the referendum the electorate is given an opportunity to vote on a measure passed by the legislature, either approving or rejecting it. A second effective check is that of the executive veto. The veto is fre-

quently used on defective measures which escape the scrutiny of the legislators. In writing of the effectiveness of this check Professor Senning in his book *The One-House Legislature* states, "The old presumption that the second house corrects and checks the mistakes of the other is one of the shibboleths which must be discarded. The Governor, with his veto power, checks the careless and hasty legislation which the bicameral state assembly has passed."

A third effective check is that of judicial review. The courts have the power to declare measures passed by the legislature unconstitutional when they conflict with the fundamental law as expressed in the constitution of the states; this ruling has proved very effective. A fourth check characteristic of unicameralism is that of public opinion, perhaps the strongest check possible. With publicity given to the introduction of bills possible only in a small house the volume of worthless legislation would be materially reduced. We contend that legislation is sufficiently and effectively checked without the second house; therefore, the check of the second house is unnecessary.

Not only is this check unnecessary but it is undesirable. Why? In the first place because it is not effective. It is common knowledge that the great majority of important acts of the legislature in states do not pass before the last ten days of the session. This is due to the operations of the committee system. In New York, where a detailed study has been made of the effectiveness of the second house check, it was found that only 19 per cent of the bills passed by one house were killed by the other; of the 967 bills passed in a single session, 505 received the approval of both houses without change and 102 were vetoed by the Governor mainly because of legislative error. Not only is this check ineffective, it is actually detrimental to efficient legislation. Instead of acting as a check, the two houses cause delay and permit bargaining in both houses through trading of votes and the shifting of responsibility. Thus, this second advantage claimed for bicameralism falls because it is not needed, it is ineffective, and undesirable.[14]

In planning for defense before the debate, prepare a broad outline of your case on a sheet of paper or cards, allowing space between points to record refutation material that opponents present against your arguments. This outline provides a clear chart for counterrebuttal material. It may be necessary to use a separate sheet or card for incidental rebuttal points; by combining these sheets, you can tear down your opponent's arguments and build up your own case by a well-organized plan.

Charting the debate as it progresses constitutes another important part of rebuttal organization. To chart the debate effectively, outline the opposing case as your opponents present it; leave space in

---

[14] Classroom debate recorded and transcribed for study.

the outline for notes on material to be used in refutation. Use a two-colored pencil, say red and blue, so that statements to be refuted and statements to be made in refutation can be distinguished easily. This procedure gives a clear chart of the direct rebuttal material.

Some debaters prefer to record both destructive and constructive rebuttal work on the same sheet. This plan calls for sheets of paper with lines drawn vertically through the center of the page as shown by the diagram on page 185. On the left side, you may outline the opposing case and record arguments to be made in refutation. On the right side, write a broad outline of your own case and leave space for recording opposing arguments used in attacking your case. This plan enables you to determine at a glance the status of an argument at any time.

Summary

Rebuttal may be defined as the process of destroying opposing arguments and building up one's own arguments; refutation is the tearing-down process in debate, a part of both the constructive and rebuttal speeches. Rebuttal points may be listed under three heads: (1) attacks on opposing arguments, (2) defense of own arguments, and (3) attacks on minor points used to introduce a rebuttal speech or to weaken the authenticity of the opposing case.

Opposing arguments may be weakened or destroyed by attacking either the reasoning process or the evidence used in support of a contention. Errors in the reasoning process are known as fallacies. The principal fallacies applicable to debate are: (1) fallacies of deductive reasoning, (2) fallacies of inductive reasoning, (3) fallacies of ignoring the question, and (4) fallacies of begging the question. There are four methods of attacking evidence: (1) show that evidence is insufficient, (2) show that evidence is misapplied, (3) show that evidence is inaccurate, and (4) show that evidence is obtained from an unreliable source.

There are six special methods of refutation: (1) reduce an argument to an absurdity, (2) use the method of residues, (3) point out a dilemma, (4) expose inconsistencies, (5) turn the tables or appropriate arguments, and (6) expose irrelevant arguments.

Preparation for rebuttal work consists of cultivating the ability

Rebuttal Chart [15]

RESOLVED, THAT A ONE-HOUSE LEGISLATURE SHOULD BE ADOPTED.

Opponents' case: Negative	*Our case: Affirmative*

I. *Advantages of bicameralism warrants its retention.*
  A. *Provides diversity of representation.*
    No differences in interests to justify diversity.
  B. *Serve to check hasty legislation.*
    This check is unnecessary and undesirable.
II. *Propose to modify present system.*
  Admit failure as the plan actually operates.
  A. *Elect one-house by districts—other by population.*
    No useful purpose is gained.
    Plan keeps two houses—the source of the evils.
    Plan does not correct evils.
  B. *Propose smaller houses—salaries paid per annum.*
    Counter to diversity of representation argument.
	I. CHANGE NEEDED BECAUSE OF EVILS OF TWO HOUSES.
	Admits evils—deny change in system necessary—not inherent.
	  A. ATTRACTS WEAK MEN.
	    Corrected by negative proposal.
	  B. COMPLEXITY OF PROCEDURE.
	    Corrected by negative proposal.
	  C. COMMITTEE SYSTEM SUSCEPTIBLE TO OUTSIDE INFLUENCE.
	    Agree—propose abolition.
	II. ONE-HOUSE LEGISLATION WILL REMEDY EVILS.
	Agree—but not best plan.
	  A. ATTRACTS QUALIFIED MEN—FIXES RESPONSIBILITY AND PROVIDES CONTINUOUS SESSIONS.
	    Same.
	  B. SIMPLIFIES PROCEDURE.
	    Same.
	  C. ABOLISHES CONFERENCE COMMITTEE.
	    Same.
	III. ADVANTAGES OF ONE-HOUSE WARRANTS CHANGE.
	Agrees to advantages but denies change necessary to gain them.
	  A. LESS EXPENSIVE.
	    Same under negative proposal.
	  B. LESSENS POLITICAL CORRUPTION.
	    Not possible to eliminate—.
	    Negative plan good as affirmative's.
	  C. PREVENTS FRICTION AND DEADLOCKS.
	    No answer (hit this hard).

---

[15] The material printed in caps and small caps was prepared before the debate; that in italics designates the opponents' remarks; and the regular cap and lower case material indicates the debater's own notes.

to reason and acquiring a fundamental knowledge of the question. Careful preparation of specific points should be worked out prior to the debate, but the final organization of rebuttal arguments must be made during the debate. The rebuttal arguments should be as carefully organized as the constructive speeches.

Oral Assignment

1. Divide the class into panel groups in the same manner explained in the exercises for Chapter 10.
2. Discuss "The Negative Case" on the proposition selected for class debates.
3. Hand in a summary of the discussion.

Collateral Readings

Ehninger, Douglas, and Wayne Brockriede, *Decision by Debate,* Ch. 16. New York: Dodd, Mead & Co., 1963.

Ewbank, Henry Lee, and J. Jeffery Auer, *Discussion and Debate,* Ch. 27. New York: Appleton-Century-Crofts, Inc., 1951.

Freeley, Austin J., *Argumentation and Debate,* Ch. 16. Belmont, Calif.: Wadsworth Publishing Co., 1961.

Kruger, Arthur N., *Modern Debate,* Ch. 17. New York: McGraw-Hill Book Co., Inc., 1960.

McBath, James H., ed., *Argumentation and Debate,* Ch. 11. New York: Holt, Rinehart & Winston, Inc., 1963.

Murphy, James J., and Jon M. Ericson, *The Debaters' Guide,* Ch. 5. Indianapolis, Ind.: Bobbs-Merrill Company, Inc., 1961.

IV

Presenting
the Debate

12
Presenting the Debate Case

Part III took you step by step through the process of preparing to debate—analyzing the proposition to discover the main issues, selecting the best evidence to support the arguments, reasoning from evidence to logical conclusions, arranging the arguments, and using refutation to uphold your case and weaken your opponents' case. Your task still remains unfinished. You must now consider how to present the case orally. Although a great deal of argumentation in our society is presented in written form, almost all educational debates take the form of oral argument. A textbook in argumentation cannot treat all the fundamentals of oral communication; we can, however, examine the principles applicable to oral argument.[1]

Principles of Oral Argument

What constitutes effective oral argument? Consider how the following principles of oral communication apply to argumentation and debate.

Direct, conversational, and communicative presentation

Effective presentation enables you to accomplish your purpose—to persuade an audience to accept your contentions. Look upon presentation skills as a means of communicating ideas, information, reasoning, and emotions to your audience—not as a means of exhibiting

---

[1] For a full development of the fundamentals of delivery, see the textbooks listed at the end of this chapter. Parts of this chapter are based on Glenn R. Capp, *How To Communicate Orally* (Englewood Cliffs, N.J.: Prentice-Hall, Inc., 1961), pp. 177-283.

your voice, bodily action, or language. If your speaking calls attention to your presentation skills, you will fail to communicate your ideas or persuade your audience. If your audience remains unaware of how you speak but comprehends your ideas and accepts your arguments, you are making effective use of delivery skills.

Communicative speaking presents a special problem for the debater since his emphasis on analysis, evidence, and reasoning often causes him to neglect presentation skills. Mastering the principles of argumentation in a course in argumentation and debate leaves little time for a study of the fundamentals of speech. Furthermore, the procedures for intercollegiate debate present limiting factors. Because of the time element, debaters often race through their speeches attempting to include all the major arguments with adequate supporting evidence. The emphasis on tournament debating during the past forty years has added to the problem. The audiences for tournament debates usually consist of a well-informed judge, a timekeeper, and an occasional additional auditor. This artificial audience situation causes the debater to adapt to a highly specialized listener and to omit much of the explanation and support essential for effective presentation to a public audience. He often acquires a bombastic, rapid-fire manner of speaking seemingly designed to overwhelm his opponents and judges.

Actually, the debater is more effective when he utilizes conversational and communicative speech designed to persuade listeners rather than to force arguments upon them. Realization of the advantages of direct and conversational speech will help you acquire a communicative delivery. The following factors should enable you to avoid the undesirable features of presentation often associated with debaters.

Dividing Your Case Properly. Debaters sometimes divide their cases unevenly and thus leave insufficient time to develop them in a communicative manner. As discussed in Chapter 3, an effective affirmative case must prove that (1) a problem exists in sufficient severity to demand action, (2) the affirmative's proposal will remedy the problem, and (3) the affirmative's plan will result in an advantageous condition—its attendant evils will not outweigh its advantages. The negative side must negate one or more of the issues; the usual practice is to counter each issue.

The affirmative speakers must first decide upon a division of their case. The logical adequacy of the case should receive first attention, but the breadth of the case must also be considered to permit time for developing it in a communicative manner. The first affirmative speaker should present a significant part of the case so as to leave his colleague enough time for refutation before completing the constructive arguments. However, the first speaker should not rush his analysis of the proposition, for the analysis serves as the basis for the case.

The issue of need is usually of utmost importance to the affirmative case; on most questions the analysis and the need issue will require the full time of the first speaker. Some affirmative teams do not spend sufficient time in developing the need issue and as a result speak much too rapidly and forcibly. Some affirmative teams attempt to present their entire case in the opening speech—such procedure does not allow them sufficient time to support the specific evils with adequate logical proof. In such cases, the constructive phase of the debate stops after the first affirmative speech, and the remainder of the debate consists largely of a rehashing of arguments. Excessive repetition prevents the debater from developing his constructive arguments fully and in a communicative manner. No standard answer can be given to the question of what constitutes sufficient proof, but too much is better than too little. The degrees of proof required will vary with different propositions, but ordinarily the first affirmative speaker cannot develop more than the issue of need adequately if he gives the proper analysis and introduction to the debate.[2]

In short, the first affirmative speaker introduces the question, gives the necessary analysis for its understanding, and develops the issue of need. The second speaker re-establishes the need and shows that the affirmative proposal will correct existing evils and result in an advantageous condition. The first negative speaker negates the need, and the second negative speaker shows that the affirmative's proposal is impractical and will result in disadvantages that will outweigh the advantages. To perform these necessary duties, the debaters must divide their cases so as to restrict the scope of the debate. Each speaker should assume part of the responsibility for both constructive and rebuttal work. A case properly restricted and divided

---

[2] For a more detailed discussion, see Glenn R. Capp, "Debating the Affirmative," *The Forensic* (January, 1955), pp. 44-47; and Glenn R. Capp, Robert Huber, and Wayne C. Eubank, "Duties of Affirmative Speakers—A Symposium," *The Speech Teacher*, VIII, No. 2 (March, 1959), 139-49.

will permit time for direct, conversational, and communicative delivery.

Selecting Only the Best Arguments and Evidence. The number of the arguments and the amount of evidence on many national debate topics may seem almost inexhaustible, but because of the time limits of educational debates, the debater must be selective. It is better to develop a few of the best arguments fully and with a communicative delivery than to race through a multiplicity of points without adequately developing them.

For example, the first affirmative's duty consists of showing that certain evils prove the need for a change. This speaker should concentrate on the strongest evils, those that can be corrected by his proposal and that he can develop adequately in the allotted time. A long list of evils, without proper arrangement and development, may represent such a scattered attack that the audience and judges fail to see any fundamental weakness in an existing order—fail to see the forest for the trees. In one debate, on the subject of discontinuing direct economic aid, the first affirmative speaker advanced the following evils in the order listed:

1. Direct aid creates ill will among neutral nations.
2. Direct aid sometimes results in a give-away race between the United States and Russia.
3. Direct aid is expensive to the American taxpayer.
4. Direct aid tends to create a false economy in the United States.
5. Direct aid is detrimental to the incentive of undeveloped countries.
6. Direct aid is harmful to internationalism.
7. The direct aid program has failed to contain communism.

The judge criticized the debater's development of the need issue on three counts: (1) He had too many isolated evils and as a result did not have time to develop the philosophy and background of each evil. It is not enough to list and briefly explain the indictments of the status quo—each indictment must be developed in sufficient detail to demand an answer by the negative. (2) The indictments were not well arranged. The speaker skipped back and forth from one idea to another to the extent that it was difficult to isolate any concentrated attack on the aid program. The multiplicity of points with their jumbled arrangement and hasty presentation made it difficult for the critic to retain them. (3) The arrangement of points did not indicate a difference between main points and subpoints. Some separate evils were parts of a larger indictment contained in the list. The critic suggested the rearrangement of points into three principal indictments, as follows:

I. The present program has failed to contain communism, for
   A. It has created ill will of neutral nations for the free-world concept.
   B. It has resulted in retaliatory grants by Russia, thus precipitating a give-away race.
II. The present program has had detrimental economic effects, for
   A. It has been a burden to the American taxpayer.
   B. It has created a false economy in the United States.
   C. It has kept undeveloped countries from developing by lessening their incentive.
III. The program is harmful to internationalism.

In short, the tendency to include too many points and too much evidence in a disorganized arrangement causes the debater to rush his presentation, to speak too forcibly, and to decrease his effectiveness. The grouping of the indictments under main headings saves time because the philosophy of many evils stems from the same cause. One background explanation thus suffices for each particular category. The debater should limit the scope of his arguments and group them under main headings to allow for a concentrated attack.

Proper attitudes

Debaters are sometimes said to be arrogant, bombastic, conceited, and unsportsmanlike. Not all debaters deserve these epithets, but some do. Some debaters acquire the idea that opponents are enemies that must be defeated at any cost, that judges are necessary evils standing in their way to becoming champions, and that the audience should not be seriously considered. Establishing proper mental attitudes is essential to effective delivery, for attitudes are reflected in the total impression that a debater makes on his audience. Debaters should acquire the proper mental attitudes toward their subjects, their opponents, their audiences, and their judges.

Toward Subject. Some critics of educational debating question the ethics of debating both sides of a proposition. They claim that this practice encourages sophistry, fosters intellectual dishonesty, and causes students to disregard their convictions. Although such students may go through the process of developing logical arguments, their lack of conviction will be shown by subliminal signs of which both the audience and the debater may not be aware. Is there a justifiable rationale for debating both sides of a proposition?

We must start with the premise that certain factual arguments exist on all sides of a question and on both sides of a resolution. There is no such thing as "the truth" relative to questions that propose a change in an existing social, political, or economic policy. Truthful arguments and valid evidence exist on either side, and equally intelligent men may evaluate these arguments and facts and come to different conclusions. Otherwise, how can we account for political parties with varying beliefs, religious organizations with differing doctrinal principles, and nations with conflicting ideologies?

The same principle involved in debating both sides of a debate proposition applies to the lawyer deciding whether or not he should accept a case. He may be asked, "Can you ethically defend a person whom you know to be guilty?" The obvious reply is, "How can you know that he is guilty prior to the trial? If guilty, of what is he guilty?" A person may take the life of another and receive a verdict that ranges all the way from "not guilty" to "death." The purpose of the trial is to determine the guilt or innocence of the defendant. Unless both sides are represented by able advocates, injustice may result. The lawyer's obligation can be satisfied only by presenting the strongest case possible for his client consisting of sound arguments and factual evidence.

In much the same way, the debater marshals the best arguments and most valid evidence for his side of the proposition. In doing so, he does not infer, "This is the side in which I believe"; rather he says, "Here is the most valid case that I have been able to devise for this side of the proposition."

An important question of public policy deserves careful study from all points of view. There must be two sides, and they may have an almost equal balance of arguments and evidence. In championing either side, simply recognize the existence of fundamental pro and con arguments. Do not attempt to "prove beyond the shadow of a doubt" the affirmative or the negative side; present the best arguments for either side. When you come to the platform with this attitude, you will usually deliver a sincere, intelligent, persuasive case because you will not feel that you are being intellectually dishonest in debating both sides of the proposition.

Toward Opponent. If you look upon your opponents as enemies or as untruthful simply because they oppose you, your presentation will lack conviction. Instead of allowing the personal element to enter, consider opponents simply as those expressing a different point of view; but for the element of chance, the sides might have been reversed. Your task is to develop your side as objectively as possible, and your opponents' duty is the same. Deal with facts, arguments, and fallacies, not in personalities. It is the argument, not the opponent, that must be destroyed.

Debaters sometimes show discourtesy toward their opponents, either intentionally or unintentionally. This discourtesy takes such forms as loud whispering between colleagues while the opposition speaks, reacting with surprise or dismay at what the opponents say, exhibiting smugness or arrogance while sitting at the table or walking to the platform, or engaging in sarcasm or ridicule while speaking. Such reactions reflect on the character of the debater; they indicate a lack of fair play and good manners. As such, they count heavily against the speaker in the total impression that he makes upon an audience.

Toward Audience. Debating consists of more than a weighing of arguments and evidence. It includes persuasion, inducing an audience to accept your contentions. Delivery is a two-way process between the speaker and the audience; unless the debater considers the audience as an integral part of the total speaking situation, communication will prove ineffective.

Do not look upon your audience as incapable of understanding the finer points of a well-developed argument. Such an attitude defeats itself because it antagonizes your listeners. Ignoring the audience and talking only to the judges, in terms that the average listener, unfamiliar with debate tactics and language, does not understand, is poor psychology; the presence of the audience is assurance in itself of interest in the question. Therefore, consider the right of the hearers to the courtesy of being addressed. The good speaker establishes mental contact with his hearers and makes them understand his case.

Toward Judges. The judges selected for college debates are sometimes criticized on the basis that being untrained in educational debate, they cannot properly evaluate the students' performance. The argument states that the debater may be trained by an expert and then evaluated by a nonexpert; he may be graded down for doing what he has been trained to do. The answer to this criticism lies in the fact that debaters should learn to adapt their presentation to varying types of listeners, the types they will encounter in life situations of advocacy.

The average debate judge is in many ways superior in ability to members of the jury in a court trial, the electorate in a political campaign, or the participants in a policy-determining body. Educational debate is in part an exercise in persuasive speaking. If your judges are well-trained forensic directors, you can assume that they probably know as much about the topic as you do. Thus, they will not require the detailed background explanations and careful documentation that would be expected by the nonexpert.

The forensic director is well acquainted with the strategical devices sometimes employed by debaters. For example, "I presume that the affirmative is waiting until the last rebuttal to answer this important argument" is a commonly heard stratagem. The inference desired by the debater is that his opponents have taken unfair advantage by such delay. The nonexpert judge might give the debater an advantage if he made such a claim, but the forensic director would realize that the affirmative cannot cover all refutation in the first rebuttal speech and furthermore that the affirmative has the right to use the last rebuttal speech to full advantage—since the affirmative side must initiate the argument, debate procedure gives it the advantage of closing the debate. Thus, a strategic device that might serve to advantage with one judge might act as a disadvantage with another.

Many forensic directors resent comments by debaters on debate procedure; others might welcome such instructions. The ideal debate judge disregards his personal feelings about the proposition and any extraneous matters that might interfere with his evaluation of the debate. The debater must realize, however, that not all judges are ideal. His approach to a judge favorably disposed toward the proposition should differ from his approach to one opposed to the proposition. The lay judge offers a more realistic listener, in many ways, than the expert judge. The debater should analyze his judges and adapt to their training and experience, because such adaptation prepares him for life situations of advocacy.

An able advocate

It has become almost a truism in oral communication that a speaker is no better than his intrinsic worth as a person. Writers since the Classical period have stressed the character or ethos of the speaker as a part of the total speaking situation. The "able-man theory," as this theory is called, encompasses the principle that you develop yourself as a whole. When you speak, you reveal yourself, the type of person you are, your qualifications to speak on the subject, your experience and training, your soundness of judgment, and your skills in presentation. Aristotle stressed that an able speaker is a man of intelligence, character, and good will.

Intelligence. The able-man principle applies to the debater just as to any other speaker. As the debater speaks, listeners form impressions of whether or not his intelligence, general background knowledge, and preparation qualify him to appraise the subject properly. They accept the debater's contentions in part because they consider that he knows and properly interprets the facts and opinions he presents. Abundant evidence, sound reasoning, and mature judgments affect, not only the logical adequacy of the debater's case, but also his ethical adequacy as a person.

The documentation of your arguments indicates the care that you have exercised in preparing the subject. A variety of sources gives evidence of research; citing substantial sources indicates that you have done your research from primary source materials and not secondary sources or debate handbooks. Giving facts about the qualifications of a supposed authority shows that you are not quoting persons affected by bias or prejudice. When you refrain from making sweeping conclusions and extravagant claims, you reveal maturity of judgment and the ability to reason logically.

Matters that affect the ethics and judgment of the debater count more heavily than many debaters think. Exposure of questionable strategic devices affects not only the argument itself but also the debater's intellectual honesty and worth as an individual. For example, some debaters make overzealous claims of what they have done and what their opponents have failed to do. In one debate, an affirmative speaker began his rebuttal speech by summarizing an important issue and stating that the negative had remained significantly silent on the point. This claim would probably have made a more favorable impression on the judge had not the preceding negative speaker spent half of his rebuttal speech on the point. The judge was curious to know whether the affirmative speaker simply had not listened to the preceding speaker or whether he thought the judge had not.

Psychologically, most people respond more favorably to understatement than to overstatement. Yet many debaters make sweeping claims for themselves and distortingly minimize what their opponents have done. What actually transpires in the debate usually makes more of an impression on the judge than the sweeping claims of opposing speakers. More important, extravagant claims reflect on the competency and judgment of the debater; such practices indirectly affect the listeners' impressions of the debater's intelligence.

Character. Your audience and judges will accept your arguments in part because of the impressions that you make on them as a person. Indications of your character may be revealed in many ways. The enthusiasm with which you approach your debates indicates your real interest in developing yourself rather than simply winning victories. The friendliness that you show to your opponents and to the audience indicates your disposition toward debate as an educational activity. Your sincerity indicates that you would not purposely mislead your audience, that you desire to present the best possible case and support your arguments with the most valid material. A degree of self-confidence indicates that you are in a good emotional state and are prepared to evaluate properly what you talk about. Through these and many subliminal signs the audience and judges form impressions of your character, trustworthiness, and worth as a person.

Occasionally debaters present conflicting testimony or other conflicting factual data during the course of a debate. Seemingly, both sets of data came from reliable sources, yet the judge knows that both sides cannot be correct—someone has misinterpreted the evidence. Which side should the judge believe? Perhaps without realizing that he does so, he believes the debater who has made the greatest impact on him as a person. The character of the speaker as revealed by his enthusiasm, friendliness, sincerity, assurance, and knowledge has made the difference.

Good Will. As explained in the discussion of attitudes, fairness and accuracy in presenting arguments indicate a person with an attitude of good will toward his audience and toward debate as an educational activity. Questionable strategic devices, overzealous attempts to expose an opponent, and attempts to deceive an audience indicate too much emphasis on winning and too little emphasis on giving an accurate evaluation of the case.

Statements that "the negative has remained silent on this point" when it has not, that "the affirmative is withholding this argument until its last rebuttal" when it used its first affirmative rebuttal speech wisely, that "the affirmative has given a trick interpretation of the question" when it defined the terms fairly, that "the negative has asked questions to get us off our case" when the questions were pertinent, exemplify the type of questionable tactics that indicate a lack of good will toward the audience.

By keeping the debate centered on the arguments, avoiding personality clashes, and striving earnestly to give an accurate representation of your side of the proposition, you create good will among your listeners and add to your ethical appeal.

Rhetorical skills

The rhetorical principles of oral presentation taught in speech courses will help the debater convince his listeners. Although a textbook in argumentation cannot include a full discussion of these principles, a brief review of them should prove helpful. Communicative speech requires the use of language, voice, bodily action, and poise in coordination with the mind.

Language. The debater's choice and arrangement of words help determine his effectiveness in oral argument. Use language to help you communicate effectively, not to impress your listeners with your large vocabulary. Oral language differs from written in that it is more repetitious, informal, and direct. The writer uses titles, subtitles, paragraphs, summaries, and transitions. The reader can re-read difficult passages or materials not fully understood, but the listener must comprehend instantly. The debater should observe audience reactions as he speaks to determine whether or not he is being understood and whether or not the audience accepts his arguments. His observations may indicate that his explanations need further elaboration or his arguments additional support.

Oral language should be adapted to the audience and the occasion. For example, argumentation lends itself to more forceful language than does exposition. Language used in debates before audiences or over television should be more formal and show more restraint than language used in tournament debates.

The aggressive tempo of college debates often causes debaters to think faster than they can speak. They therefore tend to vocalize their pauses with "uhs" and "ahs" or with such rest phrases as "ladies and gentlemen," "first of all," "so we see," and "now then."

Such phrases may be repeated constantly without the debater being aware of it. If he would pause instead of using such mechanical phrases, his presentation would be more effective.

Rapid speech often results in poor articulation. For example, the following errors were noted in one debate: cidy for city, hist'ry for history, jist for just, inny for any, acshully for actually, ginnlemum for gentlemen, gineral for general, Amurican for American, ev'ry for every. The accent was also misplaced in several words; for example, de'-tail for de-tail', re'-search for re-search', and in'-sur-ance for in-sur'-ance. Many debaters have words in their reading and writing vocabularies that have never been added to their speaking vocabularies, and as a result, they attempt to pronounce these words as they are spelled. More often, errors in pronunciation are caused by carelessness.

We can improve our use of language by reading good literature, by associating with cultured people, and by speaking and writing. Debating offers an excellent activity for improving oral style. Conversely, care in the use of language improves the effectiveness of the debater.

Voice. A good voice helps the debater communicate his arguments to an audience; it is never an end in itself. If the debater uses his voice simply to impress his audience, he detracts from effective communication.

What goals should the debater seek for the proper use of his voice? First, he should attempt to be intelligible—to be understood clearly in the room or auditorium. A flexible voice aids intelligibility. It varies in keeping with the content of the speech. If the debater speaks in a monotone, in a sing-song pattern, or with a constant rate and volume, he impedes effective communication. He should strive for a conversational manner and vary the rate, volume, pitch, and inflection to bring out shades of meaning.

The debater should also attempt to cultivate a voice pleasing in quality and free of affectations. A voice that is raspy, harsh, guttural, breathy, thin, or monotonous is unpleasant. Desirable qualities include animation, flexibility, modulation, and controlled rate, force, pitch, and melody. Above all, a debater should not use overly precise diction, artificially rounded tones, or any affectations that call attention to the voice. A warm and pleasant voice results largely from proper attitudes—a person with a healthy attitude toward debate, his subject, and his audience will usually reflect those attributes in his voice. Voice quality can also be improved by proper training, such as that available in courses in voice and diction.

Bodily Action. A debater uses both visual and auditory means to get his arguments accepted. If your words and actions are congruous, your audience will likely accept what you say; if they are incongruous, your audience will usually accept what your actions reflect. An uninhibited person usually uses bodily action, gestures, and facial expressions to reinforce what he says. Meaningful bodily action will help you convey meaning, hold attention, and generate energy and self-confidence.

Bodily action includes movements of the whole body and gestures, or movements of parts of the body. These types work in coordination with facial expressions and posture for total body expression.

Purposeful movements on the platform will assist you in effective delivery; random movements detract from what you say by calling attention to themselves. Avoid aimless pacing back and forth or from one side of the lectern to the other while speaking. A movement forward to emphasize a point, backward to indicate the conclusion of an idea, or laterally to denote a transition from one point to another reinforces meaning. Move when you feel the inner urge to reinforce your ideas with bodily action; avoid planned movements because they will appear artificial.

Gestures consist of movements of the arms, hands, head, and shoulders to emphasize oral expression. When used in coordination with the whole body, they help to communicate ideas. If improperly used, they detract from effective presentation. Some improper uses of gestures by debaters consist of the following: (1) They may appear planned or unnatural. Gestures must come from an inner desire to share ideas with others; they must not be forced or planned in advance. (2) They may be poorly timed. Poor timing usually results from planned gestures or when the debater fails to think the thought as he speaks. Focus attention on the thought, not on the gesture itself. (3) They may appear indefinite, only slight movements, when the debater desires to gesture but is inhibited from doing so. Gestures will usually be vigorous and fully made when the debater loses himself in the idea he seeks to convey and forgets to think about whether or not he should gesture. (4) They may fail to show variety. Avoid using a single gesture excessively. Some gestures are used to emphasize ideas, others to describe the size and shape or distance and movement of objects by imitation. Attempt to use a variety of gestures to reinforce different meanings. Coordinate gestures with other bodily movements to indicate total body expression.

Poise. Reasonable self-assurance and poise also aid the debater in oral presentation. Beginning debaters sometimes feel tense in appearing before an audience or in participating in a tournament largely because they fear that which they do not fully understand. With increased knowledge about debate procedure and with practice in debating, these feelings become less noticeable. Experienced debaters may also feel anxiety, especially when encountering a new audience situation or engaging in an unfamiliar type of debate. Such feelings are entirely normal and may actually be beneficial since controlled anxiety increases a debater's desire to do well, prods him to prepare adequately, causes him to be alert and energetic while speaking, speeds up his thinking processes, and causes him to be sensitive to audience reactions.

The simple realization that some nervous feelings are a natural reaction of conscientious debaters paves the way for bringing apprehensions under control. The following factors will also help: (1) Realize that excessive anxiety can be controlled. Attempt first to control the outward signs of tenseness; then, as you become more familiar with debate procedures and gain experience at tournaments and before audiences, your feelings of anxiety will become less severe without your being entirely aware of the change. (2) Prepare thoroughly for your debates. No other factor gives most debaters a greater feeling of assurance than the fact that they know their subject thoroughly and have a well-planned case. The procedures discussed in Part III, if followed conscientiously, will result in proper preparation. (3) Keep rested and physically fit. Many debaters put off preparation until the night before a tournament and then stay up most of the night to prepare their cases. This loss of sleep together with the tiring travel to the tournament and the activities of the meeting cause the debater to become exhausted before the tournament begins. Such physical exhaustion is often reflected in nervous tension that mars effectiveness of presentation. The plan of cooperative group preparation outlined in Chapter 2 will make such last-minute activities unnecessary. (4) Think in terms of success. If you have chronic feelings of anxiety, try giving yourself a mental pep talk. Do not dwell on the seriousness of the occasion and magnify it out of proportion. Think in terms of your successful experiences in debate, not about those occasions when you felt that you did not do well—you earned the right to represent your school or you would not have been chosen. Adopt an attitude of success and attempt to do your best.

Stage Conduct and Delivery Mannerisms

Some problems of delivery have special application to debaters. They may be grouped under the headings of stage conduct and delivery mannerisms.

Stage conduct

The way a debater conducts himself before and during the debate makes an impression on his listeners and thus affects his over-all effectiveness. Some of the more noticeable factors of stage conduct will be considered.

Actions on the Platform. Your reactions during the debate affect the total impression you make on the judge and audience. Do not sit on the platform as if you were either ill at ease or bored. The person who sits rigid with both feet planted firmly together on the floor makes as poor an impression as the one who slumps in his chair. Assume a natural position and avoid drumming on the table, clasping and unclasping your hands, or any other distracting activity. Do nothing while sitting on the platform that will call attention to your actions.

You also impress an audience by the way you walk to the lectern when it becomes your time to speak. By slouching up to the speaker's stand, you give the impression of a poor attitude toward debate and disregard for your listeners. Conversely, if you hurry from your chair and charge to the stand, the audience may consider you overly anxious or excessively competitive. If you lower your head, avoid eye contact with the audience, and walk hesitantly, your audience will probably think that you lack assurance. Walk to the platform with a firm step, an erect body, a pleasant expression, and a direct and confident look at the audience.

The manner in which you walk away from the stand is also important. Using the last fraction of time allowed, grabbing notes, and rushing from the stand shows little concern for your listeners. A faltering finish is likely to affect whatever good impression you have made. To clinch your remarks, complete what you have to say, pause momentarily, and return to your chair with the same poise that characterized your taking the floor. Never seem to apologize for what has been said by your manner of leaving the platform.

Using Notes and Materials. The improper use of notes and other materials that the debater takes to the platform mars effectiveness of presentation. Particularly objectionable is the practice of making notes on large artist pads that require both hands to hold; such notes decrease the proper use of bodily action and cause the debater to focus attention on his notes to the exclusion of his listeners. Armloads of books and pamphlets taken to the platform have a similar effect, besides requiring too much time to arrange and thus prolonging the debate. Actually the debater would make a better impression if he gave the gist of the quotation or the statement of facts in his own words; this would leave him more time for reasoned development of his arguments.

Cards or sheets are improperly employed when a debater plays with his notes, folds and unfolds them, or puts them in and takes them out of his pockets. Some debaters read from the card, look at the card, speak to the card, and do everything but let the card serve its real purpose.

Perhaps the greatest objection to the use of notes is the too frequent reference to them; an occasional glance should suffice. You cannot project yourself to an audience if your eyes are focused on your notes. Talk with the audience, not merely about a subject. Looking at notes too often leaves the impression that you are interested only in your material and care little about communicating with people.

Notes, properly used, should be an aid rather than a hindrance. They relieve the necessity of committing to memory quotations, tables of statistics, and the exact sequence of supporting material. Through skillful handling of notes, quotations and statistical tables may be used without breaking eye contact with the audience. To do this, the debater must "think through" his arguments as he communicates with his listeners. If the attention of the audience is focused on the argument, brief references to notes can be made without diverting attention.

Occasional glances may be made at notes without taking them from the stand if a speaker's desk is provided. If the notes are to be held, type them on stiff cards. Waving large sheets of paper distracts the audience and decreases communication.

Explaining Charts, Diagrams, and Drawings. Charts, diagrams, and blackboard drawings are valuable aids if properly made and displayed. Consider the following suggestions:

1. Stand to one side of the blackboard or diagram so that the audience's view is not obstructed and contact with the listeners is not lost.

2. If you illustrate by drawing, explain the drawings as you make them. Such explanation saves time and keeps up interest. If the drawings are complicated, draw them on large sheets of cardboard and display them when you present the explanation.

3. Make drawings and letterings large enough to be seen by all members of the audience. A visual aid that cannot be seen confuses rather than clarifies.

4. Use a pointer to indicate special features of the drawing or chart. A general reference confuses the listener.

5. Do not display charts or drawings before time for using them. They will distract attention from what you say.

6. Remove the chart or erase the drawing when you finish with it. Otherwise your listeners may continue to study your visual aid after you have finished with it.

7. Check the auditorium before the debate begins and remove visual aids that may distract from your speaking.

Delivery mannerisms

Peculiarities of delivery vary, but all have one characteristic in common—they call attention to the speaker and divert attention from what he says. Often the debater may be unaware of his mannerisms until they become habitual. The following mannerisms, cited by critic judges, are among the most common for debaters.[3]

Taking Pencil or Pen to Platform. Debaters sometimes take pencils or pens to the platform, hold them, wave them about, put them behind their ears, or use them as pointers. The audience may follow the movements of the pencil instead of giving

---

[3] The ballots observed were from judges in the Baylor University forensic tournaments.

their attention to the arguments. Before going to the speaker's stand, put your pencil in your pocket or leave it at your desk.

Misusing Hands. Continuously putting your hands into and taking them out of your pockets, clenching and unclenching them behind the back, rubbing them together, clasping and unclasping them, or placing them on the desk or on the hips distracts from your delivery. The use of the hands in the ways mentioned cannot be objectionable if done occasionally; frequent repetition calls attention to the movement and away from subject matter.

One critic wrote on his ballot that a debater put his right hand into his pants pocket and withdrew it thirty-five times in a single rebuttal speech. The critic's count indicates that he found this peculiarity of the delivery distracting. To avoid this mannerism, begin your speech by resting your hands on the lectern. As you continue, use them to gesture or to hold your notes. As you become engrossed in your speech, you will tend to forget about your hands and use them naturally to help express your ideas.

Improperly Using Speaker's Stand. Some debaters rest a leg on the base of the stand, lean heavily on the stand, cling to it, pull it toward them, or push it away. There is no objection to resting one or both hands on the stand occasionally, but do not lean upon it excessively or otherwise use it as a crutch. The speaker's stand may be used to advantage by (1) placing notes on it together with any other materials that may be needed, (2) standing directly behind it or slightly to one side, (3) varying the position occasionally, and (4) refraining from pacing from one side of the stand to the other.

Adjusting Eyeglasses or Clothing. This mannerism may consist of taking your glasses off and putting them on, placing them on the table and withdrawing them, or cleaning, adjusting, and using them as pointers. An occasional touch of the hand to your glasses may not be objectionable, but excessive adjustments decrease effectiveness of delivery. To adjust ties, hoist trousers, button and unbutton coats, or make other similar movements frequently while speaking diverts attention of listeners from the arguments. These are nervous mannerisms that tend to disappear as the speaker concentrates on subject matter, but they become annoying to listeners if used too often.

Indirect Eye Contact. Instead of looking out of windows, at the ceiling or floor, or at some object in the room, look directly at your listeners. Not to look at the audience invites loss of interest. Some debaters seem to look beyond the audience. This practice prevents direct eye contact and leaves the debater without the advantage of facial expression. Looking directly at the audience and occasionally shifting the glance from one section of the auditorium to another increases audience communication.

Moving Head. Constantly shifting the head up and down or from side to side is disturbing. Head gestures may serve a useful purpose; excessive head movements do more harm than good.

Swaying Body. Equally distracting is the swaying movement or actions where the speaker bends his knees and constantly rises up and down on the balls of his feet. A speaker naturally leans forward for emphasis and slightly backward during transitions of ideas. Such movements aid in delivery; mechanical swaying movements mar speaking effectiveness.

Resting Weight on One Leg. If the weight of the body rests entirely on one leg while the other hangs limp, the debater presents a slouchy appearance. A natural and graceful position lets one foot rest slightly forward with the greater weight of the body on the ball of the forward foot. Changes of position naturally occur and help the debater avoid an ungainly stance.

Playing with Watch Chains and Coins. Displaying medals on watch chains and fumbling with them frequently seem to call attention to past accomplishments. This mannerism and the jingling of coins in pockets mar effective delivery.

Addressing Remarks Too Often to the Opposing Speakers. You naturally turn to opponents and speak directly to them from time to time, but too much direct attention to the opposition tends to inject a personal element into debate and also suggests neglect of the audience. Unless issuing a challenge or asking a question of your opponents, address your arguments to your listeners. Your duty is to convince your judges and listeners, not your opponents.

Speaking Too Fast. Rapid speaking that allows little time for pause seems to be characteristic of many debaters. Transcriptions show that the rate of speaking in debate sometimes exceeds 250 words per minute. An effective rate for most speakers is between 120 and 150 words. The rate of speaking should vary with content, type of occasion, and temperament of speaker. For example, the rate used to describe a horse race or a dash for the goal line would be more rapid than that used to describe poverty in a slum district. Vary the rate, but do not race through point after point. A few points well developed and explained are more effective than many points inadequately and hurriedly given.

Using Too Much or Too Little Volume. A bombastic tone or explosive force throughout a speech proves irritating to listeners. The audience may not be able to hear what is said because of the noise. Conversely, a speech delivered in tones that cannot be heard throughout the speaking hall proves equally ineffective. A judge who has to strain to hear what you say will soon give up and think about something else; the listeners will think that you are not convinced of the importance of your material nor concerned with your desire to communicate with them. Variety in force aids directness of communication.

Presenting an Ungainly Posture. Posture means the stance of the speaker, his bearing on the platform. To stand rigid, with both feet immovably fixed, is as undesirable as to slouch from apparent lack of energy. A good posture allows one to keep his head erect, his chin in, his chest out, and his shoulders relaxed. Do not maintain one posture throughout a speech; change occasionally to emphasize meaning and relieve tension.

Using Too Many or Too Few Movements. Aimless and frequent movements prove as objectionable as lack of movement. Some debaters fan the air, pound the table, or pace the floor constantly while speaking, and such movements make a poor impression and direct attention to the mannerism. Little or no bodily action makes one appear sluggish and fails to arouse interest. Controlled movements are effective; meaningless movements detract. Moving the body forward, backward, or to the side indicates thought transition and aids clarity. Use the arms, head, and shoulders for specific gestures to bring out distinctions in meaning and for emphasis. Above all, gestures and movements must be natural and spontaneous, not mechanical.

Showing Poor Facial Expression. The insincerity of the fixed smile of professional good will in debaters is easily detected. Equally objectionable is the arrogant look, the scowl, the overly anxious look, or the bored appearance. Faulty expressions are best remedied by a right mental attitude. If you have proper feeling for listeners and opponents and an interest in the subject, you will evince these things in your face.

Resorting to Name Calling and Loaded Words. Calling something bad does not make it bad. Do not label a proposal as communistic or anything else without offering proof. Those who lack information often appeal to the emotions and prejudices of audiences by using emotionally loaded words. Such words stir up hate and fear; they often get a quick reaction, but it is hardly honest to use them. Such phrases as "fellow travelers," "egghead," "do gooders," "scheming politicians," and "money-mad bankers" stir up emotions rather than intellect. They are not substitutes for logical reasoning.

Summary

Effective oral presentation is essential to the training for educational debate. The following principles apply: (1) Effective presentation is direct, conversational, and communicative. Presentation skills are not ends within themselves, but are the means of communicating ideas and persuading listeners. (2) Effective presentation requires proper attitudes toward your subject, your opponents, your audience, and your judges. They are all necessary factors for training in a worthwhile, educational activity. (3) Effective presentation requires an able advocate—a person of intelligence, character, and good will. (4) Effective presentation utilizes rhetorical skills—a coordinated use of mind, language, voice, bodily action, and poise.

Some problems of delivery applicable to debaters include achieving proper stage presence and avoiding delivery mannerisms. Stage conduct relates to your behavior while on the platform, how you handle your notes and materials, and how you explain charts and diagrams.

Delivery mannerisms applicable specifically to debaters include: (1) taking pen or pencil to the platform, (2) misusing the hands, (3) improperly using the speakers' stand, (4) adjusting eyeglasses or articles of clothing, (5) indirect eye contact, (6) continually moving the head, (7) constantly swaying the body, (8) resting weight of the body on one leg, (9) playing with watch chain and coins, (10) addressing remarks too often to the opposing speakers, (11) speaking too fast, (12) using too much or too little volume, (13) presenting an ungainly posture, (14) using too many or too few movements, (15) showing poor facial expressions, and (16) resorting to name calling and loaded words.

Oral Assignment

1. A legislative debate should be conducted on the topic selected for classroom study.
2. The class should be divided into three groups: pro, con, and neutral.
3. The pro group should introduce the resolution with an opening speech of eight minutes. Thereafter, the chairman should alternate in recognizing speakers from each side for speeches limited to five minutes.
4. The neutral group may ask questions but may not participate in the debate.
5. Toward the end of the class period, the chairman should bring the resolution to vote. Members of the neutral group should vote with that side which they consider has done the most effective debating.

Collateral Readings

Capp, Glenn R., *How to Communicate Orally,* Chs. 10, 11, 12, 13. Englewood Cliffs, N.J.: Prentice-Hall, Inc., 1961.

Crocker, Lionel, *Argumentation and Debate,* Ch. 14. New York: American Institute of Banking, 1962.

Dickens, Milton, *Speech: Dynamic Communication,* Chs. 9, 10, 11. New York: Harcourt, Brace & World, Inc., 1963.

Ehninger, Douglas, and Wayne Brockriede, *Decision by Debate,* Chs. 17, 18. New York: Dodd, Mead & Co., 1963.

Murphy, James J., and Jon M. Ericson, *The Debaters' Guide,* Chs. 6, 7. Indianapolis, Ind.: Bobbs-Merrill Company, Inc., 1961.

White, Eugene E., *Practical Speech Fundamentals,* Chs. 4, 5, 6, 7. New York: The Macmillan Company, 1960.

13
Adapting Debates to Public Audiences, Tournaments, and Television

In educational debate, each team attempts to convince the audience that it has upheld its side of the proposition better than has the opposing team. The debate should be evaluated on the basis of which team does the most effective debating, not which side the judge personally favors. Your task is nonetheless more than building a logical case; you must persuade your listeners to accept the reasonableness of your arguments. To persuade your listeners, you must analyze their interests, attitudes, and knowledge of the subject. Three types of audiences—those for public, tournament, and television debates—require varying types of appeal and methods of procedure.

Public Debates

Public debates provide the most realistic audience situation for educational debate because they attract the type of listeners most often encountered in life situations of advocacy. To convince public audiences, you must keep your specific listeners in mind as you choose your arguments, supporting material, and elements of interest. A case that will appeal to one type of audience may not convince another.

Audience interest

Audiences vary according to the community of their interests. If members of your audience come from the same profession or business, they will have common primary interests to which you may appeal. For example, if you should debate socialized medicine at a meeting of the local medical association, your choice of arguments and supporting material would appeal to all members of the audience in much the same way. If you debated the same topic before an invited audience at your university, you would likely encounter listeners of varying interests and beliefs. Your basic appeals would, therefore, be more general with a heterogeneous audience than with a specialized one.

If your listeners do not have common primary interests, determine if they may have similar secondary interests to which you may appeal. For example, if you should debate at the local Rotary Club, you would encounter leaders in the community from many professions and businesses. Although their primary interests would vary greatly, they would have common secondary interests regarding civic affairs and fraternal matters as shown by their membership in the same club.

Audiences for debates open to the general public may have neither primary nor secondary interests in common. Local happenings in the community may be of such importance, however, that they will appeal to all listeners. If your topic relates to slum clearance, for example, choose your supporting material from conditions in the local community, not from those in other cities. If your topic concerns presidential succession, illustrate your points by the events of President Lyndon B. Johnson's succession to the presidency following the assassination of President John F. Kennedy. Such momentous events appeal to all listeners.

Audience attitude

Almost all policy questions chosen for educational debates relate to controversial subjects on which sharp disagreement may exist. The approach made by each debate team should depend on whether a particular audience favors or disapproves of its position. For example, let us suppose that the proposition calls for a program of socialized medicine and the audience consists of the local chapter of the American Medical Association. The affirmative team faces an audience strongly opposed to its position, whereas the negative enjoys an audience favorable to its stand. The affirmative must use psychological principles designed to create an open-minded attitude that will insure a fair hearing. The affirmative might, for example, refer to the basic democratic principle that calls for a consideration of all points of view, compliment the medical profession on its scientific advances, quote men from the medical profession revered by the audience, or inject well-chosen humor. The affirmative should be careful to support each point with adequate evidence and logical reasoning; it should omit quotations or other evidence that might antagonize members of the audience, such as statements prejudicial to the medical association's cause. In short, the affirmative faces a psychological problem in persuasion as well as a logical problem in developing an adequate case.

The negative in this case has public sentiment working in its favor. It should attempt to strengthen existing beliefs by a logically arranged case that includes only the strongest arguments against socialized medicine. It should be courteous to the opposition and make no obvious play to exploit the favorable attitude of the audience. The extent of logical proof will be less for the negative than for the affirmative, however, because of existing beliefs.

Listener background

The more you know in advance about your listeners, the better you will be able to adapt to their interests and beliefs and choose effective logical and emotional proofs. Determine their approximate age level and educational background. If your audience consists largely of young people, for example, they will usually be more favorable to new ideas than older people, as well as more open to suggestion. Listeners with a broad background of training and knowledge will usually require a higher degree of logical proof than persons without such backgrounds. The interest in the subject and the ability to understand an argument will vary with your listeners' prior knowledge of the subject and their training in reasoning. Chapter 7 discussed how these same factors affect the sufficiency of your evidence; they affect both your choice of supporting material and your manner of presentation.

In short, consider educational debate as an activity that calls for both logical development of arguments and persuasive presentation. Adapt your cases to your listeners' interests, attitudes, and social and cultural backgrounds.

Tournament Debates

Elements of persuasion and logical argument have always been integral parts of the processes of argumentation, but the advent of tournament debating in the 1920's was largely responsible for the change in emphasis in educational debating from persuasive speaking to logical development of cases. The typical audience in tournaments consists of a well-trained critic or judge and a timekeeper. The critic judges largely on the adequacy of the case—the analysis of the proposition, the organization of the case, the logical adequacy of the arguments, the validity of supporting evidence, and the ability at refutation. In short, the critic evaluates the debate according to how well the debater performs these functions, not according to which side is more persuasive.

The tournament has largely replaced the public audience in educational-debate activities. Many colleges and universities restrict their forensic programs largely to tournaments; some report attending as many as 15 to 20 tournaments each year. The result has been to extend intercollegiate competition to an increasing number of students. Before the advent of the forensic tournament, the average size of the debate squad was from four to six students who participated in from eight to ten public debates per year. Professor Paul Hunsinger of the University of Denver made a survey of the forensic activities of 53 representative colleges and universities for the academic year 1961–62; he found that these schools used an average of 29 students in intercollegiate competition and attended an average of 12 tournaments. Twelve universities reported that 40 or more debaters participated in tournaments, and 16 universities reported attending 15 or more tournaments.[1] The directory of forensic tournaments, published by the American Forensic Association, lists 123 tournaments in the United States for the academic year 1964-65, and it makes no claim to complete listing.[2]

To realize maximum educational advantages from tournament debating, consider the following suggestions.

Preparation for life debates

The emphasis on tournament debating, although having a beneficial effect of extending forensic activities to many students at a minimum cost, has tended to decrease the importance of educa-

---

[1] Paul Hunsinger, "Comparative Studies of Forensic Budgets," mimeographed report of survey, 1962.
[2] *Journal of the American Forensic Association,* I, No. 3 (September, 1964), 116-19.

tional debate as a persuasive activity. To offset the emphasis on the mechanics and logical adequacy of case construction, consider the tournament as a training activity, not as an end in itself. Although the declaring of championships provides strong incentives for thorough preparation, the ultimate purpose of forensic training is to prepare for life situations of advocacy. After you have become proficient in tournament debating, your training is not yet complete—you must learn to adapt your acquired skills to actual life audiences. Seek occasions to put your training to realistic use through participation in public debates.

Limiting tournament participation

Eligibility for participation in the West Point National Debate Tournament and some regional programs is based upon the successes in tournaments held earlier in the school year. To increase their chances for qualifying, some schools send the same students to a large number of tournaments in hopes of making a good showing in at least some of them. These applications sometimes show that the same two students participate in as many as 80 debates in 15 tournaments on the same subject. This overemphasis on winning leads to serious criticism of intercollegiate debate as an educational activity. Some critics aptly ask what the students could possibly have learned in the eightieth debate on the same subject that they had not already learned by the fortieth debate. Overemphasis on qualifying a team leads to a disproportionate expenditure of time, effort, and money on a few students. It also raises questions about the educational values of forensic programs that put such a great emphasis on winning and that take students away from the campus so often.

The tournament can serve a useful purpose by enabling a large number of students to participate in intercollegiate competition within the limits of many forensic budgets. These values cannot be attained, however, if almost all the funds are spent on a few students. Some forensic directors have imposed limits on tournament participation. For example, one university with an extensive program limits participation for any one student to four tournaments and six days' absences from classes per semester. This university attends some 15 tournaments each year, but it permits 40 or more students to alternate in attending them. Such self-imposed limitations must be made if the tournament is to realize its maximum educational potential.

Learning from each tournament experience

Attending several tournaments on the same question can be an enriching educational activity only if you profit by each tournament experience. The practice of using the same case under similar conditions in tournament after tournament has doubtful values. Fortunately, the enterprising student can learn a great deal by utilizing features of tournaments made available to him. The majority of tournament debates are judged by capable critics. Some of the tournaments provide time for oral critiques following each debate; others provide ballots, with carbon copies for each team, on which the judge may write his criticisms. The debater can learn a great deal from these criticisms for improving both his case and his presentation for the next tournament.

The debate case should always remain flexible; make corrections, deletions, and additions to the case as indicated by the critics' suggestions, by what you learn from your opponents, and from weaknesses you detect in using your case. Make each tournament experience serve as a basis for improving your case for the next tournament; engage in practice debates between tournaments to test your corrected cases. Tournament participation can be a real educational enterprise for improving your skills in debating.

Variety in tournament experiences also has educational advantages. Instead of debating with one colleague throughout the year, change colleagues occasionally to improve your ability to work with other people and to learn new approaches to the question. Attend tournaments that employ different forms of debates and other types of speaking contests. The variety will help prepare you for the many types of speaking occasions encountered in life activities.

Continue to read new materials on the debate topic throughout the debate season, especially before important tournaments. Unless you continue to acquire ideas and new ways of stating old ideas, you will become stale on the subject. Fresh ideas renew interest and generate enthusiasm for the debate subject. Between each tournament, revise your case, add new ideas, and refine your methods of presentation. Only through these procedures can you realize the full advantages of tournament debating.

Television Debates

In recent years efforts have been made to adapt educational debate to television. Interested organizations hoped that these debates would gain public favor sufficient to attract commercial sponsors. Although these aims have not yet been fully realized, progress has been made. The American Forensic Association, in conjunction with the National Broadcasting Company and the American Student Foundation, sponsored a series of seventeen debates known as "Championship Debating" during the academic year 1961–62. These debates, carried as a public service, culminated with an hour-long debate between North Texas State University, the champion American team, and a British team representing Oxford University. A similar series was carried over the National Education Network in the spring of 1964.

Regional and state organizations have also been active in sponsoring television debates. For example, the Southwest Conference Forensic Association arranged the debate series "Young America Speaks," which was sponsored by the Sinclair Oil and Refining Company and carried over WFAA-TV, Dallas, Texas. Television debating requires an entirely new technique, which probably accounts for the difficulties encountered in getting public acceptance for such programs. Let us consider some of the adaptations that must be made.

Adapting the case

The time usually allowed for television debates is slightly less than thirty minutes. For example, "Championship Debating" used the following format:

Affirmative constructive speech	5 minutes
Cross-question affirmative speaker	3 minutes
Negative constructive speech	5 minutes
Cross-question negative speaker	3 minutes
Negative refutation and summary	4½ minutes
Affirmative refutation and summary	4½ minutes
Total	25 minutes

The speakers that cross-questioned the opposing speakers also gave the closing speeches.

The format for "Young America Speaks" called for four constructive speeches of three minutes each, followed by a cross-fire period in which the members of each team questioned the other team for four minutes. One speaker on each team then gave a closing speech of two and one-half minutes.

Such time limits prevent a full development of the traditional issues—need, practicability, and desirability. You must select no more than two or three of the strongest and most appealing arguments for the case. Time does not permit the detailed development of a plan; concentrate on the need for a change and the desirability of the proposal. Support each point with evidence that applies directly, takes little time to present, and has universal appeal. Do not read evidence from books or pamphlets—put it in your own words or commit it to memory. Besides being time consuming, reading from books breaks your eye contact and direct communication. Plan your constructive arguments in detail, especially the phraseology. Strive for economy of wording, clarity, and action. Television debating must provide a good show as well as a logical argument. It must be entertaining as well as instructive if large audiences are to be attracted.

The cross-question period can do much to popularize television debating because it dramatizes thought in rapid action. Plan provocative questions on arguments that you anticipate may be advanced by your opponents. Once begun, the line of questioning should be pursued until your point becomes obvious. Questions may serve (1) to reveal fallacies in your opponent's arguments, (2) to show weaknesses in your opponent's evidence, (3) to reveal inconsistencies in the opposition's case, (4) to lay the groundwork for arguments that your side plans to present, and (5) to give your side a psychological advantage by injecting humor or clever repartee into the debate. Unless your series of questions reveals an obvious weakness in the oppositions' arguments, you may either state the weakness immediately or wait until your rebuttal speech to capitalize on it. Make the cross-question period an integral part of your case, and follow through on your questions to insure a strong over-all line of attack.

Adapting to the audience

We learned in Chapter 12 that such factors as listeners' interests, attitudes, and backgrounds can be pinpointed with a high degree of accuracy for public and tournament debates. Potential listeners for television debates, however, have a greater diversity of interests and attitudes than other audiences. Unfortunately, many of these potential listeners also have less motivation to listen. The members of public audiences are usually too courteous to walk out; the judge in a tournament must see the debate through regardless of his desires in the matter. The television viewer, on the other hand, has no pressures to prevent his changing channels. The television debater must therefore give careful attention to the elements of interest and dramatic appeal.

Make your appeals as universal as possible. Because of the diversity of ages, cultural and social backgrounds, and education, your listeners will not have a community of primary and secondary interests. You must appeal to matters of unusual concern, momentous events in which all people will be interested. Make psychological appeals a part of your presentation. Without resorting to emotionalism, appeal to basic motives such as self-preservation, economic well-being, power, authority, sentiment, reputation, and affection. Link your cause with those impelling motives that command the attention of people. Make your refutation more direct and personal than you would in a tournament or public debate.

In choosing your supporting evidence, make liberal use of illustrative material. Use specific instances, comparisons, and life experiences that show action. Avoid technical and theoretical discussions that require lengthy explanations; use a simple pattern of organization that can be easily understood. Begin each speech in an interesting manner—ask a provocative question, relate a striking illustration, tell an unusual experience, or quote an impelling statement. Decide on a central theme for your case; state it in a brief, slogan-like phrase and repeat it often throughout the debate. State your main issues in short sentences and re-state them frequently. In short, make it easy for your listeners to understand your central theme and your sequence of ideas.

Adapting the presentation

The principles of effective presentation already discussed in Chapter 12 apply to television debating. In addition, several other factors peculiar to television debating should be considered.

Adjustment to the microphone includes the following factors:

(1) Be careful not to move outside the range of the microphone by moving about, by turning your head to speak directly to your opponents, by swaying movements, or by changes in stance. Such movements cause variations in volume that prove irritating to audiences. (2) Speak in an animated, conversational manner. Avoid the grand manner usually associated with unusual force, sweeping gestures, and elaborate style. Strive for a direct, conversational, communicative manner. (3) Beware of causing extraneous noises by pounding or drumming on the table, by rustling papers, or by shuffling your feet. The microphone will pick up these sounds and they will mar your presentation. (4) Look directly into the live camera as indicated by the tally light, a small red light just below the lenses of the camera. When the cameraman changes cameras, vary your position slightly so that you always face the live camera.

Several distracting delivery mannerisms apply with force to television presentation; especially on close-up shots: (1) looking away from the camera; (2) observing notes too frequently; (3) showing a lack of animation in facial expression; (4) adjusting clothing, glasses, or materials on the lectern; (5) making large and sweeping gestures; (6) shuffling about; and (7) sitting or standing in a slouchy position. Attempt to maintain a relaxed but poised appearance free of such distracting mannerisms.

The technical aspects of producing a television program often prove distracting, especially to inexperienced performers. The bright floodlights generate considerable heat. The debater should wear light clothing and avoid accessories, such as tie clasps and jewelry, that reflect light. White shirts or blouses and clothes with prominent stripes and figures should also be avoided. Pastel shades of blue or gray appear as white on cameras and do not reflect the bright lights. The activities of the cameraman, the director, and the timekeeper may also prove distracting. Although you must heed the instructions of these technicians, attempt to visualize your listeners as you concentrate on the substance of your arguments. If a studio audience is present, direct your arguments to them much as you would in a public debate.

Summary

Presentation must be adapted to different types of audiences. In adapting to public audiences, consider their interests and attitudes toward the subject and their age and background. The audiences of tournament debates consist of highly specialized listeners who are interested more in the training aspects of debate than in the success of the persuasion. Although tournaments have extended debate training to an increasing number of students, some schools have overemphasized winning at the expense of training. To realize the full potential of tournament debating, consider tournaments as preparation for life debates, limit the number of tournaments attended, and learn from each tournament experience. Television debating requires special adaptation of presentation skills, including: (1) adapting the debate to a limited time that cannot include the traditional case—need, practicability, and desirability, (2) adapting to an unseen audience, and (3) adapting to special techniques of presentation. Although television debating includes all principles of effective presentation, it encompasses special skills applicable only to television.

Oral Assignment

1. The class members should be arranged into two-member teams for a class tournament. Members of the class may choose their colleagues if they have a preference; the instructor should pair those class members who have no preference.
2. A schedule should be drawn up to provide four debates for each team and permit sides to be alternated.
3. Two or more debates may be held each day depending on the size of the class and the rooms available.
4. Those members of the class who do not debate on a particular day should serve as judges. The instructor should alternate as judge among the debates so that he will have heard each team at least once during the series.
5. Each team should be provided with a ballot after each debate. If possible, use ballots with carbon copies that provide space for written criticisms, such as the American Forensic Association ballot.
6. If time permits, the four high-ranking teams should be selected for a semifinal and final debate.
7. This assignment should extend to the end of the semester.

Collateral Readings

Capp, Glenn R., *How to Communicate Orally*, Ch. 4. Englewood Cliffs, N.J.: Prentice-Hall, Inc., 1961.

Crocker, Lionel, *Argumentation and Debate*, Ch. 13. New York: American Book Co., 1944.

Ewbank, Henry Lee, and J. Jeffery Auer, *Discussion and Debate,* Ch. 13. New York: Appleton-Century-Crofts, Inc., 1951.

Huber, Robert B., *Influencing Through Argument,* Ch. 14. New York: David McKay Co., Inc., 1963.

McBath, James H., ed., *T.V. Championship Debates.* Portland, Me.: J. Weston Walch, Publishers, 1964.

McBurney, James H., and Glen E. Mills, *Argumentation and Debate: Techniques of a Free Society,* Ch. 11. New York: The Macmillan Company, 1964.

V
Appendix

A National
Television Debate[1]

Resolved, That gambling should be legalized in all states.
WNBC-TV, New York, Channel 4

ANNE HODGES: Attempts to abolish gambling have been unsuccessful in solving the problems that gambling creates. We think it's time to try a new approach.

SHELDON MIXSON: I'm opposed to any proposition predicated on the premise that crooks are clever people and also gamblers who find ways to get around the laws. Therefore, we should do away with the laws.

JOHN SWANEY: The legalization of gambling will be one of our most effective weapons against organized crime.

MICHAEL HENKE: I'm opposed to any government program that preys on the weaknesses of its citizens.

(*Music*) ANNOUNCER: The National Broadcasting Company, in association with the American Forensic Association and the American Student Foundation, presents "Championship Debate." Our moderator is Dr. James H. McBath, Professor of Speech at the University of Southern California and Chairman of the National Debate Board of the American Forensic Association. (*Applause*)

DR. JAMES H. MCBATH: Should gambling be legalized in all states? To argue this provocative question, Championship Debate brings to its platform two great teams from Texas: North Texas State University in Denton and Baylor University in Waco. This is their quarter-final round in New York City for the Southern Championship. Sides were assigned by the American Forensic

---

1 This television debate is one of the series entitled "Championship Debate" held over the NBC networks during the academic year 1961-62. The debate was transcribed from a recording and is published with permission of NBC and the debaters.

Association. Naturally the views expressed aren't necessarily those of either the schools or the network. In a few minutes each team will hear the other's arguments for the first time. But first let's meet our debaters. From North Texas State University, on the affirmative—John Swaney and Anne Hodges. Their opponents from Baylor University, on the negative—Mike Henke and Sheldon Mixson.

The rules for "Championship Debate" provide these students a balanced opportunity to convince us. Each side presents its main case, can interrogate the opposition, and then can summarize its case. Immediately after the last speaker has concluded, we consult our judges for their decision. Our three critics today are prominent speech directors and debate critics. They are: Jack Lynch, St. Anselm's College; Clayton Schug, Pennsylvania State University; and Wofford Gardner, University of Maine. Now to launch the affirmative, Anne Hodges speaks for legalized gambling. Anne.

ANNE HODGES: Last year the American people spent fifty billion dollars on gambling and forty-seven billion of that was spent on illegal gambling. Therefore, whether we approve or disapprove of gambling, it's rather difficult to deny that the American people want to gamble. So the real question today is not between gambling and no gambling, but under what conditions gambling is going to exist. Now, of course, John and I realize that gambling does create some problems in our society. But those problems have occurred because gambling has been forced to operate outside of the law. So our case today is going to take the form of three indictments against illegal gambling.

And the first indictment is that illegal gambling is a major support of organized crime. The United States Senate Sub-Committee on Gambling and Organized Crime last year pointed out that forty-seven billion dollars last year was gambled illegally. The profits from illegal gambling went into the pockets of organized crime. Yet if we would legalize gambling and cut off that supply of funds, we would injure organized crime. Attorney General Robert Kennedy in the April, 1962, issue of the *Atlantic Monthly,* tells us that when we reduce the gambler's income, we have reduced a major source of revenue for organized crime.

Secondly, we find that illegal gambling leads to the corruption of public officials. Mr. Goodman A. Sarrison, who is the chairman of the New York Commission of Investigation testifying before that Senate Sub-Committee, tells us that illegal gambling cannot exist without the protection from local law-enforcement officials.

He further says that one-half of the profits from illegal gambling are used to buy protection and bribe public officials.

And thirdly, the present law is not consistent with public morals. Now John and I think that the purpose of law is to reflect social attitudes, not to create them. Even Elliot Ness could not stop the sale of illegal liquor simply because the American public wanted to drink. And John and I think that even if Elliot Ness and all the "Untouchables" were on NBC instead of that other network, they still couldn't solve the problem because the law is inconsistent with American morals. And so it is with gambling. The American people want to gamble as evidenced by the fact that they spend so much money doing it. And if they can't do it legally they're going to do it illegally. So in order to remedy these problems, we proposed that gambling be legalized in all states.

We would say that all gambling should be allowed in state-owned and operated establishments under state supervision, much as the states now own and operate liquor stores throughout the country in some particular states. For you see, with the state managing the gambling business, the American public is going to be able to satisfy its desire to gamble without the stigma of breaking the law and without perpetuating the evils that I have already discussed with you.

I think we can see that, by legalizing gambling, we are going to gain three obvious and important advantages. First of all, we are going to cut off the supply of money which goes from illegal gambling to organized crime because the state is going to get the profits from gambling. Secondly, we are going to be able to do away with corruption of state officials for it would no longer be necessary to bribe the public officials and the local law-enforcement officers because illegal gambling will be gone and the states will be getting the profits. And thirdly, the states can use the money for education, welfare, and highway construction that they receive from legalized gambling. Florida now finances scholarships; New York and New Mexico finance welfare programs and highway construction. And in all three of these instances the money comes only from legalized horse racing while millions of dollars still go down the drain in other forms of illegal gambling.

John and I are certainly in favor of fighting crime, but the present laws against gambling are forcing many American people unwittingly to become partners in crime. As long as illegal gambling exists, a part of every dollar that goes to the bookie is going into the hands of organized crime. As long as illegal gambling exists, a part of every dollar that goes down the drain is going to buy protection for that illegal gambling. And as long as gambling exists, the American public's respect for the law is diminished. The American public has proven that it wants to gamble and, if it can't do it legally, it's going to do it illegally. So we say that the best solution to the entire problem to stop the crime—to do away with the corruption—is to legalize gambling.

DR. McBATH: Thanks, Anne. (*Applause*) Baylor's Sheldon Mixson now subjects this argument to cross-examination. Sheldon.

MR. MIXSON: Thank you, Dr. McBath. Just a couple of questions, Anne, if you don't mind.

MISS HODGES: I don't mind.

MR. MIXSON: I assume, from your proposition, that you're going to have gambling going on in areas where it doesn't at the present time?

MISS HODGES: That's true. All states don't now allow gambling.

MR. MIXSON: In other words, there will be an increased incidence of gambling, and necessarily an increased number of participants in gambling.

MISS HODGES: Gambling will be legalized and if people want to do it legally or want to gamble they can do it. If it increases, it is just an indication that people want to do it.

MR. MIXSON: All right, fine. The next question would be this: I suppose the same officials on the local and state level will be checking the control of gambling under your program as they do under the existing laws which outlaw gambling?

MISS HODGES: State officials certainly will be regulating gambling, but we don't think that the necessity for corruption and buying off those officials is going to be necessary because gamblers won't need the protection that they now need.

MR. MIXSON: I see. In other words, you believe your program will eliminate the criminal element from gambling?

MISS HODGES: We certainly think it will. The only way to corrupt is to corrupt the state government.

MR. MIXSON: All right. You pointed out here that the people seem to want gambling and the figure you used to substantiate this point is the total number of or total amount of money that goes into gambling each year. Do you know how many people are responsible for this total income to gambling?

MISS HODGES: Well, Sheldon, the Senate Sub-Committee on Gambling and Organized Crime pointed out that it was very, very difficult to determine exactly how many people gamble every year. But to give you an indication, legally at Aqueduct in one day, twenty-six thousand people went out there and gambled. Think about all the people who do it illegally at the present time. It's probably a number that cannot actually be calculated. Millions of people do it.

MR. MIXSON: All right, let's take another example then in this particular aspect. Do you think that because people want to do something this is any reason why the government should permit them to do something? For instance, your statement would indicate that you believe that gambling seems to be some sort of urge that people have, that they can't fight it and they're going to gamble legally or illegally. Well now, using this logic, would you advocate legalizing all urges that all people have?

MISS HODGES: I certainly would not, but I think that gambling is an instance in which the public morals reflect the fact that people want to gamble.

MR. MIXSON: Well, why not? Isn't the logic the same here? People want to gamble and they're going to gamble anyway, so why not let them go ahead and do it legally. What about robbery? Why don't we say, "people want to rob, they have an urge to rob . . ."?

MISS HODGES: Because the morals of the society say there aren't enough people in the country who want to go out and rob everybody . . .

MR. MIXSON: Oh.

MISS HODGES: . . . to demand that it be legal.

MR. MIXSON: Well, in other words, if I had an uncontrollable urge to throw that book at you now, the morals of society would prohibit my doing it?

MISS HODGES: Good taste would also prohibit you from doing it, don't you think?

MR. MIXSON: I see. The next question might be this: Why don't we go to President, rather Attorney General Kennedy's article here in the *Atlantic* which you quoted and read this conclusion.

MISS HODGES: I've read it.

MR. MIXSON: All right. Do you agree with this conclusion that we don't need to legalize gambling, merely to make the penalties for gambling today more stringent to solve your problem?

MISS HODGES: We certainly don't.

MR. MIXSON: How would this solve your problem?

MISS HODGES: We think that the American people are going to gamble. If you don't legalize it, illegal gambling is going to continue to exist. Billions of dollars are still going into the hands of organized crime. Officials are still going to be corrupted. Legalize it and solve the problem.

DR. MCBATH: Thank you very much. Now Sheldon's colleague, Mike Henke of Baylor, presents the negative side of this issue. Mike.

MR. HENKE: Thank you, Dr. McBath. You know, as my colleague and I have been researching this topic, we have been repeatedly impressed by the unanimity of expert opinion in the area of gambling. For example, the foremost comprehensive surveys of gambling in the United States since 1940—that would be the Kefauver Committee investigation, the investigation by the Massachusetts Citizens Council, the California Governor's Commission report, and the Chicago Crime Commission report have all been unanimous in their conclusions against legalized gambling. Not only that, but in many, many states in the United States today—Iowa, Minnesota, Wisconsin, Idaho, Montana, Florida, and Louisiana, to name just a few—present anti-gambling statutes are the results of long and disastrous experience with legalization.

Why has legalization of gambling proved undesirable? Why should it not be adopted? I think the answer is quite clear. The legalization of gambling inevitably results in an increase in the incidence of gambling. Now the lady of the opposition, in answer to a question that my colleague put to her along these lines, said if it increases it means the people want it to. She didn't commit herself as to whether it would or not. But the point is, and the fact is, that gambling will increase whether that lady agrees with this conclusion or not. State sanction is given to the process of gambling. Promotion increases, slot machines are placed everywhere, tickets to horse race tracks are distributed on every corner; gambling is made more accessible and more desirable, and consequently it increases. As Charles G. Caldwell of Iowa State University points out in his textbook, *Criminology*, "History shows that legalization advertises gambling, makes it more attractive and convenient, and thus leads inevitably to an increase in it." So first of all, gambling is going to increase.

Now this in itself, we would maintain, is not inherently bad; but what we are inveighing against today is the fact that there's also going to be a correlated increase in two evils which are inherent within gambling in a professional and organized manner. What are those two evils? First, there is harm to the individual; and second, harm to society. Now it's inevitable that gambling exacts its heaviest toll from those who are least able to pay. It is an axiom in gambling that those individuals in the low and lower-middle income groups are disproportionally attracted to gambling. These are the individuals who today are saddled with

195 billion dollars' worth of installment indebtedness. These are the very individuals who can least afford to gamble on their financial future, and yet they're going to be most allured by the affirmative program. That's the reason I said a few minutes ago that I was opposed to any government program that preyed on the weakness of its citizens as a revenue measure. I think harm to the individual dictates rejection of that affirmative proposition.

But how about this idea of corruption? Well it's even more important, I think, than the harm to the individual and certainly it's just as inherent. The United States Guaranty and Trust Company of Baltimore has pointed out that as much as 75 per cent of the 400 million dollars that's embezzled each year in this country is directly attributable to gambling indebtedness. In Philadelphia, in the last seven years, 200 members of the police force have been fired because of taking bribes from gamblers. Attorney General Robert Kennedy, in the report that's been referred to by the lady of the opposition, has stated that practically every narcotics operation in this country is financed by gambling revenue. Now the question arises, "Will crime and corruption in gambling decrease as a result of legalization?" I think the answer is obviously no. The reason—because criminals are attracted to gambling; not because it's illegal today, but because gambling is profitable to them. And, as a result, legalization is not going to decrease the profitability of gambling; legalization is not going to decrease the criminal element in it. You're going to have the same law enforcement officials under the affirmative proposal that you have today. If these individuals today are unable to cope with gambling when it's illegal, how much more incapable will they be of dealing with it under the affirmative proposal of controlling it because you still have to have some controls whether it's legal or not. As Dr. Caldwell states once again, "The legalization of gambling would not take it out of the hands of criminal elements." Past experience demonstrates that legalization has never succeeded in doing this. The underworld is interested in gambling, not because it's illegal, but because it's a highly lucrative business and offers opportunities for getting easy money. So what were those negative objections then? Harm to the individual and harm to society.

Now in the last thirty seconds, let me summarize the negative objections to the affirmative contentions. First, that illegal gambling finances organized crime; it still would with the affirmative. Second, that bribery and corruption results; it still would with the affirmative because there would be bribery and corruption as regards the control of gambling. Third, that it's not consistent with public morals. I pointed out that state after state in the United States has rejected legalized gambling in spite of the fact that it had been legalized before.

DR. McBATH: All right. There's the negative proposal. Coming to the rostrum now, North Texas State's John Swaney. John.

MR. SWANEY: Thank you, Dr. McBath. Mike, do you think that we should eliminate all forms of gambling?

MR. HENKE: All organized, professional forms of gambling, yes.

MR. SWANEY: Well then you don't think we should eliminate all forms of gambling. For instance, should we eliminate church bingos, church raffles, and gambling conducted for other such charitable purposes?

MR. HENKE: Yes, I do.

MR. SWANEY: You think we should eliminate those forms, too.

MR. HENKE: Yes, I do.

MR. SWANEY: Well now, while your particular church which supports your University does not feel that these forms of gambling should be allowed, isn't it true that other religious groups do approve of them and actually practice them and encourage them?

MR. HENKE: Oh, I can't deny that.

MR. SWANEY: Well then apparently you would be trying to force your religious beliefs on these groups by law. Is that correct?

MR. HENKE: I'm not trying to enforce anything on anybody by law. I'm merely stating that our opinion as the negative team in this debate is that gambling has these two evils . . .

MR. SWANEY: I understand that; so then even to the extent of church bingos and raffles you would force your religious opinion on these other groups by law. Is that correct?

MR. HENKE: Yes, because I still feel that it harms the individual, the little man, the individual who can least afford to lose money.

MR. SWANEY: All right. Thank you. Now isn't it true that illegal gambling provides great amounts of money for organized crime?

MR. HENKE: Yes, both teams have agreed on that.

MR. SWANEY: That's right and you want to keep gambling illegal, don't you?

MR. HENKE: We want to perhaps enforce more stringent penalties but certainly not to legalize it.

MR. SWANEY: But you want to keep it illegal?

MR. HENKE: That is correct.

MR. SWANEY: Well then, apparently you are in favor of continuing the support of organized crime. Is that correct?

MR. HENKE: No, this is not correct. I think Mr. Kennedy, according to the quotation that Anne read in her speech, said that this revenue for organized crime would decrease as gambling revenue decreased. If we imposed more stringent penalties, what better way to get at the decrease in gambling revenue?

MR. SWANEY: Mike, do you think the law has ever been able to stop any practice which a majority or at least a great percentage of the American people want to indulge in?

MR. HENKE: Well, now that is a point I contradicted in my speech also. I don't believe that a majority of the people want legalized gambling as illustrated by the vast number of states who have rejected proposals for legalization.

MR. SWANEY: Prohibition wasn't very successful, was it? As hard as the Federal Government tried, it could never completely stop the illegal sale of liquor, could it?

MR. HENKE: Let me stop right here to show a very basic dichotomy between the example of liquor and the example of gambling.

MR. SWANEY: Why don't you let Sheldon show that in his speech?

MR. HENKE: Well, I think it is in answer to your question, if you don't mind?

MR. SWANEY: Well, okay.

MR. HENKE: The distinction is simply this. That the legalization of alcohol tends to drive out the criminal elements because they can't compete with legal breweries and distilleries. The legalization of gambling on the other hand tends to entrench the criminal . . .

MR. SWANEY: Okay, I think we understand the point. Let me ask you this: Gambling is quite a large-scale operation, isn't it?

MR. HENKE: Yes it is.

MR. SWANEY: And do you think an operation of that magnitude can go on without the knowledge of public officials?

MR. HENKE: No, I think that's obvious from the reports that you've given us.

MR. SWANEY: Then there is quite a serious problem in corruption and we agree on that, don't we?

MR. HENKE: Yes, we do.

MR. SWANEY: Isn't it true that in New York State you can bet money at a race track, but if you live in another city where there's not a track you can't legally bet on that race. Is that right?

MR. HENKE: That's true. And in many states you can't even bet at a race track.

MR. SWANEY: Don't you imagine the average citizen finds it a little hard to see any logic in a law such as that?

MR. HENKE: Well, the citizens have enacted such laws; I hardly see how they could propose . . .

MR. SWANEY: And the citizens also provide the bookies with billions of dollars every year, too, don't they?

DR. McBATH: Thank you, gentlemen. Let's hear the final summation for the negative. Sheldon Mixson, Baylor University. Sheldon.

MR. MIXSON: Thank you, Dr. McBath. One important admission that Anne made in her question period was that her proposition almost inevitably, or if I may use that phrase, would lead to increased incidences of gambling. You're going to have more people gambling under the affirmative proposal than you have under the present system. And Mike pointed out to you that this increase is going to be detrimental for basically two reasons. It will simply aggravate the problems that the affirmative team has sought to bring to our attention in the present system. Let's see how this is going to take place. Anne pointed out we must reduce gamblers' income. Illegal gambling supports organized crime. Well, you're not going to be able to get rid of the criminal element in gambling. Anne said she thought the affirmative proposition would, but she has not gone back into history and showed us where legalized gambling anywhere has gotten rid of the criminal element. Mike did this for you in his speech. You can't get the criminal element out of gambling. Why not? Because gambling is the quickest way to fast money and fast money, as a matter of fact, always attracts the criminal element. So by increasing the incidences of gambling and not being able to get the criminal element out of gambling, you're just going to be increasing the revenue that pours into the underworld treasury—the very evil the affirmative team has sought to remedy under the present system.

The next idea was that it leads to corruption of officials. She's going to be using, under her proposition, the same officials that we are using today—the same officials that she alleges are corrupt today. We want to know exactly where the difference is going to be. If these people are corrupt today with what money is pouring into gambling, how much more corrupt are they going to be when you increase the flow of money that'll be falling into the hands of the gamblers who will be controlling the affirmative proposition?

She says it's not consistent with the public morals. This is a very big part, I think, of the affirmative case; but they can't tell us how many people in the United States, they can't even prove that a majority of the people in the United States, want legalized gambling. If we look at the states that have gambling and the states that have illegalized gambling, we might assume that the converse was the case. She can't demonstrate to me that the majority of the people in this country want it. Maybe all of that fifty billion dollars is spent by fifty thousand people. It doesn't prove anything about how many people in the United States want legalized gambling.

All right, the point here is this: Mike brought out the idea that by increasing the incidence of legalized gambling, by putting gambling in every city and town in the United States or at least making it legal there, you're going to make gambling appeal to people who never thought about spending their lunch money on it before because it's going to be right there in front of them. The temptation will be strong. Mike pointed out to you that the evil in gambling is this: it appeals to those people who can least afford it, those people who are looking for a way out of a financial situation. Those people will be the ones harmed by the affirmative proposal. The affirmative team in today's debate has never controverted this contention.

The general harm to society will be as Anne herself pointed out. We have corruptness today with fifty billion dollars. What are we going to do about it? We are going to increase the money that pours into gambling enterprises. Well the states are going to check it but the states are already corrupt today, Anne tried to tell us in her first speech.

The revenue benefits—I think Governor Dewey said that it was indecent for a state to prey on the weakness of the citizens. We are not going to call the affirmative team indecent, we are just going to call them mistaken. I think we have a very definite reason here for rejecting this affirmative proposal: harm to the individual, harm to society. If there are problems today, then let's just increase the penalties on gambling. Let's make it so expensive for a person to gamble; that is, send him to jail if he does. The people aren't going to want to do it. The only argument which can be given about this is to prove that all, or at least a substantial portion of the citizens in this country want gambling. If so, I submit we already have it today. The affirmative team has offered us no statistics, no reason for change.

DR. McBATH: Thank you, Sheldon, for the negative summation. Returning now to the platform, John Swaney, North Texas. John.

MR. SWANEY: Thank you, Dr. McBath. I think the first thing we need to do is look back at these affirmative need issues and see what the gentlemen from Baylor have had to say about them. We told you that gambling today is the major support of organized crime, illegal gambling. On that point both teams have agreed, but the gentlemen have said that legalization of gambling will provide even more funds for organized crime. Pardon me, but I cannot see the logic in that negative position because, under the plan which Anne presented, the state is going to own and operate all the gambling establishments. In which case, all the profits from gambling would go directly into the funds of the state. We can see no method in such a plan that the funds would be able to be channeled into organized crime unless organized crime itself controls the state government. And if that's the case, we may as well give up on a lot of things. So I think we can say that this first affirmative contention, that illegal gambling supports organized crime, has gone undenied.

What about Mr. Kennedy's proposals for stricter law enforcement? All we can say is that, throughout the history of the United States, the strictest law enforcement we could muster has not been able to stamp out illegal gambling. In fact, forty-seven billion dollars' worth of illegal gambling still goes on every year. We don't think strict law enforcement is the answer. It hasn't been the answer yet. We say, let's try a new approach.

We told you, secondly, that illegal gambling leads to the corruption of public officials. The gentlemen said, "Well, that's true so there's no disagreement on that point"; but then they told you that under our proposal, the officials could still be corrupted. Once again, we fail to see the logic. What possible reason would there be to corrupt the local law enforcement officers under our plan when the state government will own and operate the gambling establishments—no gangsters involved here, no one to bribe the local officials, no reason to bribe the local officials. So we've removed that evil from the present system.

Point No. 3—the laws are inconsistent with public morals. Well, what did Sheldon have to say? He said, "Well, should we legalize everything which someone has an urge to do?" No, I'm afraid he's missed the point. You see we said the laws should reflect social attitudes, not create social attitudes. Now he made the analogy to a law against robbery. Let me point this out: A law against robbery does reflect social attitude because the overwhelming majority of American people are opposed to robbery; so such a law reflects their attitudes. Laws against gambling do not reflect social attitude; they attempt to create social attitudes. So the analogy is a false one. We don't think that the gentlemen have been able to deny that the laws are inconsistent with public morals.

In relation to this point, they said, "Well, how many people do gamble? The figure fifty billion dollars isn't really indicative of how many people actually gamble." Well, all we can say is this: fifty billion dollars is indicative of the fact that either a lot of people gamble moderately or a few very, very, very rich people gamble quite a bit. We would say that one indication of how many people want legalized gambling is that twenty-four states now do have some form of legalized gambling. Well, that's half the states in this country. We think that's a pretty good indication.

They said gambling will increase under our plan. We said that if it does, that's simply proof that people want to gamble. So for all the time the gentlemen have taken to prove that gambling will increase, we think all they have done is prove that people want it. They said, "Well, that's harmful to the individual." Well, Mr. John Scarney, an expert on gambling, who incidentally has appeared on the Jack Paar show several times, said if they had something where they could play legally it would cut down every phase of organized crime there is. Mr. Scarney thinks it would cut down organized crime.

And finally they said gambling is profitable to crime. Why? Because the gamblers run the illegal establishments. Under our plan the state would run all gambling establishments. It could no longer be profitable to crime. We should legalize it. Thank you.

DR. MCBATH: Thank you. Legalized gambling for all American states—well, there are the arguments pro and con. Ready now for the verdict of the judges. First, let's turn to Professor Lynch.

PROFESSOR LYNCH: I would certainly like to congratulate both teams on their excellent presentation and clear analysis. I did think that this was a very close debate. It seems that generally on logic and evidence that I would have to declare for North Texas State.

DR. MCBATH: All right. Professor Schug.

PROFESSOR SCHUG: Well, I thought, too, that this was a very close debate, indeed. I thought the North Texas State team did a very good job in establishing the need; however, I am going to have to disagree with my good friend Professor Lynch here. I believe the disadvantages, as presented by the team from Baylor, outweighed the advantages; so I would cast my vote for the Baylor team.

DR. MCBATH: All right, a split decision, and the crucial one—Professor Gardner.

PROFESSOR GARDNER: There comes a time when a decision must be rendered. I would like to say this with regard to the debate itself. I think both debaters did a fine job, both teams did a fine job. I'm concerned and impressed with the appeal which I think the North Texas team had in terms of the general effect on the debate as a whole. Consequently, my decision would go to North Texas State.

DR. MCBATH: Thank you. So the decision is two-to-one for North Texas State University. Coming to the stage now Professor Bill DeMougeot from North Texas State and Glenn Capp of Baylor University. Congratulations Bill, and here is the Southern Championship Trophy presented by the American Student Foundation. And our best wishes to Baylor University for their very excellent opposition today. To the winning school "Championship Debate" awards $500, and $250 to the losing school. Our winners and losers have already won sets of the Encyclopedia Britannica. Now "Championship Debate" awards to each student a two-volume set of the Britannica World Dictionary. And thanks to our critics for their expert judgment. When George Eliot remarked "blessed is the man who having nothing to say abstains from giving us wordy evidence of the fact," he certainly didn't have today's four debaters in mind. Their arguments were soundly grounded and certainly crisply presented. And just as important, I think, you could share with us in New York the high excitement of "Championship Debate."

Index

A

Able-man theory, 196-99
Actions on platform, 203-4 (see also Delivery)
Admitted issues, 85
Admitted matter, 93
Affirmative:
  contentions, 98-99
  obligations, 49-50
  position of, 49
  proposition, 60
  rights, 46-70
Alternate solution, 45-46
Alternative syllogism, 145-46
Ambiguous terms, 61-62
American Forensic Association, 54, 214, 217
American Student Foundation, 217, 238
Analogy:
  as evidence, 108-9
  figurative, 129-30
  literal, 129
  as reasoning, 128-31
  suggestions for use, 108-9
  tests of, 130-31
Analysis, 82-101
  explained, 82
  illustrated, 86-88
  plan of, 86-88
  preliminary steps, 88-100
  purpose of, 82
Antecedent, 143-45 (see also Syllogism)
Anxiety, 202-3
Argument, 122-51 (see also Reasoning)
Aristotle, 102
Attacks on opposing arguments, 168-69 (see also Rebuttal)

Attitudes:
  of audience, 212-13
  toward audience, 195
  toward judges, 195-96
  toward opponents, 194-95
  in research, 75-76
  toward subject, 193-94
Audience:
  attitudes of, 212-13
  beliefs of, 119-20
  effect on evidence, 119-20
  interests of, 211-12
  listening, 213
  public, 211-13
  television, 218-19
  tournament, 213-16
Authority:
  as evidence, 109
  quotations of, 109

B

Background knowledge, 68-69
Baylor University, 225, 238
Begging the question, 173-74 (see also Fallacies)
Benson, Sarah, 168-69
Blackboard drawings, 205
Bodily action, 201-2
Brief, 152-66
  outline distinguished, 153-54
  purpose of, 152-53
  rules for, 154-64
  specimen introduction, 160-61
Bruner, J. W., 67
Burden of proof, 41-44
  application of, 43
  explained, 41
  on counterplan, 45-46, 51

Burden of proof (cont.)
  requirements of, 42
  rights of, 46-47
Burden of rebuttal, 44-46
  explained, 44
  illustrated, 45-46
  shifts in, 44

C

Caldwell, Charles G., 230, 231
Capp, Glenn, 238
Catalogue of Public Documents, 74
Categorical syllogism, 139-43
Causal reasoning, 132-35 (see also
    Reasoning)
Cause to effect, 133-35 (see also Reason-
    ing)
Case:
  adapting to television, 217, 220
  constructive, 167
  definition, 103
  formulation of, 13
  prima facie, 42
  proper division, 190-92
  selecting best arguments, 192-93
  selecting best evidence, 192-93
Chain of reasoning, 149
Chairman of discussion, 33-36
Championship Debating, 16, 217
Charting the debate, 183-85
Charts, 205
Circumstantial evidence, 110-11
Communicative speech, 189-93
Conceded matter, 93
Conditional syllogism, 143-45
Conferences, 69-70 (see also Discussion)
Congressional Digest, The, 75
Congressional Record, The, 74
Consequent, 143-45 (see also Syllogism)
Consistency of evidence, 117-18
Constructive case, 167 (see also Case)
Contentions:
  affirmative, 98-99
  issues distinguished, 162
  negative, 99-100
Contrasting issues, 98-100
Correspondence, 70-71
Counterplan, 45-46, 51
Cross-questions, 218

D

Debatable proposition, 59-60 (see also
    Proposition)

Debate:
  areas of application, 7-10
    in courts of law, 8
    in educational institutions, 10
    in everyday activities, 10
    in legislative assemblies, 9
    in political campaigns, 9
  as conflict-resolving process, 7
  educational, 3-4, 10-11
  handbooks of, 75
  legal, 4, 8
  of legalized gambling, 225-38
  legislative, 5, 9
  political, 4, 9
  practice, 16
  procedure, 48
  proposition, 54-56
  public, 211-13
  requirements for, 14-17
  specimen, 225-38
  television, 10, 217-20, 225-38
  tournament, 213-16
  values of training in, 11-14
Decision making, 11-12
Deductive reasoning:
  enthymeme, 146-49
  inductive distinguished, 122-23
  sorites, 149
  syllogism, 138-46
Defense of arguments, 169 (see also Re-
    buttal)
Definition of terms:
  authority, 94
  etymology, 94
  exemplification, 94
  explication, 94-95
  negation, 95
  requirements of, 95
Delivery:
  able-man theory, 196-99
  attitudes, 193-96
  mannerisms, 205-9
  rhetorical skills, 199-203
  stage conduct, 203-5
Delta Sigma Rho-Tau Kappa Alpha, 54
DeMougeot, Bill, 238
Diagrams, 205
Dilemma, 179
Discriminating attitude, 77
Discussion:
  areas of application, 7-10
  attitudes of participants, 31-32
  chairman, 33-36
  explained, 19

Discussion (*cont.*)
  leader, 33-36
  outline, 23-24
  participation in, 30-33
  pattern for, 19-22
  as preparation process, 6, 72
  as problem-solving method, 6
  series for preparation, 26-30
  types, 23-26
Disjunctive syllogism, 145-46
Distributed term, 140-41

E

Effect to cause, 132-33 (*see also* Reasoning)
Eliot, George, 238
Emotional proof, 103
Encyclopedias, 72-73
Enthymeme, 146-49 (*see also* Reasoning)
Ethical proof, 103
Ethical standards, 14
Evidence:
  analogy, 108-9
  attacks on, 174-78
  characteristics of, 105-9
  classifications of, 109-14
  example, 107-8
  expert opinion, 109, 111-12
  explained, 103
  misapplication of, 175-76
  statistics, 105-7
  tests of, 114-20
  types, 105-9
Examples:
  corroboration of, 128
  as evidence, 107-8
  generalization, 124-28
  negative, 127
  number of, 125-26
  as reasoning, 124-28
  representative, 126-27
  suggestion for use, 107-8
  tests of, 107-8, 124-28
Expert evidence, 109, 111-12
Extraneous matter, 92-93

F

Facial expression, 208 (*see also* Delivery)
Fact propositions, 56
Factual evidence, 95-109 (*see also* Evidence)

Fallacies:
  begging the question, 173-74
  of deductive reasoning, 138-49
  ignoring the question, 170-73
  of inductive reasoning, 122-28
  meaning, 170
Federal Reserve Bulletin, 75
Figurative analogy, 129-30
Fishbein, Morris, 177

G

Gardner, Wofford, 226, 238
Generalization, 124-28 (*see also* Reasoning)
General knowledge, 68-69
Gestures, 201-2
Governmental documents, 74-75

H

Hance, Kenneth G., 10-11, 19-20
Handbooks, 75
Hearsay rule, 104
Henke, Mike, 225-38
History of question, 90-92
Hodges, Anne, 225-38
Humphrey, C. J., 67
Hunsinger, Paul, 214
Hypothetical syllogism, 143-45

I

Ignoring the question, 170-73 (*see also* Fallacies)
Imperfect induction, 124
Inaccurate evidence, 176-77
Inconsistencies, 180
Inductive reasoning:
  deductive distinguished, 122-23
  generalization in, 124-28
  imperfect, 124
  perfect, 124
Inference, 122, 124 (*see also* Reasoning)
Informal discussion, 23-24, 27-28
Information Please Almanac, 75
Inquiring attitude, 75-76
Insufficient evidence, 175
Intercollegiate Debates, 16
Interpretation of proposition, 46-47, 93-96 (*see also* Proposition)
Interviews, 69-70
Irrelevant arguments, 180-81
Irrelevant matter, 93

Issues:
  contentions distinguished, 162
  contrasted, 98-100
  declaration of, 47
  new, in rebuttal, 49
  types of, 82-86

J

Jackson, Robert, 78
Johnson, Lyndon B., 212
Judges, 195-96

K

Kefauver Committee, 230
Kennedy, John F., 212
Kennedy, Robert, 226, 229, 231
Kent, Calvin, 169
Korzybski, Alfred, 77
Kruger, Arthur N., 16

L

Language, 199-200
Leading discussion, 33-36
Lecture forum, 26, 28-29
Lee, Irving J., 77
Library of Congress, 74
Limiting tournaments, 215-16 (see also
  Tournaments)
Lippmann, Walter, 8
Listening:
  audience background, 213
  in discussion, 31-32
Literal analogy, 129
Loaded words, 209
Logic, 122 (see also Reasoning)
Logical pattern of discussion, 19-22
Logical proof, 103
Logical reasoning, 12-13
Lycidas, 130
Lynch, Jack, 226, 237

M

McBath, James H., 16, 225-38
McBurney, James H., 10-11, 19-20, 146
Main contentions, 98-100, 162 (see also
  Contentions)
Main issues, 82-86 (see also Issues)
Major premise, 138-46 (see also Syllo-
  gism)

Major term, 139-43 (see also Syllogism)
Mannerisms:
  in delivery, 205-9
  in television debates, 220
Material:
  handling of, 203-4
  recording of, 78-80
  sources of, 68-75
Middle term, 139-43 (see also Syllogism)
Mills, Glen E., 146
Milton, 130, 168
Minor point, refutation of, 169-70
Minor premise, 138-46 (see also Syllo-
  gism)
Minor term, 139-43 (see also Syllogism)
Misapplied evidence, 175-76
Mixson, Sheldon, 225-38
Modifications of status quo, 51
Monthly Catalogue, 74
Movements on platform, 208 (see also
  Delivery)

N

National Broadcasting Company, 217
Name calling, 209
Negative:
  contentions, 99-100
  examples, 127
  position of, 50-51
  premises, 141-42
  propositions, 60-61
  rights of, 47-48
New material in rebuttal, 49
Nichols, Egbert Ray, 16
North Texas State University, 217, 225,
  238
Notes:
  recording of, 78-80
  specimen cards, 80
  use of, 204-5

O

Objective attitude, 31
Omitted matter, 93
Opinion, in evidence, 109
Oral argument, 189-210
Oral presentation, 13 (see also Delivery)
Ordinary evidence, 111-12
Outline for discussion, 23-24, 27-28
Oxford University, 217

P

Panel discussion, 24, 29-30
Paradise Lost, 168
Participating in discussion, 30-33
Particular term, 142-43 *(see also* Syllogism)
Pattern for discussion, 19-22 *(see also* Discussion)
Perfect induction, 124
Phelps, Ralph, 67
Philosophy of proposition, 96-98
Phi Rho Pi, 54
Phrasing the proposition, 59-63
Pi Kappa Delta, 54, 169
Plan for analysis, 86-88
Poise, 202-3, 208
Policy propositions, 55
Poole's Index, 74
Posture, 202-3, 208
Potential issues, 84-85
Prejudiced terms, 62
Preliminary steps in analysis, 88-100
Premises, 138-46
Preparations for tournaments, 214-16
Presentation, 189-210
    oral, 13
    on television, 219-20
Presumption of argument, 42
Prima-facie case, 42
Private documents, 74-75
Probability, 117
Problem-solving stages, 5-7
Procedure in debate, 44-46, 48
Processes of debate, 102-3
Proof, 103
Proposition:
    affirmative resolution, 60
    ambiguous terms, 61-62
    analysis of, 82-101
    central idea, 61
    characteristics, 56-59
    examples, 55-56
    interpretation, 46-47, 93-96
    philosophy, 96-98
    phrasing, 59-63
    prejudiced terms, 62
    restricted scope, 63
    selection of, 54
    types, 54-56
Public debates, 211-13
Public Law, Nos. 88-246, 74
Pure refutation, 50

Q

Qualifications of authority, 115-16
Quality of evidence, 116-18
Quantity of evidence, 118-20
Questionnaires, 70-72
Quotations, 109 *(see also* Authority)

R

Rate of speaking, 207-8 *(see also* Delivery)
Reader's Guide, 74
Real issues, 85-86
Reasoning:
    analogy, 128-31
    causal relation, 132-35
    deduction, 122-23, 138-49
    enthymeme, 146-49
    explained, 122
    fallacies, 170-74
    generalization in, 124-28
    induction, 122-28
    logical, 12-13
    sorites, 149
    syllogism, 138-46
Rebuttal:
    explained, 167
    organization, 182-85
    preparation, 181-82
    steps in, 182-83
    types, 168-70
Recording notes, 78-80 *(see also* Notes)
Reductio ad absurdum, 178
Reference Shelf, 75
Refutation:
    briefing of, 164
    general methods, 170-78
    minor point, 169-70
    pure, 50
    rebuttal distinguished, 167-68
    special methods, 178-81
    types, 168-70
Representative examples, 126-27 *(see also* Examples)
Research:
    attitudes in, 75-78
    debate preparation, 72-78
    sources, 72-75
Residues, 179
Rhetorical skills, 199-203
Romney, George, 94

Roosevelt, Franklin D., 3-5
Rosson, Frank M., 67

S

Sarrison, Goodman A., 226
Scarney, John, 237
Schug, Clayton, 226, 237
Self-assurance, 202-3
Significance of subject, 89-90
Sophistic devices, 14
Sorites, 149 (see also Reasoning)
Source, unreliable, 177-78
Source book, 73
Southwest Conference Forensic Association, 217
Speech Association of America, 54
Spoken evidence, 111
Stagefright, 202-3
Statesman's Yearbook, 75
Statistical Abstract of U.S., 74-75
Statistics, 105-7 (see also Evidence)
Status quo, 50-51
Steps:
    in analysis, 88-100
    in discussion, 19-22
    in rebuttal, 182-83
Stock issues, 83-84
Storey, Ellis, 177-78
Strife as conflict resolving, 7
Subordinate points, 103
Swaney, John, 225-38
Syllogism, 138-46
    alternative or disjunctive, 145-46
    categorical, 139-43
    conditional or hypothetical, 143-45
Symposium discussion, 25-26, 30

T

Television debates:
    adapting to audience, 218-19
    adapting presentation, 219-20
    adjusting to microphone, 219-20
    Championship Debating, 16, 217
    cross-questions, 218
    Kennedy-Nixon, 10, 16
    mannerisms, 220
    specimen, 225-38
    technical aspects, 220

Television debates (cont.)
    time limits, 217-18
    Young America Speaks, 217
Teller, Edward, 94
Tentative attitude, 76
Tests:
    analogy, 130-31
    categorical syllogism, 139-43
    cause-to-effect reasoning, 133-35
    disjunctive syllogism, 145-46
    effect-to-cause reasoning, 132-33
    evidence, 110-11, 114-20
    fallacies, 122-28, 138-49, 170-74
Toulmin, Stephen E., 102
Tournaments:
    learning from, 216
    limiting participation, 215-16
    preparation for life, 214-15
    variety in, 216
Turning the tables, 180
T.V. Championship Debates, 16

U

Undistributed term, 140-41 (see also Syllogism)
University Debater's Annual, 16
Unreliable source, 177-78

V

Value propositions, 55
Voice, 200-201
Volume, 208 (see also Delivery)

W

Waived matter, 93
Webster's New International Dictionary, 94
Weighing attitude, 77-78
WFAA-TV, 217
Windes, Russel R., 16
WNBC-TV, 225
World Almanac, 75
Written evidence, 111

Y

Yearbooks, 72-73
Young America Speaks, 217